Charles Duff was born in 1949. He is an actor, a lecturer in Shakespeare and theatre history, and a contributor to the national press on arts-related subjects. He has lived between Los Angeles, London, Paris and Tangier and he is now a Brother of the London Charterhouse. His memoir, *Charley's Woods: Sex, Sorrow & a Spiritual Quest in Snowdonia* was published in 2017.

Edith Evans and Sybil Thorndike in
Waters of the Moon by N.C. Hunter in 1951

The Best of the West End

The Life and Work of Frith Banbury

Charles Duff

ZULEIKA

First published (as *The Lost Summer*)
by Nick Hern Books 1995

This edition published 2022 by Zuleika Books & Publishing
Kemp House, 152-160 City Road, London, EC1V 2NX

British Library Cataloguing in Publication Data

A catalogue record for this book is
available from the British Library.

ISBN: 978-1-8380324-9-4

Printed in the United Kingdom by CPI Books.

Cover: Costume design by Cecil Beaton for Mercade
(Charles Gray) in *Love's Labour's Lost*, Old Vic
1954. © National Portrait Gallery, London.

Contents

Illustrations

For Barbara Jones

Acknowledgements

For the interest they showed, and for the help and time they gave throughout the writing of this book, I would like to thank:

Joss Ackland; the late Rodney Ackland; Sam Beazley; Jeremy Blake; the late Robert Bolt, C.B.E.; the late Richard Carey; Enid M. Collett; Allan Davis; Clarissa Dennison; Dr. Diana Devlin; the late Robert Flemyng, O.B.E., M.C.; Moyra Fraser; Janet Glass; the late Ronald Gow; Lady Selina Hastings; Dame Wendy Hiller; Michael Hucks; Benjamin Jackson; Griffith James; Louisa Lane Fox; Sean Lydon; Ruth McNicoll; Brian Manly; Edward Morgan; Joan Morley; the late Robert Morley, C.B.E.; Professor Charles Nolte; William Osborne; the late John Perry; the late Dorothy Primrose; Nancy Seabrooke; Paul Scofield, C.B.E.; Marjorie I. Sisley; Patrick Spottiswoode; Christopher Taylor; Terry and Debbie Todd; Michael Wickham; Elizabeth Winn; Geoffrey Wright.

Gerald and Lucy Cadogan kindly let me stay for long periods at their house in Northamptonshire where, with three writers working in different rooms, the atmosphere was both peaceful and stimulating.

The late Robert Flemyng gave me permission to include an unpublished article (written in 1962) about his involvement with the first production of John Whiting's *Marching Song* (Appendix III). It is an important account for any student of Whiting, and I am glad it can now be read.

I am grateful to the following for allowing me to quote from correspondence to which they hold the copyright: Robert Bolt, C.B.E., for his letters to Frith Banbury and Sir Michael Redgrave; John Casson, O.B.E., for letters from his mother, Dame Sybil Thorndike, C.H.; Clarissa Dennison for letters from her father, Wynyard Browne; Bryan Forbes for letters from Dame Edith Evans; Rachel Kempson for letters from her husband, Sir Michael Redgrave; and Terry Todd for a letter from Rodney Ackland.

I am indebted to Dr. Jeanne T. Newlin, Curator of the Harvard Theater Collection, for permission to use photographs by Angus McBean from the Harvard College Library, and for her friendliness and encouragement.

The Trustees of the Victoria and Albert Museum gave me permission to reproduce the photograph of *Love's Labour's Lost* by Houston Rogers from the collection in the Theatre Museum.

My deepest gratitude must be reserved for Barbara Jones, who, out of the goodness of her heart alone, typed, re-typed and disked-up this book. During the many hiatuses, when I had to leave off writing and earn my living, her enthusiasm kept my motivation alive. It is as much her book as mine, and to her it is dedicated with my fondest love.

Every effort has been made to obtain permissions from the owners of copyright material both illustrative and quoted. If there have been any omissions in this respect, the publishers and author offer their sincere regrets and will be pleased to ensure than an appropriate acknowledgement will appear in any future edition.

* * *

I would like to thank my student and godson Henry Young, for his assistance in the preparation of this updated edition. And I remember Christopher Taylor (1928-2008) who, suffering from Alzheimer's survived Frith by just three months.

C.D.
London, 2021

Preface

i

In 1983, Frith Banbury, having directed a play in America, returned with a cassette tape of an interview he had given for a radio station in Minnesota. This interview, which largely concerned the relationship between director and playwright when working on a new script, had obviously crystallised many of his thoughts about the task of directing plays and, for a man who seldom looked back, stimulated his memory and rekindled interest in his past work. Wanting to expand on what he had said in the short American interview, he asked me if together we could record some conversations which would cover both his past career and present feelings about actors, writers, and the theatre in general. His interest in himself, and my fascination in what he had to say, exceeded our initial expectations, and soon there were twelve hours of taped reminiscence.

Concurrently, in 1983, I was asked by one of the London drama schools to work with their students on some scenes from modern plays. The year concerned in this exercise was divided into two groups, and as the director of the other group had already chosen all the obvious scenes from Osborne, Wesker, Pinter, Beckett, Delaney, Orton, Stoppard and Ayckbourn, with a certain trepidation I decided to go back before *Look Back in Anger*, and take some scenes from Wynyard Browne, N.C. Hunter and Terence Rattigan. What astonished me was that where my generation would have found these writers and their world dated, students of the 1980s found an easy emotional identification with the characters' situations and made little distinction (besides the obvious one of social class) between the worlds of N.C. Hunter and Arnold Wesker. When I told them about the West End-Royal Court divide they seemed quite puzzled.

It struck me then how long students of the theatre had accepted the English Stage Company's verdict on the state of writing in the then contemporary West End: that the plays were cosy, middle class, seldom telling the truth about real problems, and never challenging an audience. A theatre dominated by light comedies and thrillers. I wondered whether such an opinion had become outmoded; if the pre-Royal Court playwrights could be re-assessed, and whether that re-evaluation could be combined with an account of the life and work of a man connected with nearly every theatrical protagonist of that period: Frith Banbury.

I am of the generation influenced by the Royal Court, as indeed are most of the drama critics now writing, but these critics, because of a new interest during the 1990s in the plays of Rattigan – and, to a lesser extent of Rodney Ackland – are beginning their own reassessment. The critic of *The Daily Telegraph*, reviewing Enid Bagnold's *The Chalk Garden* – not, in my view, a particularly distinguished example of a 1950s play – conceded that the production offered 'further persuasive evidence that there was far more vitality in the English theatre before the arrival of the angry young men and the Royal Court revolution than is generally acknowledged'.

My premise is simple: without underrating or denigrating the importance of any writer of the English Stage Company, many of their hypotheses about the state of the West End were wrong; that the standard of individual acting was very high, and that its playwrights knew more about the human heart and wrote with greater literacy than many of their successors of the late 1950s and 1960s.

As early as 1968 the theatre historian Allardyce Nicoll was writing in *English Drama, A Modern Viewpoint;* 'It is, therefore, certain that future historians will find themselves forced to consider more than what the New Wave authors have offered during the period between 1956 and 1966.' In other words that there was another theatrical movement running alongside the angry young men. Playwrights, the most notable being Robert Bolt, who knew their Brecht as well as any; whose left-wing credentials were just as unassailable, but who preferred to have their work staged in the Commercial Theatre. The founding of the two big subsidised companies may have taken away the power of the West End managements, but interesting new plays were still to be found in the West End, and can sometimes be seen there still.

Why choose Frith Banbury as exemplifying the kind of theatre I am considering? Although relatively unknown outside the profession, he was an archetype of that era. An actor during the 1930s, an important director and manager of the late 1940s, '50s and '60s, Banbury is now, in his eighties, that theatre's sole *active* representative. Representative because he was never assimilated into the national companies, never directed films, and always found his place of work in the unsubsidised West End theatre. He played a leading part in every movement within that movement, and has been a close friend as well as colleague of every famous manager, writer and actor connected with it. Bryan Forbes, in his biography of Dame Edith Evans calls him 'a man who has never received proper recognition for his significant contribution to the post-war theatre', and Sam Walters of the Orange Tree Theatre, Richmond said publicly that his name was synonymous with West End excellence. Indeed to read in a published playscript, 'The Play Produced by Frith Banbury', does encapsulate a world of Binkie Beaumont and glittering first nights at the Haymarket.

Therefore, as a book, *The Best of the West End* is a hybrid: neither formal biography nor straight narrative theatre history. I have used Frith Banbury's career as a focus for the kind of theatre about which I wish to write; as a means of observing the London stage from 1930 to the present, and therefore I only discuss plays with which he was connected either as actor, director, or manager, although many plays in which he appeared and many productions he directed or mounted are necessarily omitted. I deal with what I consider to be the most representative. The benefit of this scheme is that I can concentrate more fully on a smaller number of plays, but in so doing the book becomes necessarily selective. If I lose out by omitting Charles Morgan, Enid Bagnold, or the later works of R.C. Sherriff, I hope I gain by being able to spend more time considering two of the best English playwrights of the century: Wynyard Browne and Rodney Ackland.

Frith Banbury was not a director on the world stage like his hero Tyrone Guthrie, nor an innovator of theatrical forms like Peter Brook. Yet any glance at the commercial theatre of the twentieth century will find him somewhere. He has always been connected with the best. Not a leading actor, but one never out of work; a very good rather than a great director, and one whose skill and insights have been trusted by some of the most considerable artists of the age: under his aegis they were able to produce some of their finest work. As a manager he was, most notably, a spotter of new playwrights but he also had the boldness to follow his own enthusiasms rather than the dictates of commercial profit. His lifelong love – indeed obsession – with the theatre has made him an absolute connoisseur of good acting and truthful writing. His life is the thread that runs through this book, and although I tell it with selectivity, I tell it with enthusiasm and as a celebration. The theatre of the last sixty years would have been a much poorer place without him.

I have drawn, perforce fairly extensively, on contemporary newspaper criticism, especially from the two great critics of *The Observer* and

The Sunday Times. One of the surprises I have had while preparing and writing this book was how my admiration for the judgements of the late Kenneth Tynan declined in inverse proportion to my ascending respect for the opinions of the late Sir Harold Hobson. Hobson's enthusiasms were to my generation something of a joke, while Tynan was a god. Yet Hobson seems to view the theatre from a more elevated vantage-point and to write about it with a love that, in hindsight, has made his opinions – and his predictions – more often right than wrong; while Tynan, supremely elegant writer of prose though he undoubtedly was, was so relentlessly fashionable and proselytising, that his perceptions were often limited and his assessments sometimes obsolete. Hobson was more universal because he was free from the stricture of being in the vanguard of fashion, and he had by far the greater insights into the workings of humanity. So it will be found that more weight is given to his opinions than has been usual in books about the recent past of the British theatre.

I am also aware that it is not strictly correct to refer, as I have done, to the producing firm of H.M. Tennent Ltd, as 'Tennents', but as this is what it was nearly always called by those inside the theatre, I have chosen the colloquial course. Because it seemed less pedantic, I also often refer to theatres informally: the Phoenix, the New, the Queen's etc. without the noun 'theatre' attached.

My gratitude to Frith Banbury for allowing me to write a book, many of whose opinions he is bound to question, is immense; just as his influence on my life and thought has been immeasurable. I stress: the story I tell will be his; the analysis and conclusions mine.

ii

Where the Royal Court or Joan Littlewood and her Theatre Workshop did certainly leave their mark was in bringing back to the theatre an audience which was unfamiliar with life as it was lived in drawing rooms: a working-class audience newly educated by the post-war Welfare State. For the previous century, plays had usually dealt with themes particular to the middle class, because such was the audience for which they were being performed. Although that audience was prepared to laugh at, or even sympathise with its inferiors, the people it wanted to see on stage were its social equals or betters, and actors were needed who could play them convincingly. As early as 1831, the Garrick Club had been founded with the intention of putting players and patrons onto the same social footing, and later Sir Henry Irving (the first Theatrical Knight) had recruited 'deeply interested and earnest young men of good education and belongings' from the two major universities into his company at the Lyceum, so by the end of the nineteenth century the theatrical 'profession' had become middle-class and respectable. It was also one of the only professions where a woman could have a successful career, which led to many of the most interesting women of the time becoming actresses.

The social order depicted in most plays had not changed by 1930, and the theatre still required middle or upper-class actors and actresses, or that those born into the lower-middle or working class should develop the accents and manners of ladies and gentlemen.

Looking at the paternal occupations of many young actors at the end of the 1920s or the beginning of the 1930s, it seems that the paradigm of the kind of young man who entered the theatre at that date had a father in one of the Services or Professions. A father who, although he may have been unsympathetic to his son's choice of career, would have had to admit that the theatre now harboured gentlemen leading prosperous lives. Although homosexuality was illegal, the young actor was entering a profession where it was fairly tolerated, because of the increasing number of homosexuals who seem to have entered the theatre since the First World War:

'The fact that he was homosexual and went into the theatre,' said Robert Morley about Frith Banbury, 'was a protest against his father. Most people in my day went on stage to annoy their parents.' Well, yes; and having made that protest and annoyed their father they wanted to prove the father's disapproval wrong by doing well and finding security. Also, because most people deep-down want their parents to be proud of their achievements, they then strive to prove to them that their choice of life is respectable and sound, and so reassure those parents.

My paradigm was born at Plymouth Hoe in Devon, on May 4th 1912 and was christened Frederick Harold Frith Banbury; his father a Captain in the Royal Navy, his mother a rich Australian Jewess. The story of the London Theatre from 1930 to 1960 and after, can be seen through his life and work.

Introduction

Deeply Interested and
Earnest Young Men

Both Frith Banbury's grandfathers were crooks; his paternal, rather a pathetic 'bad lot', served a six year prison sentence in Australia for forging a cheque for four pounds; his maternal, B.J. Fink, with more aplomb, went bankrupt for two million pounds, which in 1892 was the largest figure then recorded by the Australian receivership.

Both men, who naturally never met, may have drifted to Australia to commit their misdemeanours, but their backgrounds could hardly have been more markedly unlike. The Banburys had originally been Warwickshire yeomen who distinguished themselves in a moderate way; for instance one of them became Mayor of Coventry. By the middle of the last century they were living in London, in the middle-class respectability of Westbourne Grove. Frith's grandfather Banbury wished to marry a Miss Tippetts, of Highbury. Many years later Frith discovered a letter from his great-grandfather to her father: '. . . my son is no good. He is an idler and a drinker. If he has led your daughter to believe, my dear sir, that he is to inherit money, I regret to inform you . . . ' Notwithstanding this ominous warning, Miss Tippetts did foolishly marry Mr Banbury, and they had a son who was Frith's father. Soon he left his wife and child; drifted to Australia where he served the aforementioned prison sentence, and on his release, rather surprisingly ran a magazine connected with the church; but his father had been right, he was No Good. There were other short terms of imprisonment, and eventually he killed himself. Back in England, Mrs Banbury brought up her son alone. As a boy of twelve she sent him into the navy as a midshipman (a 'snotty'), and his whole life was to be spent in that Service, completing his successful career as a Rear-Admiral. As a child, Frith never once remembers Admiral Banbury mentioning his own father.

His mother's family, the Finks, could not have been more different. The brothers Moses and Hirsch Fink were Jews from Lvov, then in Russia, who, in the 1840s walked across Europe, one of them earning money by playing the fiddle. Arriving in St Peter Port, Guernsey where there was already a community of Jewish tradesmen, they opened a tailor's shop. In 1856 they unsuccessfully set up their business in London, and in 1863 went to Australia to Geelong near Melbourne, Victoria, where they had much more luck. Their children married each other: Moses's son B.J. marrying his first cousin, Hirsch's daughter, Catherine.

B.J. initially did very well and made a great deal of money. He seems to have been an astute and cunning man with no ethics in his business dealings. He clearly foresaw his bankruptcy; for when the crash came he was only required to repay his creditors a halfpenny in the pound. Nearly all his assets were in his wife's name. He was known as 'Farthing Fink'.

When, one infers, there were not many people left in Australia prepared to do business with him, he came back to London and continued his shady dealings; always remaining just ahead of the law, and thus holding on to most of his money.

B.J. and Catherine had a daughter to whom they gave the very un-Jewish name of Winifred, who in 1910 decided to spend some of her inheritance on a trip around the world.

Wintering in Jamaica, she went to a dance and met Lieutenant Commander Banbury. She accepted his proposal of marriage because he was a straight Englishman, as far removed as could be from all the Jewish emotionalism of her upbringing. There were two children from the marriage; Frith, and six years later, a daughter, Joan.

It was not a love-match, the difference in their backgrounds and outlooks providing very little in common. It is intriguing to find in Frith's letters to his mother how free he felt to mock and ridicule his father, so he must have assumed that she at least half-shared his views; but she would apparently always say with loyalty if no great originality: 'He is as honest as the day is long.'

Frith's feelings for his father were obviously deeply complicated. Without laying on psychology too heavily, it must have been his early sense of inadequacy at being so unlike the son his father expected to have, that made him cast Admiral Banbury as a character from a farce: a bigoted, philistine buffoon; full of quarterdeck expressions, completely baffled when up against any view remotely different from his own. This is a defensive act put up by many adolescent boys. A stage they go through of despising their father and making him and his values into a joke. In his eighties, Frith still holds on to this stage and the joke, and his imitation of the Admiral, with the ludicrous observations he made when faced with the theatre and its participants is very funny. A contemporary of Frith's just remembers the Admiral as 'red faced and bluff'.

But his father exerted a strong influence as well: on Frith's voice, his manner to subordinates when exasperated, on his chin-up-and-let's-get-on-with-it attitude to setback, and, according to Marjorie Sisley, his secretary for many years, 'his really frightening temper'.

On one hand there was a genuine wish to rebel and get as far away from his father and all he stood for as possible, on the other, there was a desire, however subconscious, to emulate that father and to be approved of by him.

In 1914, two years after Frith's birth, his father went off to the War where he saw active service at the Battle of Jutland, after which he was posted to the Far East. On his return, when the war was over, he found a namby-pamby little boy who had been brought up by his wife and mother-in-law: two Jewish ladies, who he considered had 'spoiled' his son by teaching him all the wrong things. Frith, however, considers his father's absence to have been his salvation: 'Had he been around for my first six years and tried to have me brought up his way, I might have turned out a mess.'

Did he want Frith to follow him into the navy? Frith says no: 'He thought it would be a great disadvantage to the navy. He had too much respect for the navy to want this boy to go into it.'

Unlike her husband, Winnie Banbury was genuinely artistic and the 'wrong things' taught to Frith included piano lessons, which he began at five and at which he showed promise, for he was to develop into a gifted amateur pianist; the piano remaining to this day his greatest recreation and comfort. At six he was taken to his first play *Joy Bells*, at the Hippodrome and at seven given a toy theatre. On receiving this present, 'I knew what I wanted to do. From then on the theatre's been a religion to me. Some people have got Christianity. I've got the theatre.'

At his prep. school, he was an oddball, bad at games and consequently bullied, so the theatre became his consolation.

'The intensity of my obsession was a secret between me and myself. There was something to look forward to that 'these people' knew nothing about. I knew absolutely and for certain where I was going to end up. This knowledge carried me through my childhood. It could be said to have had a religious dimension to it – still has.'

Because prep. school had not worked, the Admiral decided to send

Frith to Stowe, the new liberal public school in Buckinghamshire whose headmaster was the flamboyant J.F. Roxburgh. There he found another like-minded boy to discuss Life, Death and the Theatre. His name was Geoffrey Wright, and later he became the composer of many successful songs for revues including the popular "Transatlantic Lullaby".

Geoffrey Wright had theatrical antecedents; his great-grandmother, Mrs Theodore Wright, had created Mrs Clandon in *You Never Can Tell,* and was the first English Mrs Alving in *Ghosts.* At Stowe he and Frith rivalled each other in female roles; Frith's greatest triumph playing Celestine, the maid, in a French farce. Geoffrey also designed sets and costumes and wrote songs, of which one was a number for seven matrons called "Matrons 'til Judgement Day".

There were other friends: Peter Willes, later mentor of Joe Orton when Head of Drama at Associated Rediffusion, and Patrick Beech, grandson of the famous Mrs Patrick Campbell. The school did a production at the Steiner Hall in London, and afterwards Mrs Campbell, large and *decoltée,* took Patrick and Frith out to dinner. Some months later she said to her grandson,

'What happened to that strange boy? He seemed to laugh every time I opened my mouth!'

One of Roxburgh's reports read: 'He ploughs a lonely furrow.' At this the Admiral summoned Frith to his study:

'You know what this means? It means that the other boys don't like you.'

'But, Father, I thought it meant that I didn't like the other boys.'

*

Frith was lucky that then, as later, he had the support of a doting mother, but during his early adolescence, his bad relationship with his father, and his unpopularity with many at school, were obviously making him unhappy.

Fortunately for him at this time he met his first real actor, Mrs Campbell being considered simply a friend's grandmother.

A family friend, knowing of his adoration of the theatre, introduced him to the son of her local Rector in Muswell Hill, an actor in his mid-twenties called Denys Blakelock.

From his autobiography *Round the Next Corner*, and from all accounts, Blakelock seems a most sympathetic man. He was then in a play called *Insult* at the Apollo Theatre and Frith used to go into his dressing room and 'grizzle about my father, and say the only thing I wanted to do was be an actor. Denys was so sweet to me and nice.'

He was also an excellent actor, better than anybody, Frith thinks, as Pinero's *The Magistrate,* but he was emotionally tortured. He suffered cruelly from claustrophobia which forced him to leave the stage in his forties, and become a successful and much loved teacher at R.A.D.A. He later directed Frith in *A Trip to Scarborough,* and wrote of him in his autobiography:

'In the Sheridan, Frith Banbury gave a highly amusing and accomplished performance of Lord Foppington. I remember Frith as almost the only actor I know to whom one could speak the absolute truth without beating about the bush, which made directing him doubly pleasurable. Some years later, after the war, positions were reversed. Frith Banbury, by then manager and producer, directed me, when I took over from Ernest Thesiger in *Always Afternoon,* by Dido Milroy at the Garrick Theatre. I hope he found me as easy to deal with.'

He did. Those early heart-to-hearts between the fourteen-year-old boy and twenty-five-year-old professional actor had created a bond.

The other reason for Blakelock's emotional torture was that he was both a devout Roman Catholic convert, and a homosexual. He had a *nostalgie de la boue,* but his excursions into that gutter caused him great guilt and shame. That was not a subject they discussed however and it would not have been a conflict that Frith shared.

However hard I have tried to find otherwise in Frith's view of himself as emotionally secure sexually, I cannot. He truly seems to be a most un-neurotic and well adjusted homosexual man. Unlike Denys Blakelock he has never been attracted to sleaziness, and has never gone 'cruising'. All his sexual relationships have been the result of social contact followed by friendship.

Why was this? While at prep. school, the headmaster mildly interfered with him and some of the other boys. Instead of causing a trauma, Frith says that afterwards he felt sex to be neither wrong nor dirty. It seems to be one of the few things in his schooldays that he accepted because it was sanctioned by authority. And, of course, considering that homosexuality was illegal for a large part of his active sex life, Frith was lucky to be in a profession where it was tolerated.

By now the Banburys lived in London, renting houses in the country for the summer holidays, and Frith began to go to the theatre in earnest and to record his visits in scrapbooks, leatherbound and green. Not just the programmes and paraphernalia of his own theatre-going, but meticulously cut-out and pasted newspaper articles, reviews and press photographs; assiduously listed records of tours; West End openings and lengths of runs, all in a small, neat, dip-penned hand.

The plays are largely light comedies, thrillers, and musicals, with some visits to the Old Vic, and to Stratford which was near Stowe.

The literary standard of the theatre in the twenties was not generally very high, apart from Maugham, Lonsdale and the young Coward. Even Shaw had passed his peak. The provincial public, on the whole, seemed to prefer Matheson Lang in *The Chinese Bungalow* or *Carnival* to anything more substantial, while, in London, there was always Sir Seymour Hicks, who Frith remembers as a fat decrepit *flâneur,* leching after nubile young girls whom he chased around the stage.

At Stowe, Frith's strongest academic gift was for modern languages, and he later became almost fluent in French and German. On trips to Paris, and later staying with a family in Germany, he saw some contemporary European Theatre, although I suspect the greatest impression was left on him by the French *diseuses, chanteuses,* and *flâneurs* like Mistinguett, Alice Delysia and, most of all, Charles Trenet, whose songs he would use in his own revue career.

The reaction against the Admiral did, however, produce one act of defiance which became a moral conviction: at fourteen he refused to join the Officer Training Corps.

A former army chaplain called Rev. Dick Sheppard, who had become a convinced pacifist after witnessing mutilation and death in the trenches, had started a movement whose spirit was beginning to influence the generation brought up in the twenties, many of whose fathers or even elder brothers had been killed in the Great War. Over the next few years, Frith's moment of rebellion became a fundamental belief. When Sheppard founded the Peace Pledge Union in 1935, Frith became one of the original members, carrying the signed card renouncing war. Later as a Conscientious Objector, Frith's early and official association with pacifism was to carry some weight; for his sincerity could hardly be questioned.

Like many who became authority figures themselves, Frith does not take kindly to authority in others. If serving under Military Law was rejected because of the Admiral, so also, was God.

Religion is strongly associated in Frith's mind with the organised Christianity of his childhood, whose hierarchy and dogma were obviously distasteful to him. He does not like other people giving him moral rule books.

Prayer has an even worse association. As a small boy he had to kneel and pray while his nursemaid Goodie, sat on the bed; 'I'm afraid she had a smelly cunt, so I never liked saying my prayers,' he says.

It could be argued here that his adolescent dismissal of what was held to be received truth has been less happy. He has the humanitarian's disinterest in spiritual belief. If anyone he likes or admires has a deep religious faith, or worse still becomes involved with any form of mysticism, then it is treated as an aberration; a 'silly side' to be gently laughed at and not taken into serious consideration when assessing that person's character or work. I think Frith feels only those disappointed with this life need a belief in the next.

He is not by temperament an introspective man. On his own admission he is an instigator and taker of action rather than a ponderer. The benefit is that he has more certainties than most, fewer doubts and very little melancholy. A single-minded love of the theatre is all he has found necessary. This may be a passion but it is a limited faith. Frith has never moved on from God as a judgemental authority figure. His teenage rejection of God was too tied up with rejection of his father.

The Admiral did do one thing pleasantly, however, and that was to ask him to go to Oxford, when Frith was impatient to enter the theatre. 'I went to Oxford because my father asked me nicely,' he says. Although not nicely enough it seems for him to stay there for very long.

At Hertford College he was due to read Modern Languages, but after half the Michaelmas term he was in trouble for doing too little work and was sent for by the Dean who, trying to be helpful, suggested he might be happier living out of college. That was a great mistake. Frith took rooms in St Giles and now did hardly any work at all. When asked how he spent his time, he says, 'I went to parties.'

It was Oxford of 1930, at the end of the Depression and just after that period we think we know from *Brideshead Revisited*. At these parties he met a more successful undergraduate called Terence Rattigan. They were in a production of Flecker's *Hassan* together, with Frith doubling as the Fountain Ghost and Willow, the servant.

At the end of his first year, in the summer of 1931, he came down for good, and in the autumn enrolled at what people who went to it before the war still call *the* R.A.D.A.

Training with Joan Littlewood

Kenneth Barnes, the fifty-three-year-old Principal of the R.A.D.A., was the younger brother of the two successful and distinguished actresses, Violet and Irene Vanbrugh. The Academy had been founded in 1904 by Sir Herbert Beerbohm Tree, to give young actors the technical training that, coming from Amateur Dramatic Societies, he felt he lacked himself.

Violet Vanbrugh had been Tree's Queen Katherine and Lady Macbeth at His Majesty's, and her brother's appointment as Principal in 1909 may have owed something to this connection.

Violet Vanbrugh had her critics, especially the young, who laughed at her enormous feet and her tendency to sentimentalise on stage; and so too did her brother. They claimed – and this was to last until the 1950s – that he ran R.A.D.A. like a finishing school with far too much emphasis on articulation, 'the R.A.D.A. Voice'. Yet Barnes was an educator, not just a trainer. During the seven term course, there were classes in art history and acting in French, as well as in the more usual subjects, such as speech, poetry and dancing. There was only one other drama school of any note, Elsie Fogerty's Central School for Speech Training and Dramatic Art, so Barnes's control over who entered the theatrical profession was enormous. He did his job honourably if not imaginatively, and few begrudged him his knighthood of 1938.

For many years the staff of the R.A.D.A. consisted for the most part of reasonably successful actors and actresses, some out of work, some in plays running in the West End, with visiting stars giving what today we would call masterclasses: Sybil Thorndike on Greek Tragedy for instance.

The member of staff Frith seems to remember best was Stella Campbell, daughter of Mrs Pat and mother of his Stowe school friend, Patrick Beech. She was a moderately successful actress whose most noted performance had been in a play about Napoleon called *A Royal Divorce*, ('Not Tonight Josephine', is a curtain line).

'Fetch me me sable tippet,' she would intone from this play, 'that I may receive her as befits a Queen!'

Frith's year at R.A.D.A. was rather distinguished. Stephen Haggard was considered the greatest talent; Shaw, and others, thought Haggard the best actor of his generation and his Marchbanks in *Candida* and Fool in Granville Barker's production of *King Lear* are still spoken of highly. His early and mysterious death in a train going to Damascus in the War was considered a great loss. His memorial, *The Craft of Comedy,* which he wrote with Athene Seyler, is one of the best books ever written about acting.

There was also Joan Littlewood, who remained a friend, although many people must have thought that the Theatre Workshop represented the exact opposite of all that Frith was seen to stand for in the 1950s. Leueen MacGrath was another friend for life, and also a 'bouncy English girl', the daughter of the Headmaster of Dartmouth Naval College, called Rachel Kempson. The Academy was so short of boys, that in an internal exercise Rachel played Horatio to Frith's Hamlet.

'She was very pretty, and got taken almost at once to Stratford where she played Juliet – not very well in my view. The interesting thing about Rachel's acting is that she didn't come into her own until well into her middle age. She is now a very much better actress. No she didn't play down her career, it was to a certain extent played down for her. She had three children to bring up.'

His schoolfriend Geoffrey Wright remembers Frith's traumatic death scene in Ibsen's *The Pretenders,* 'It seemed to last forever,' and Nancy Seabrooke the actress and stage-manager, who was in the following year, thought highly of him as the murdered husband in *Thérèse Raquin,* and very funny in a duologue with Julia Crawley, in a students' entertainment, which was written by themselves, and which won a prize.

The Academy gave a plethora of these prizes and medals, which were listed in *The Times* as if they were university degrees. In the final term the Bossom Prize for English speech was won by Joan Littlewood and Stephen Haggard, and the Irene Vanbrugh Prize for Acting in French, by Stephen Murray and Frith.

R.A.D.A. retained its influence on Frith's life. It was Sir Kenneth Barnes asking him to direct there in 1946 that led to his changing over from actor to director; and, for over twenty years, from the early 1960s, he was a member of the Council.

Frith left R.A.D.A. in the early summer of 1933. Was he still a paradigm for the young actor of the 1930s? In one sense he was, and remained, very untypical: he had more money than most. Not, in those days, great riches, but an allowance from his Fink grandmother which paid the rent, and ensured the next meal. That he has never known the poverty which is the lot of most young actors meant that a most disagreeable pressure and worry was removed. Removed too was the shared experience with the majority.

Of course he was not unique. Friends like Peter Bull and Robert Morley were in roughly the same position with small allowances from their families. Also, because during his fourteen years as an actor he was seldom out of work, and because he never lived over-ostentatiously, his financial good fortune was not that noticeable.

Theatre people are not usually envious of others having their own money if they are good at their job, and generally Frith has not been resented; but all the people I talked to when writing this book, mentioned him having money, and the subject needs to be dealt with now.

Only one actor actually said, 'He bought his way into directing,' and the answer is that yes he did, but with a sum of money most working actors could have afforded in 1947: a hundred pounds for a six month option on Wynyard Browne's *Dark Summer*.

Afterwards in 1949, when he wanted to go into management and present Basil Thomas's *Shooting Star,* his mother gave him ten thousand pounds. That money, which was invested in further productions and kept Wynyard Browne on contract, lasted until he inherited more at her death in 1960, after the period when some people had considered him so rich. Money may have eased his way in, but clearly he would not have been the West End's most important director for a decade, and one of its most senior for twenty years after that, if he had been no good.

There was also a rumour in the past that he was personally mean: unwilling to put his hand in his pocket, and it certainly led to some stories: Robert Flemyng meeting Peter Bull in the street said he was off to dinner with Frith Banbury, which elicited the reply, 'I hope you're taking iron rations'.

The rumour seemed so false to me that I wondered how it could have originated. His secretary of those days, Marjorie Sisley, thinks it could be because in the heat and bustle which surrounds a first night he forgot to tip the stage staff which was then common practice, and at the end of the run people like the stage-door keeper, 'He was always in too much of a hurry'. When Marjorie realised this was arousing adverse comment she would give the Company Manager an envelope containing money of Frith's for distribution. That is surely an understandable oversight from a man who was usually manager or part-manager as well as director.

The truth is that Frith has shown very marked generosity with money during his life. Not a soft touch, and Jewish enough to be carefuland sensible, he has nevertheless given money to countless people undergoing bad patches; and, furthermore, given it surreptitiously. He has also lent a lot of money which has never been repaid and remained ungrudging. If he has had more financial security than many, he has always spent it on the theatre, which is wise, and on his friends, which is kind.

From photographs of that time he was obviously not a *jeune premier*, but his face looks animated and expressive, full of good humour and good nature: his forehead and eyes his best feature, his mouth his weakest; a Jewish face, clearly more Fink than Banbury. Just above average height, and slender, the narrow shoulders give the impression of a physical lightweight. On his own admission, his voice was light too; but he worked hard improving its tone and range and it had a natural flexibility. His delivery was slightly camp, and his accent upper-middle-class theatrical. His voice has always been individual, and many people have imitated it with varying degrees of success.

Like many actors, his character was and is contradictory: sometimes so self-centred that all self-knowledge stops and awareness of his effect on others is non-existent; sometimes so in tune with those around and so sensitive to others' feelings that his perceptions are acute and heightened.

His curiosity is also a driving force. He said recently, 'All my life I've wanted to see what's around the next corner'. When he does not immediately understand and grasp, especially in matters theatrical, the resulting frustration goads him on to even greater curiosity and burrowing for enlightenment. Professionally and privately he is one of nature's deconstructionists.

Because he is not an introspective man he was not, until old age brought time for reflection, a very deep one. But his energy was prodigious and in his passion to share his enthusiasms, nothing was allowed to stand in his way. Like most men with one-track minds, he was very competitive and has remained so in old age, although he harbours the delusion he is not. If he takes offence it is not for long and he. never holds grudges, which denotes basic emotional security. Although not shy he can be socially insecure; talking too much and shouting others down through nerves and self-absorption. But he is sensitive too, easily sheds tears, and, since a bad case of food poisoning after the war, can suffer from stomach cramps when under stress. When his companions and colleagues of those early days remember him it is for being great fun. It is a good way to be remembered.

Part One

An Actor in the Thirties

The Worst Unicorn I Ever Had

Frith Banbury did not spend his early years as an actor with provincial repertory companies, but as a small-part player in grand productions, and a leading actor in smaller club performances. There were, it is true, three summer seasons at Perranporth in Cornwall, but that was a thing apart: a repertory of plays performed with a group of friends, and with what we would now call a profit-share at the end of the season rather than a weekly salary. Later on as an influential manager and director he was to advise many young actors to 'Go into rep. and get some experience', but it was not a path he took himself. This was partly because there was no need: jobs in the West End arrived regularly, and partly because his one effort to join a major provincial theatre came to nothing.

There was, of course, an enormous provincial theatrical network, and some theatres like William Armstrong's Liverpool Rep., or Sir Barry Jackson's Repertory at Birmingham exerted influence by providing the West End with new acting talent but not, by the early thirties, with many new plays of note. Repertory Theatres usually made do with the year-before-last's West End successes because last year that success had been on an extended provincial tour with the play's copyright unreleased. What was new in the theatre of the 1930s happened in the West End, and the British Theatre became increasingly centralised.

Gladys Cooper had relinquished her tenure of the Playhouse Theatre in 1933, the year of Frith's *début,* and with that the du Maurier era was really brought to an end; when acting was done thoroughly, professionally and without fuss. For recreation there were weekend tennis parties in Hampstead Villas, or rounds of golf at houses near Sunningdale. Sometimes there were three matinees a week and no performance on Monday night, and the impression is somehow one of professionalism and dilettantism at the same time.

Sir Gerald du Maurier must have been the supreme sophisticated naturalistic actor; twin master of both authority and repose; but he was also a snob: he liked public school men in his company and he was not over fond of homosexuals. Earlier in his career he had been associated with some fine new writing: his Dearth in J.M. Barrie's *Dear Brutus,* and mute butler in the same author's *Shall We Join the Ladies?* displayed a range of characterisation and a depth of emotion that he hardly needed for *Bulldog Drummond.* Gladys Cooper too had presented and played in Maugham's *The Letter* and *The Sacred Flame* at the Playhouse as well as in frivolities like *Cynara.*

These two were fundamentally Edwardians; but Barrie, Maugham and Lonsdale had really had their day. The hope of the Commercial Theatre was Noel Coward, just as John Gielgud, since his Old Vic Season of 1929, was the hope of the Classical.

Ten days after leaving R.A.D.A., at the beginning of June 1933, Frith was at the Shaftesbury Theatre rehearsing for a play whose slightness was belied by its original title: *Hard To Be a Jew.* This was written by Sholom Aleichem (whose short stories were to become the basis for the musical *Fiddler On the Roof),* and was being mounted as a vehicle for Gus Yorke, one half of the American double act in *Potash and Perlmutter.* On becoming a straight actor he had grandified his first name to Augustus. Now Hitler was in power, it was pointed out that the title suggested a more serious political piece, and might thus lose the audience who came for light entertainment; so it was changed to *If I Were You,* which meant nothing at all and it closed after ten days. Frith was little more than a walk on; the Banbury career had not exactly started off with a bang.

It did, however, bring him the friendship of another walk-on; a heavily built young man of his own age, the brother of a baronet, of pugnacious countenance, aptly called Peter Bull. His nature, though, was much gentler and funnier than his appearance. Robert Morley remembers Bull as 'an extraordinarily nice man; a sort of archetypal friend. He had more friends than almost anyone and kept them separate which was sensible.'

Frith's second job, through the mischance of one leading to the good fortune of another, placed him, albeit at a junior level, into the mainstream fashionable theatre where he was to remain for the next thirty years. *Richard of Bordeaux,* by Gordon Daviot *(nom de plume* of Elizabeth MacKintosh who was also the thriller writer, Josephine Tey) was a costume drama about the life of Richard II and his marriage to Anne of Bohemia, with John Gielgud both directing and playing the lead; it was this play that enabled Gielgud to bridge the gap between the Classical and Commercial theatres, and made him a box-office draw. In January 1934, the manager Bronson Albery decided to send it out on tour with Glen Byam Shaw who had understudied Gielgud in London both playing the King and directing, with his wife, Angela Baddeley as Queen Anne.

Frith could still sometimes be self-effacing, and after his first audition he was recalled to be heard again. Before he said his piece, Barney Gordon, the stage-manager, took him aside and advised him to walk onto the stage with more confidence: advice he must have taken, as he was successful playing Sir John Montague and understudying Glen Byam Shaw, as Richard. In the company, there was a large and portly young actor called Robert Morley playing the Duke of Gloucester. It was the beginning of their close but not always tranquil friendship.

After fifteen weeks on the road, Frith had his good fortune. Albery had booked the King's Theatre Hammersmith for a final week and just before it started Glen Byam Shaw became ill and thus Frith played for every performance. On the first night, after his first entrance, he saw a glint of light reflected from an eyeglass in the front row. Rather touchingly, the Admiral had turned up all by himself to see how 'the young one' was coping. Beforehand, Glen Byam Shaw had sent him a note saying; 'Don't worry about the clothes at all,' but Morley clearly thought that he ought to have worried more, considering Frith 'Awful. He couldn't even manage the sleeves. He used to flap them about.'

'Well, what did he *expect*,' said Frith crossly when I told him. 'I was a twenty-one-year-old understudy.'

*

Bronson Albery was pleased enough by what he saw to offer Frith Marcellus in the *Hamlet* which he was presenting for John Gielgud at the Queen's Theatre; but Gielgud thought he was much too young and demoted him to the Courier who announces Laertes's insurrection:

Save yourself my lord,
The ocean, overpeering of his list,
Eats not the flats with more impetuous haste
Than young Laertes, in a riotous head,
O'erbears your officers . . .

'Banbury don't be so prim', said Gielgud the first time he rehearsed it. 'Jack, take the rest of that speech.'

Jack Hawkins as Horatio immediately took up the next seven lines . . . 'The rabble call him lord . . .' Banbury's humiliation was complete.

He put up a black mark again at the technical dress rehearsal, when at the start of Act I, Scene II, the lights went up on the council chamber revealing

Frank Vosper and Laura Cowie, enthroned as Claudius and Gertrude and Gielgud seated downstage, and *in character,* as Hamlet. The Motleys' multi-level set; costumes based on Dürer and Lucas Cranach, was framed by a row of halberd-bearing switzers behind the thrones upstage left, and another of the same downstage right. Banbury, as one of the latter, had missed his entrance:

Though yet of Hamlet our dear brother's death
The memory be green . . .

Frith, unexpectedly, appeared at the topmost level ('I thought I'd be less conspicuous') made his way down a staircase behind the thrones and pushed his way through the court until he had taken up his position. Gielgud took it all in and was very displeased.

For six months; eight performances a week, John Gielgud played *Hamlet,* and for Frith, 'Johnny G's *Hamlet* is a yardstick. It's only when *Hamlet* is so far away from John Gielgud's, like David Warner, that his shadow does not come over it.'

Gielgud himself was only thirty at the time but the younger actors like Frith and Sam Beazley, who was the Player Queen, would stand in the wings night after night, awestruck at the reality of the situation, energetic rhythm and beauty of sound and shape of Gielgud's performance.

'The space between actor and audience was electric,' says Sam Beazley. 'The silence was brilliant.'

*

At this time, there were a number of small theatres which produced plays banned by, or not submitted to the Lord Chamberlain. They circumvented the Licensing Act by turning their premises into private clubs, with membership obtained forty-eight hours in advance. The best known of these was the 'Q' Theatre at the north end of Kew Bridge run by Jack and Beattie de Leon, which produced West End plays, if possible with the London cast; the Torch Theatre, where the Berkeley Hotel now stands, which was known as the Torture because of the discomfort of its seats, and, most influential of all, the Gate in Villiers Street.

There were groups, also, who operated 'Sunday Clubs', playing Sunday night, and sometimes a Monday matinee at any theatre willing and available. These were usually of esoteric plays, either with no likely commercial future or whose subject matter would not pass the Lord Chamberlain's strictures. One of these groups called itself the 1930 Players. Frith lent his talents to them for a play called *Dath, a Study of Early Man*, written by Bertha N. Graham, who had financed the production herself and hired the Fortune Theatre for two performances on Sunday and Monday afternoon. It was set in early Britain with Frith as a Chieftain in woad and skins, with Peter Bull as his retinue.

'Banality beyond belief,' says Frith now. 'The leading lady called herself Emmlienne Terry, in the hope, no doubt, that people would think she was Ellen Terry. We were paid three guineas a performance.'

This piece was directed by Frederick Mellinger, a German refugee, at that time trying to establish a foothold in the English Theatre: 'Mr Banbury,' he implored, 'please! Do not make nonsense with yourself.'

Another refugee was the cabaret singer Valeska Gert, whose strange act had been particularly targeted by the Nazis as the epitome of Jewish decadence: her photograph appeared in Goering's anti-semitic propaganda books. She had been rescued by Robin Anderson, who ran another Sunday Night Club called The Tempest Theatre, who offered her a job in Stefan Zweig's adaptation of Jonson's *Volpone*, which he put on, again, at the Fortune.

Frith played a judge and Valeska Gert, though she spoke not one word of English and had learnt her part parrot fashion, played a prostitute, one of Zweig's additional characters. 'I vill not vear zis dress,' she screamed standing centre stage and tearing off a bunch of detachable material from her red costume.

'I vill not vear zis dress,' and off came another bit, and so on until she was standing in her underclothes. In a later entertainment she dressed up as a baby and stood on stage blowing sherbet bubbles, while Mosco Carner, the world expert on Puccini's operas, banged a gong. She soon moved to New York, where happily she was better appreciated, opening her own night-club, and becoming a figure of New York cabaret.

The Gate Theatre was a different story altogether, and was a highly professional set-up. Norman Marshall was Artistic Director and his Business Manager Enid M. Collett, always known as 'Peter' because of her rocklike reliability.

Marshall had run the Festival Theatre Cambridge, succeeding the innovative Terence Gray, and 'Peter' Collett had been his administrator. They took over the Gate in 1934, from its founder, Peter Godfrey.

The policy was for unlicensed plays like O'Neill's *Desire Under the Elms*, put on in 1931 with Eric Portman and Flora Robson Laurence Housman's,

Victoria Regina, presented there in 1935, and Lillian Hellman's *The Children's Hour,* given its first London production in 1936 with Valerie Taylor; or for translations of European drama like Pirandello's *Six Characters in Search of an Author;* and, its lasting memorial, the Gate Reviews, many of which had West End transfers.

The annual subscription was ten shillings and sevenpence, (the sevenpence for Entertainment Tax). The seats were seven shillings and sixpence at the front; five shillings for the middle, and two shillings and fourpence for the banquettes at the rear. The maximum takings at full house were thirty-two pounds; the actors were paid three pounds a week expenses, no salaries; and the largest profit ever recorded was seventeen pounds. The Gate played Sunday nights because it was then that Jewish people came.

There were theatre companies too, then as always, run by altruistic people who saw theatre as a Social Force; a legacy of William Morris's socialist folk-art: the Poor being exposed to Beauty. The most noted of these was The People's National Theatre run by Nancy Price, which had been founded in 1930, and was by now based at the Little Theatre, Adelphi.

Nancy Price feared no one; not even Mrs Patrick Campbell, whom she had famously stood up to when they had appeared together in *John Gabriel Borkman.* Nicknamed Half-Price because of her parsimony, her curtain speech in her harsh, slightly suburban voice was much mimicked:

'Now, you dear people; look at all the lovely, priceless antiques we have up here on stage,' gesturing to the load of old junk that passed for furniture. 'For an extra half a crown, you can actually come up on stage and *touch* these beautiful objects.'

She seemed to have many disciples, nearly all women of a certain age, who hung around the theatre. One of these brought her a cup of soup every morning. Miss Price was not very grateful: 'Every morning she brings me soup at eleven o'clock, and sometimes I could *throw it in her face!'* she said.

In October 1935, Frith appeared for her in a Swedish play called *The Hangman,* by Pär Lagerkvist. It was being presented by the People's National Theatre for two reasons: the first was that all the money had been put up by a Mrs van der Elst, the second that the play's theme, anti-hanging, suited Miss Price's social beliefs. For the eponymous role she had engaged Frank Vosper.

The first half was Mediaeval and was set in an ale-house where Vosper, as a hangman, felt guilty and brooded. Frith played a yokel. The second was modern and set in a low dive where Vosper, as a hangman, felt guilty and had a very long speech. Frith played an *habitué* of the night-club.

Nancy Price co-directed with Dr Lindtberg from the National Theatre in Stockholm, whither he often returned, leaving Miss Price to change everything that had been rehearsed.

'I want you to play it like *Shakespeare Clown,'* said Dr Lindtberg to Frith.

'What do you think you are *doing?'* shouted Miss Price when the Doctor went back to Stockholm yet again.

'Dr Lindtberg said . . .'

'Well, do what he tells you when he's here, but *don't do it when you come to it.'*

Frank Vosper's boyfriend was Frith's Stowe contemporary, Peter Willes. He attended rehearsals and was dispatched to the back to check audibility.

'Now you've got to speak up everybody,' exhorted Miss Price; 'because Mr Vosper's er . . . er . . . er . . . friend was in the circle and couldn't hear.'

But it was over the black jazz band in the second half, however, that she made her greatest blunder:

'Mr Goring and Mr Glenville stand up. You lot, run down the steps to the table. N***** put down your instruments. Mr Vosper, dear, come downstage.' But there had been a gasp from the whole company. In the ensuing silence the band leader went down into the stalls, had a whispered conversation with Miss Price, then resumed his place. She tried again:

'Mr Goring and Mr Glenville stand up. Musicians do you think you could *possibly* stop playing please . . .'

From photographs, though, the production appears very powerful. Atmospherically grouped and lit, with impressive and effective sets. It also looks modern, rather like a production in a German Theatre during the 1980s.

After *The Hangman,* Frith stayed on: at the Little to play the Unicorn in the People's National Theatre's perennial production of *Alice Through the Looking Glass.*

Some years later, Nancy Price and Robert Morley were guest speakers at a banquet. When Morley, who was talking about some of his contemporaries, mentioned Frith's name, he noticed Nancy Price making a note on her menu. After sitting down, he looked. She had written: 'The worst Unicorn I ever had.'

She must have remembered him differently, however, for in 1962, when in her eighties, she wrote asking him to appear in 'Our Brains Trust', which, rather quaintly was held at the Onslow Court Hotel, Queen's Gate.

She continued: 'I am constantly hearing of you and your wonderful work. I wonder if you ever imagined you would reach the heights you have and (have) such success. I can see you now and remember your *eagerness* and *concentration* on your work. It has stood you in good stead since.'

It was also the last time that he saw Frank Vosper. A while later, crossing the Atlantic with Peter, he disappeared, and his body was never recovered. He had no reason to kill himself, no one saw him fall overboard, and he was too large to have been pushed through a porthole. The truth has never been known, but the incident gave rise to the saying: *'Never cross the Atlantic with Peter Willes'*.

Eagerness and Concentration

Perranporth was the creation of Peter Bull, who sold his friends the idea of the Cornish equivalent of American Summer-stock by promising them a luxurious holiday. There were no salaries, just bed and breakfast, an afternoon meal and a profit-share at the end of the season. Obviously only people able to maintain their accommodation in London could afford to go, and some poorer actors thought the whole project too dilettante for words.

Rehearsals were in Peter Bull's mother's house in Cadogan Square. The company was strong: Robert Morley, Pamela Brown, Pauline Letts, Richard Ainley, Constance Lome, Nicholas Phipps, and Frith were the backbone, and others came and went.

One of Bull's enticements to Perranporth had been the house where, he had implied, they would all be living in 'a leafy mansion with willow trees and a river'. When they arrived they found he had taken a flat above the boot shop.

'Do you all mess together?' asked Admiral Banbury.

In later years they all lived in a villa where Richard Carey, who joined the company for the third season, had to sleep on the sofa and caught lice.

They performed in the Women's Institute Hall, and their first task was to clear out five hundred cups and saucers and wrap them individually in newspaper.

Bull and Morley shared the direction; everyone helped at the box office, and coaxed the locals into lending their furniture and possessions so they could come and see them on stage.

Morley told a story which Frith says is not quite true: 'One day Richard Ainley smashed the set up because he was so irritated by my direction, and we had to persuade the punters to stay away.' At any rate Ainley was the *enfant terrible* of the company, once eating eight eggs at breakfast to annoy Peter Bull who did the cooking.

Morley has said in print that Frith began by playing subsidiary roles, but looking at the programmes this does not seem to be the case. From the start, his parts were at the level of Granillo in Patrick Hamilton's *Rope,* and Algy in *The Importance of Being Earnest.* The plays were performed in repertoire,   .

so all rehearsing was completed early on in the season, and the rest of the list would make an interesting selection for any summer repertory company:

Benn W Levy's *Springtime for Henry,* A.A. Milne's *The Dover Road,* the melodrama, *Maria Marten* and Emlyn Williams' *Night Must Fall.*

The critic of *The New Statesman and Nation* came down to write an article on the company and gave Frith a good revue for his Granillo: 'Mr Frith Banbury has already mastered his technique enough to carry off unsuitable parts and as the weak member of the Leopold and Loeb partnership in *Rope* gave a first rate performance.'

Mrs Banbury and Lady Bull, 'The Mothers' Union', also attended, and whenever their sons appeared on stage the whole row in which they were sitting used to creak forward and the audience, thinking something greatly important was about to happen, paid extra attention.

At the end of the first season. Robert Morley decided that there was no future in acting, gave away his make-up on the last night and planned to concentrate on writing plays, while Frith had a letter from Norman Marshall of the Gate Theatre asking him to be in a play about Oscar Wilde. His character, Eustace, was based on that of Wilde's loyal friend Robert Ross and there were two effective scenes. But Morley said: 'For you of all people to do a homosexual play is very unwise. Don't mess up with it,' and when he saw Frith was going to take no notice went on, 'Your blood be on your head.'

*

The Gate had originally been sent a translation of a French play about Oscar Wilde by Maurice Rostand. Norman Marshall, who knew how litigious Lord Alfred Douglas could be, very sensibly sent him a copy with a letter asking whether he would object. He did, but hopeful as always, that there might be some money in it, replied that if a sympathetic account of his part in the story was presented he might reconsider. By now Norman Marshall was rather taken with the idea of a Wilde play, and as 'Peter' Collett knew the brothers Leslie and Sewell Stokes, he commissioned one from them which was sympathetic to Bosie. Lord Alfred was paid a salary and attended one rehearsal.

Cast in the title role because of his resemblance to Wilde, was a man who had been the secretary of the Philharmonic Society. From the start it was obvious he was going to be appallingly bad. It was a one-man play and that part was not being played.

Ten days before the opening night, Norman Marshall called a company meeting, without the leading man. He asked the cast what their opinion was, and what they suggested he should do.

Understandably, they were deeply embarrassed; but eventually someone was brave enough to say that here they were working for three pounds a week, and what for if the principal role was not going to be properly played.

Marshall thanked them, sacked the secretary of the Philharmonic Society and approached Frank Pettingell, a good fat actor who was thought the only other possible choice. He was not free, and disconsolately another meeting was called.

It was now that Frith spoke up. He had just been acting with a man called Robert Morley. At this Marshall reacted as if struck: 'No! Frightful actor.' He had played Herod in *Salome* for him at the Festival Theatre in Cambridge, 'Simply appalling. He can't do it!'

Morley had indeed been at the Festival Theatre, Cambridge and at the end of the season Marshall had given a toast 'to the worst actor I have ever met,' to which Morley had replied. 'Really, Norman you're going too far. I wasn't going to say you're the worst director, but I will now.'

Frith continued that it was not a question of acting, but a question of personality. He thought he would be amusing, and possibly even moving in the part. There were no other suggestions, so against Marshall's better judgement and because they were so desperate, Morley was telephoned. He took the play, read it over a solitary lunch at Rules, and accepted.

At the end of the first rehearsal, Norman Marshall said to Frith, 'Maybe that man *can* do it. He's got a way with him.' When he returned home, he was rung up by the new leading man: 'It's no good *me* trying to be Oscar Wilde. I must persuade people that Oscar Wilde is like *me*.'

The play was a public talking point and Morley had a personal success although the critics were predictably sniffy, *The Times* actually saying, 'Upon Wilde the artist the play has no comment of importance to make, and of Wilde the man it merely relates what is best forgotten.'

During the run, the American impresario Gilbert Miller came and the result was a Broadway transfer with Morley and a different cast that was partly American. From that came Hollywood, and Morley's subsequent splendid career. And he appreciated Frith's part in it: 'Frith got me the part. Yes, it was entirely Frith.'

*

For 1937, the second year at Perranporth, Morley had written a play for the company called *Goodness How Sad!* It was not his first effort. Two years earlier he had sent *Short Story,* a play about an unsuccessful actress, to Marie Tempest. She said she would accept if the character were changed to that of a successful actress. Morley complied and was presented with a very glamorous cast: Marie Tempest; her husband W. Graham Browne; Sybil Thorndike, A.E. Matthews; Ursula Jeans; Rex Harrison, and Margaret Rutherford; and, directing his first commercial production, an exceptionally tall Northern Irishman called Tyrone Guthrie.

Goodness How Sad! was about a film star who stumbles on a penniless touring company in their lodging house in the Midlands, where also resides Captain Angst (!) and his florid wife who have a performing seal act. The film star falls in love with Carol, the *ingenue* of the company played by Jill Furse, acts for them, saves their fortunes, and departs.

'Not a bad little play and the actors liked it,' said the author in retrospect, and he is right. It is quite amusing, rather charming, and very slight.

Frith played Peter Thropp, the company juvenile, and Morley, who had written the part for him, thought he was very good too.

The following year Peter Bull found the money to present it in London at the Vaudeville with Hugh Sinclair, a fashionable matinee idol as the film star, and with Frith and Jill Furse repeating their original roles. The most important change, and one which was to influence Frith considerably, was that it was re-directed by Tyrone Guthrie; and Morley and Banbury are on full agreement on that subject. Frith says: 'My hero. Rehearsals were always such fun. You trusted him completely and when he gave you one word of praise, which was seldom, it was better than all the good reviews of Agate, Tynan and Hobson rolled into one.'

Morley, who thought Guthrie a 'suppressed homosexual', remembered the time he took over as Professor Higgins in an Old Vic production of *Pygmalion* at a very late stage. They opened in Buxton, and Morley thought he had done wonders considering he had only had a week to rehearse. After the show Guthrie put his head around the door and said, 'Very dull, but I'm sure you'll get better.'

Guthrie became bored easily, and abandoned companies and theatres after starting them off with a bang of triumph, and he never stayed in one place for very long. '*Go home and astonish me in the morning*' was his famous exhortation to actors; inspiring, and to Morley, very sensible, although his interpretation of it was a bit eccentric.

'Actors don't want to do as they're told straight away. Guthrie was the only director to understand that. He used to let it go by and sink in, and then you came back and did what he wanted the next day – or the day after. Guthrie was a god compared to Peter Brook whom I *loathed;* messy, fussy and humourless; a real menace to the theatre. Thank God he went to Paris! But Guthrie, my God, I loved him.'

If Tyrone Guthrie was no respecter of stars, he was a natural leader of men. *Goodness How Sad!* opened on 18 October and the *News Chronicle* thought 'Mr Frith Banbury gives a capital performance,' but far more important than that was a letter from the author, by now playing Oscar Wilde on Broadway: 'Tony (Guthrie) writing of you says quote Frith is excellent and hasn't been sufficiently praised in the press. He really gives both a very sweet and charming and a very professional and efficient show . . . which coming from Tony should make you pretty proud of yourself . . . now, please don't let him, or anyone, know that I have quoted him.'

The play ran for seven months and then played at Wimbledon with Sarah Churchill taking over from Jill Furse. It was the first time Frith had been in a comparatively long run as a Principal and, beginning to feel stale, he thought of two ways to fill his days – and nights – with useful activity, wanting both to keep fresh and to expand his range.

By day he undertook further training with easily the most important figure in his field this century: Michel Saint-Denis.

*

The Compagnie des Quinze, founded by Saint-Denis's uncle, Jacques Copeau, had come to London a few years earlier, presenting the plays of their house dramatist, Andre Obey: *Le Viol de Lucrèce, La Bataille de la Marne,* and *Noé,* and had created an enormous impact on the English Theatre.

Copeau's policy at his original theatre, the *Vieux Colombier,* came from his antagonism to the well-made plays of Scribe and Sardou. This vision was to restore truth and poetry, as he saw it, to the French stage. His results were a synthesis of non-naturalistic theatre. *Noé,* (Noah) was considered remarkable for the liveliness of its actor-animals.

Saint-Denis, who had started as his uncle's stage-manager at the *Vieux Colombier* had by now become director of, as well as one of the actors in the *Compagnie des Quinze.*

Frith was one of the many who was overwhelmed by them. He wrote to Saint-Denis telling him of his fluency in French and offering his services in any capacity whatsoever. He would do anything to be connected with such a movement. Saint-Denis saw him in a tatty bed-sitting room in Kensington. Sitting on the edge of a single bed while Frith sat in the springless armchair, he had been noncommittal. That turned out to be because, after he had successfully produced *Noah* in English with John Gielgud, he was planning to transfer his activities to England where the shadow of his famous uncle, under which he somewhat laboured in France, did not extend.

He held some French acting classes in an upper room at the Old Vic attended by Vera Poliakoff, Marius Goring, Pierre Lefèvre and Frith, all French speakers. Then he opened the London Theatre Studio in Islington and it was there that Frith spent some of his days during *Goodness How Sad!*

Here, Frith says; the atmosphere of studentry 'rather got my goat'. Also there was a spirit of guruism at the L.T.S., which Frith felt Saint-Denis, great trainer of actors and philosopher of the theatre that he undoubtedly was, enjoyed far too much.

Sitting in a chair puffing his pipe and expounding, while a half-circle of young people, many of them professional actors, sat at his feet, was meat and drink to Saint-Denis, but seemed the height of obsequiousness to Frith, the anti-authoritarian.

He felt also that Saint-Denis understood some plays much better than others; so while *The Three Sisters* was the best production of that play he has ever seen, 'a great group performance', *Twelfth Night* was not good despite Peggy Ashcroft's 'lovely Viola'.

'I never worked with him to a finished production, and some people would bash me over the head to hear me talk like this, but the adulation of younger people is not always a good thing. He was too fond of power.'

The rest of his life was, in some ways unsatisfactory. The L.T.S. was closed in one day at the outbreak of war and Saint-Denis became Jacques Duchesne, head of the French Section at the B.B.C., which functioned from a studio so small that Winston Churchill had to sit on the Frenchman's knee to make a broadcast.

From 1946 to 1952, he was general director of the Old Vic Centre, which included the Old Vic School; but that went wrong when Tyrone Guthrie, who had a temporary bee in his bonnet about all drama schools being a waste of time, advised the Governors to close it when expenditure needed cutting: the closure may have been unavoidable but the behaviour of the Governors and the Arts Council was tactless, while the reaction of the school's directors, Saint-Denis, Glen Byam Shaw, and George Devine seems arrogant.

Later, Saint-Denis was appointed director of the *Centre Nationale Dramatique de l'Est* at Strasbourg and was adviser on the founding of other drama schools, including the Julliard School in New York, where, years later, Frith, as a guest director, was intrigued to find how his stock rose when he said he had known the Master: 'It was as if I had said I had known Christ.'

The Little Court that surrounded Saint-Denis was found very hard to take by others besides Frith. Like all caucuses it did not consider that any outsider could be quite serious in their work. As its members included the future directors of the English Stage Company and the Shakespeare Memorial Theatre, as well as some very distinguished actors, some still living, exclusion must have been galling, and Frith was excluded.

Charles Landstone, the Associate Drama Director of the Arts Council had dealings with Saint-Denis and wrote: 'I resented very much the attitude not of Saint-Denis but of his disciples, during the course of those abortive negotiations. It may be that the memory of that incident coloured my views on the (Old Vic) Theatre Centre for a long time.'

Frith thinks the most fruitful time of Michel Saint-Denis's career was at the beginning with the *Compagnie des Quinze,* but it must be accepted that his knowledge and ideas have influenced the way Drama Schools are run – their teaching and time-tables – all over the Western world.

*

At night, after the show, Frith Banbury took up a completely different activity.

The West End was then more like a village. Most actors lived in central London, and consequently more theatre people seemed to have a late-night life.

Earlier that year Frith had been taken to the Players, a small private theatre then situated in King Street, Covent Garden. This had been started by Peter Ridgeway and Leonard Sachs in 1936, originally only for plays. Later they had the idea of asking Harold Scott to put on a Victorian Music Hall.

Scott was a great figure around the West End and had formerly run a song-and-supper room with Elsa Lanchester called The Cave of Harmony. His Music Hall at the Players was so successful that it was decided to make it the mainstay of the evening, and that was the genesis of what came to be called *Ridgeway's Late Joys.* Leonard Sachs was the Chairman, and his largely invented alliterative way of introducing the numbers was so successful that, after the war, B.B.C. Television took the whole package still with Sachs as Chairman, and re-christened it *The Good Old Days.*

West End plays started at 8.15, or 8.30 pm, with the final curtain rarely coming down later than 11.00, so the audience arriving at the Players at about 11.15 could order food and drink and watch the Music Hall which began at 11.45. There was an interval from midnight to 12.15 am and after the second half at about 1.00 there was drinking and dancing until closing time at 3.00.

The audience, to begin with, consisted of actors, writers, artists and their friends; but soon came cafe society, and the arts were rather elbowed out by smart bohemia.

Frith had been having weekly singing lessons since leaving R.A.D.A. and thought 'hopping about' at the Players might be a good antidote to classes with Saint-Denis and acting at the Vaudeville. He paid two guineas to Wendy Toye – who had won a Charleston competition when she was twelve but who was not yet the acclaimed director she became – to stage for him two numbers with which he successfully auditioned for Peter Ridgeway.

He was very successful at the Players, and clearly a hit with customers afterwards. Very 'Cheekie Chappie' he looks too in his programme photograph.

In *Late Joys* he sang a duet with Dorothy Dunkels called 'Sweethearts and Wives', as well as the two songs with which he had auditioned. Ivor Brown of *The Observer* thought, 'Mr Banbury never puts a foot wrong in these "period" gambols.'

*

After the outbreak of war, in the first week of September 1939, all the theatres and cinemas were temporarily closed. A week later they began opening again in safe areas, (which did not include the big cities) at the discretion of local authorities, and by late autumn the West End was functioning again as usual.

It was that period known as the phoney war, with nothing ostensibly happening but some keen and patriotic people already appearing in uniform having volunteered to fight at a non-existent front.

Frith had already registered as a Conscientious Objector against the time his age group received their call up papers.

Robert McDermot and Diana Morgan put on a revue at the Chanticleer Theatre, now part of the Webber-Douglas School, with the brave little title of *Let's Face It*. Frith sang a coster duet with Billie Hill, once a successful soubrette, by then middle-aged. They were two old flower sellers and Frith appeared in drag for the first and last time since his Stoic French maid. He also sang a French solo, *C'est L'amour,* made popular at the *Casino de Paris* by the *flâneur* Charles Trenet. He wore Trenet's trade mark, a straw hat with the front brim turned back, and *Theatre World* thought he put it over with 'point and verve'. It was recorded, and very charming and stylish it sounds.

Jack Davies of the management, Archie Parnell, and Jack Davies and the director and designer, Hedley Briggs were so approving of his singing of *'C'est l'amour'* that they lifted it into their new entertainment, *New Faces.* Frith's face was perhaps not all that new but some of the others were real finds. There was a man who had been running a repertory in Worthing called Bill Fraser; Charles Hawtrey, whose speciality then was female impersonation; Betty Ann Davies, considered a brilliant comedienne who died in her forties; and Judy Campbell, who sang the show's most durable number *A Nightingale Sang in Berkeley Square* – *Vogue* called her 'a strapping creature, with a voice, a personality, a technique, and a future'.

New Faces opened at the end of the phoney war in April 1940 when the *Daily Mail* thought Frith 'an excellent light comedian of whom more will probably be heard', and closed in September at the onset of the Battle of Britain and the air-raids. It then toured without Frith, who was acting at Stratford, and briefly had a second edition at the Apollo when Judy Campbell added the well known "Room Five Hundred and Four" and Frith sang "Europa and the Bull" with words by Nicholas Phipps from Perranporth and music by his schoolfriend, Geoffrey Wright.

The theatres in the safe centres outside London stayed open during the Battle of Britain and in the autumn of 1940 the famous old Shakespearean, Balliol Holloway, took the Shakespeare Memorial Theatre, Stratford-upon-Avon for a season of Victorian plays. Frith was invited to play Horace Bream, the young American, in Pinero's *Sweet Lavender* and, for the second time, Algernon Moncrieff in *The Importance of Being Earnest.*

While he was at Stratford, Frith's age group received their call-up papers and he was summoned to a tribunal in Birmingham to explain his Conscientious Objection.

It is impossible to compute the exact degree of anyone's conscience, but the tribunals who judged Conscientious Objectors often seemed to take it for granted that the defendant was insincere: that he was motivated by cowardice rather than genuine religious or ethical belief. There were religious sects like the Quakers whom it was difficult to gainsay, their belief in pacifism being dogmatic, but theatre people who registered as being unwilling to fight were suspect.

Frith appeared in front of his tribunal well prepared. He had refused to join the O.T.C. at fourteen, was a card-carrying member of the Peace Pledge Union, and Peter Bull, serving in the navy, had written a testimonial to his sincerity. His credentials were unassailable. Also he was twenty-eight and educated. His fellows seemed much younger and in education much poorer.

The august looking gentlemen of the panel looked bored. Most of the boys just repeated the sixth Commandment; but the panel knew their Bible too and could outwit: if the Lord had said 'Thou Shalt Not Kill' in Exodus, he had said other things in other places. These young men were confounded, as their education had not fitted them for argument with august looking gentlemen. Frith had a great advantage in being able to deal with these men on their own level.

He said that he was an Objector on ethical not religious grounds; and was asked whether he was prepared to do farm work. 'Prepared but not equipped', was his reply.

He was registered on condition that he continued being an actor; the only man in the country so categorised.

Other theatre people whose objection was unconditional were much unluckier: Christopher Fry, Wynyard Browne and Michael Gough were enlisted in the Non-Combatant Corps and given a wartime of very disagreeable and tough physical work; David Markham's conscience was disbelieved and he was imprisoned; while William Douglas Home decided to join up in spite of his pacifist beliefs, later refused to obey an order when he thought civilians were in danger, and was cashiered, a misfortune he was to put to good use in prison by writing his play, *Now Barrabas*.

Conchies were not given quite the rough ride in the Second World War that they had been in the First when they had been sent white feathers by outraged Colonels' Ladies; and they were better treated in Britain than America. Also, being in Europe and nearer battle risking death firefighting in the Blitz took away most of the charges of cowardice, but not all. After the War, Esmé Percy put Frith up for membership of the Savile Club. He later heard he had been blackballed, although whether his homosexuality or his Conscientious Objection was the reason he never found out; but considering his proposer was not the only homosexual in the Club at the time, it was probably because he was a Conchie.

There was perhaps more hostility than he was aware: One story doing the rounds was that when someone said, 'Isn't it sad Rex Whistler has been killed in France,' Frith said, 'Oh? Who by?' which, as he points out, if true would make him into a complete idiot.

So he fulfilled his condition and continued acting and still considers his treatment miraculous. 'In no other country in the world would one have been treated as I was.'

Part Two

A Conchie in the
Theatre of the Forties

Revue and After

Intimate revue is difficult to re-create. Its ambitions were modest and it succeeded only when all the sketches and numbers were not only good in themselves but were correctly positioned in the running order. On the printed page, even sketches which were successful in their day, read very lamely. To a world used to *Private Eye* the targets of the satire seem trivial and unimportant and its execution too cautious and tasteful. Indeed comically and musically it suffered from a surfeit of good taste and English politeness. The internal rhyme schemes of the lyrics are sometimes quite clever and witty; the music sometimes has a moderate melodic charm or is fairly skilful *pastiche* or is jolly enough, but to anyone reading the sketches or picking out the tunes on a piano the feeling is often 'so what?' Nothing dates like topicality and slang: Intimate Revue, being full of both, has dated and been superseded by a sharper and more hard hitting television comedy. Sometimes a smile is raised by a *double entendre* so outrageous that it bypassed an innocent Lord Chamberlain's Reader; but, in hindsight, as an entertainment it seems to lack what it strove so hard to achieve: sophistication.

Yet old recordings by Douglas Byng and Beatrice Lillie are being re-issued; and the revue format, which by consensus was both absorbed into television and supplanted by it, is finding new interest with a small but significant caucus largely of young homosexual men. This is of course because of the quality of some of the performers. Byng, for instance, who wrote all his own material, was as camp as camp could be in the days when the Theatres' Act was still in force; and Bea Lillie, even to those too young to have seen her, was a clear comic genius, her inspired zaniness and surreal sense of fantasy remaining a marvel. It was the start too for many talented young people who developed into famous comic performers, and, in the case of Hermione Baddeley and Beryl Reid, into excellent straight actresses too.

The trouble was that Intimate Revue lacked the glamour and sex appeal of the spectacular revues of André Charlot and Charles Cochran – rows of chorus-girls with gorgeous legs, tits and tinsel – and also it lacked the earthiness and gusto of Music Hall, which, to a degree, it tried to incorporate. It was very middle-class, which perhaps is not a valid criticism as there was largely a very middle-class audience watching it. The actor Sam Beazley probably takes its measure best when he says that 'it was all quite fun and there was a war on'.

It had a final flowering in the fifties with the revues of Laurier Lister at the Royal Court, and West-End offerings like *Pieces of Eight* and *Share My Lettuce,* which introduced Kenneth Williams, Maggie Smith and Fenella Fielding, and had their sketches written by Harold Pinter and N.F. Simpson. But by the 1960s, it had retreated to the universities and undergraduate humour; the Cambridge Footlights being the most noted example.

Beyond the Fringe in 1961 was both the last triumphant statement of the form, and its death-knell. The four performers had, until recently, been undergraduates at Oxford and Cambridge and even this most insubstantial branch of theatre had fallen to the academically trained; two of them beneficiaries of a post-war Welfare State: lower-middle and working-class boys on student grants. *Beyond the Fringe* led to the television satire that followed. Intimate Revue and Music Hall – the latter incomparably the more important form – were the true victims of the rapaciousness of television.

*

Following Frith's career as a performer in the hotch-potch world of Intimate Revue gives us a good glimpse of its merits and failings. His next engagement in 1941, was called – wartime pluck again – *Rise Above It.*

Presented by Jack de Leon of the 'Q' Theatre, the cast, because of their subsequent success in other areas, seems star-studded. Apart from Frith, there was Wilfred Hyde-White; Joan Greenwood; Carole Lynne, later Lady Delfont; Peter Cotes, of whom more will be heard later; Edward Cooper, and Hermione Baddeley. They had, as Frith puts it, 'strange times'.

The first problem was the director and designer Hedley Briggs, for whom Frith had previously worked in *New Faces.* Briggs, who had made his reputation designing 'The Farjeon Revues' before the war, was a brilliant but unreliable little man. Self-destructive to a degree and famously adept at fouling his own nest: his twin problems were his love-life with various men and his fondness for the bottle. Five days before the pre-London tour was due to open at the Arts Theatre, Cambridge, the company arrived at the London rehearsal room to find no director. They waited.

Eventually the stage-manager rang Briggs's rooms in Beaufort Street. There was a long pause while whoever answered went to search, returning to the telephone with the news that his door was locked with sounds of sobbing coming from inside. After a discussion, Frith was deputed to go and fetch him, try to make him pull himself together, and bring him back to rehearsal. So off to Beaufort Street he went and knocked on Hedley Briggs's locked door, from the other side of which were the sounds of dreadful howls and cries.

'Hedley! We're all waiting for you!' he shouted cheerfully. After a silence the door was unlocked and as Frith entered, Briggs threw himself, Elinor Glyn-like, on a zebra-skin covered bed. After being persuaded that his art came first, his love-life second, he returned to rehearsals, but only to disappear again the next day, seemingly for good.

So they had to open this Intimate Revue without a director or designer. Revue! Which of all things has the most technically complicated production week with its altered running-order and numerous lighting cues. Somehow they managed, but were understandably furious and kept asking Jack de Leon when they were going to be given a new director. Then, to their astonishment on the opening night, as cool as a cucumber, appeared Hedley Briggs, behaving as if nothing had happened.

Briggs's end was to be sad. After a few more similar incidents the theatre gave him up. He took up cooking, and eventually killed himself. The drink had done for him.

One of the troubles with *Rise Above It*, thinks Frith, was that everybody enjoyed themselves far too much; in particular Hermione Baddeley.

'Totie' Baddeley, as she was nicknamed, was a woman of enormous heart and personality with an extreme comic talent. Later she was to develop into a straight actress of great power and emotional force. She was also a creature of the greatest kindness; often naughty but never unkind. On stage she lived a part to the full, and off stage she lived her life to the full, and brimming over. In her later years she was known to over-act, but even then she was appositely funny or moving. Sometimes undisciplined in her work, although not to the detriment of others, her life had its moments of chaos as well. She was also one of the funniest of conversationalists.

In 1941 she was very beautiful: a strong face with wide-apart features and a strong body. Her only fault can be best illustrated by the incident at rehearsal when, after doing something well, she said, 'I *love* myself in this part'. She sometimes, perhaps, loved herself a bit too much.

Also in the cast were the Tosh twins, a wholesome duo, and, there being no band, two pianists, one of whom was a very obvious lesbian known as Bezer. After a run at the 'Q' Theatre, *Rise Above It* went on tour to Liverpool, where Totie Baddeley gave a late night party in her bedroom at the Stork Hotel. Audrey Tosh of the twins, summoned unexpectedly, appeared in a lovely frilly nightdress. Totie looked at her, turned to the lady pianist and said: 'Oh, Bezer, I don't suppose when you go to bed you dress like that', to which Bezer replied, 'No, when I go to bed I go to bed naked, and what's more,' looking hard at Audrey Tosh, 'I expect anybody who goes to bed with me to be naked too!' Poor Miss Tosh had never come across that sort of talk before.

After a few more weeks with business fair to indifferent, de Leon decided to bolster *Rise Above It* with extra cast and numbers before bringing it back to London at the Comedy Theatre. Two leading men, Henry Kendall and the American Walter Crisham (catch-phrase 'Wha' d'ye know?') were brought in, as was – and it was this that made the difference – Hermione Gingold. The two Hermiones here began their famous revue partnership. The management let Edward Cooper go, and Frith had one of his numbers cut. Perhaps sensing that he was not as wanted as he had been before, and because there was another offer, he also left the company.

*

This offer was *The New Ambassadors' Revue* which was, as it claimed, a sequel to an earlier entertainment at the Ambassadors Theatre. Directed by Cyril Ritchard, the cast consisted of his wife Madge Elliott, Betty Ann Davies, Charles Hawtrey, with whom Frith shared a dressing room, Frith himself, Joan Swinstead – a most amusing actress, and later, when she lost her nerve, a successful director – and the inimitable Ernest Thesiger.

Thesiger, the original Dauphin in Shaw's *St Joan,* was tall, angular, extraordinary looking, always amusing and not always nice. He was known to spend time with Queen Mary doing tapestry work, and he was a member of the *Men's League for Dress Reform.* In this capacity he appeared daily in pink linen suits with natty little belts; and in the street people looked askance. Unconventional he may have been in one area, but in others, he was prissy and old fashioned.

Charles Hawtrey and Frith had a half-witted male dresser who, after a while, was called up. After two dresserless weeks they persuaded the management to engage a woman. Women had dressed men at the *Comédie*

Francaise for two hundred and fifty years but were then unknown in London and Ernest Thesiger was very disapproving. 'They'll be wanting a wet-nurse next!' He was even more mortified when this woman was detailed to help him with one of his changes. The poor lady had to leave the costume outside his door – like the milk – and only when she was safely out of the way did he open the door and take it in, putting his old costume out. She was then allowed to return to collect it.

Perhaps because his Royal friend's condescension had gone to his head, he was extremely snobbish. The talented Betty Ann Davies was not, and did not pretend to be, a 'lady'. Instead of finding this unaffected and endearing, Thesiger thought it disgraceful: 'She's nothing but a common little Chorus Gairl.' Which, as Frith observed, was odd coming from a professional in the theatre. Thesiger could be jealous too. One day the running order was changed and Frith was given an extra number. Notice of this was pinned up on the stage-door board. Thesiger was discovered looking at the notice with pursed lips, 'not another numb*ar* for Mr B*e*nbury'. All the cast, naturally, went about imitating that one. On stage, he was a great entertainer: funny and quirky and, as his film performances show, an individual and original actor.

The entertainment as a whole sounds undistinguished, 'rather a scrap-book, lacking overall impact', and it was only a modest success.

*

Frith's final revue appearance, again at the Ambassadors, was even less successful but far more important. This was because its writer, Herbert Farjeon was the *doyen* librettist and sketch writer of all intimate revues of the thirties and the forties.

Farjeon's talents spread very wide. The grandson of the great American actor, Joseph Jefferson, and son of the Victorian novelist B.L. (Ben) Farjeon, he considered himself foremost a Shakespearean scholar. Indeed his editorship of the Nonesuch Shakespeare has admirable learning and clarity, and his collection of essays, *The Shakespearean Scene* is second only to Granville Barker's in its marriage of scholarship and first-hand theatrical practicality. He was also a dramatic critic of distinction, as well as being synonymous with revue at its best. He was the most witty and versatile of men. His sister Eleanor was a poet and writer too. She wrote, with her brother, a verse book, *Kings and Queens,* full of useful facts presented in an amusing and accessible way, which introduced many children to history.

By 1942, Farjeon was disillusioned with the professional theatre and the way managers, Charles Cochran in particular, made him compromise much of his material. As Farjeon had mounted his own shows before at the Little Theatre (which was now bombed flat) he had the managerial confidence to take matters a step further by deciding his new venture would not only be backed by himself but would be co-written with his sister Eleanor: so it was very much a family affair. He had always considered too, that revue as a dramatic form could take serious as well as comic material and signalled his intentions by the title *Light and Shade*. His other bugbear was the star system. In the past he had found the likes of Beatrice Lillie and Cyril Ritchard intractable, as they were not inclined to do what they were told. With that in mind he wrote a letter to the company before rehearsals started, which told them in effect, to consider themselves part of the team, and to obey instructions. Frith was quite happy with that because the opening and ending numbers had been written around his ability to play the piano, with a rather charming twilit close with him alone at curtain fall.

Although Farjeon had delegated the direction to Reginald Beckwith he, his sister, and daughter – and sometimes wife and brother too – were arbiters of all decisions from their perch at the back of the stalls. If any suggestion was made, the family went into conclave before deciding whether or not to give permission. Max Adrian, who was in the company, thought they were like twittering sparrows who changed places on a telegraph wire. Frith remembers an air of slight amateurishness pervading the whole experience.

Farjeon was sometimes at his funniest when most solemn. Knowing that Frith could manage serious singing with his thrice weekly lessons from Gwyn Davies, he produced at rehearsal one day a lyric to be sung to a *pastiche* Handelian air. This went:

'Hail! Vocal Grove! Where flocks of little peers
Have lost their balls and learnt to stem their tears.'

A 'Grove' was jargon for the lavatory in some public schools, and Frith demurred: 'Bertie, I can't'. But when the *double entendre* was explained to him, Farjeon thought it most amusing.

With Max Adrian and Frith were Betty Ann Davies, again; Megs Jenkins, one of Frith's favoured actresses and part of his 'rep' when he became a director; Vida Hope, who went on to direct *The Boy Friend;* Noel Willman, successful actor and director; Geoffrey Dunn, singer and superb translator of operetta libretti, and Helen Burns, later actress in America and wife of Michael Langham. She was then aged seventeen and very keen – rather too keen for Max Adrian.

Max, who had understandably and correctly parted from his original surname of Bor – for bore he was most certainly not – was an Irish Jew; a potent and fiery combination. A strikingly individual and technically assured actor, as a man Frith calls him 'quite a card', and card is the *mot juste.* They also had a short affair. There was a trio in which Frith, Max, and Noel Willman played *matelots* in a railway carriage. At rehearsal Helen Burns was unwise enough to offer advice. There was a terrible silence, and suddenly Max Adrian shouted, 'Do you think I have been in the theatre for years to be told what to do by a little student?' It was the one moment of danger and excitement in the whole enterprise.

Frith remembers *Light and Shade* 'opening to disappointing notices'. That was an understatement. James Agate in *The Sunday Times* called it 'laboured, depressing, tedious and pretentious', while W.A. Darlington in *The Daily Telegraph* commented succinctly 'Too Much Shade'.

The biggest mistake was putting a serious Nativity Play right in the middle. This was twee and pretty, the Farjeons loved it and would not countenance its disappearance. It killed the whole show stone dead.

In a rescue bid, Farjeon brought in Joyce Grenfell, who after he had heard her mimicry at a party, had been put into *The Little Revue* in 1939, when she had made her first marked success, performing her own monologues.

Joyce Grenfell, like others in her family, was a true mimic: capturing the content of a person's speech as well as their accent and manner. She was the mistress of the *diction* of others, but in attitude she remained a gifted amateur. She treated the stage management like a Society rather than a Theatrical *grande dame,* and the wavelength of professional actors was not one to which she was attuned, nor probably did she wish to be; the tone of her published letters to her mother suggests a lady on a moderately enjoyable slum.

For Frith, Joyce was 'the absolute prototype amateur. She came onto the stage before the start of the show and looked through the curtains, 'I like to know who's in front'. Joyce had to know if Lady X was watching. Her amateurism gave me the willies.' In spite of three solo spots she could not save *Light and Shade.*

Farjeon's disillusionment with revue was now complete and he never wrote another, just as Frith never appeared in another. Frith found the atmosphere unappealingly though understandably competitive: the placing of a number in the running order meant everything for its success or failure, and he cites the case when Beatrice Lillie appeared on a bill with Flanagan and Allen. They were great comics, but Bea Lillie was an even greater upstager. She managed to have their act moved to the wrong place in the running order and they went for nothing. If the artists were not top dog, they were at the mercy of those who were, and it thus became a backbiting world with none of the company spirit to be found, as in say a musical. In Revue, everyone was out for themselves.

Perhaps it was during the war that revue served its best purpose. While 'theatre' meant Sybil Thorndike and Lewis Casson touring the South Welsh Valleys with *Macbeth* and *Medea,* or the Old Vic, evacuated to Buxton, playing *King John* for its patriotic final speech, revue could offer, almost literally, light relief, far removed from wartime tribulations.

*

Shortly after the Gate Theatre had closed at the outbreak of war, Norman Marshall met the Queen, who had politely expressed the wish it would soon again be flourishing. Using this as a lever – Her Majesty Earnestly Hopes – he approached the newly founded C.E.M.A.

The Council for the Encouragement of Music and the Arts, forerunner of the Arts Council, had been set up at the beginning of 1940 with money from the Pilgrim Trust and funding from the Treasury via the Ministry of Education. Marshall was provided with backing for four new plays and the revue *Swinging the Gate,* which transferred to the Ambassadors. After two years of Army Service, he telephoned his business partner, 'Peter' Collett, with the news that he was, again with C.E.M.A.'s sponsorship, mounting an eighteen month season at the Arts Theatre Cambridge, whence there would be dispatched extensive tours. He told her too that he had engaged a nucleus company: Geoffrey Edwards, Vivienne Bennett, Joan Swinstead and Frith Banbury.

Frith had meanwhile been giving one of his only surviving performances on film, in Michael Powell and Emeric Pressburger's *The Life and Death of Colonel Blimp.* As the charmingly named Babyface Fitzroy, *attaché* at our Embassy in Berlin, he looks boyish and engaging, an intelligent Bertie Wooster. It also gives him the chance to show off some very fluent German.

For Cambridge, Marshall offered him his best parts to date. 'Peter' Collett thought Frith a competent rather than an outstanding actor, but was pleased at his inclusion in the company for she appreciated his good humoured contributions and his easy co-operation. Even though management had, during the war, a limited choice of male actors – 'geriatrics, cripples and nancy boys', in Donald Wolfit's opinion – Marshall must have had a higher opinion of his talents, for the roles offered were unquestionably those of a leading man: the title role in *The Gay Lord Quex,* Gregers Werle in *The Wild Duck,* Muishkin in *The Idiot,* the Actor in *The Guardsman,* Sneer in *The Critic,* Adolphus Cusins in *Major Barbara,* and for the first time Joseph Surface in *The School for Scandal:* all parts, which even at a distance of fifty years, seem absolutely suited to him.

They also presented *Uncle Vanya* at the Westminster Theatre in September 1943, with Frith in the unlikely role of Dr Astrov for which he would seem to have had few qualifications, neither immediately suggesting the countryman and conservationist, nor the masculine cynosure of the two women. The *Evening Standard* review confirms this conjecture, finding Frith 'too gentle with it all. Although sensitive and understanding, [he] hangs his hat over the funnel of his trumpet like a player in a jazz band.'

Continuing as a leading man, he played Lord Foppington in *A Trip to Scarborough,* Sheridan's rewrite of Vanbrugh's *The Relapse.* This performance, which so pleased the director, his old confidant Denys Blakelock, pleased the critics too, 'a vastly magnified Backbite – an ace of complacent coxcombs', thought the *Observer.* He made guest appearances for repertory companies. At the Oxford Playhouse he was again Joseph Surface in a *School for Scandal* directed by Christopher Fry, who although the author of two plays was a year away from his first success, *A Phoenix Too Frequent,* and was thus still considered primarily a director. The rest of the cast was very impressive: Michael Gough as Charles, Hannam Clarke as Sir Peter and Joan Greenwood, Yvonne Mitchell, Jane Henderson, Winifred Evans, Nora Nicholson. Fry and Gough, also Conchies, had just been released from the Non-Combatant Corps.

At the newly formed Citizens Theatre in Glasgow, Frith played Khlestakov in Gogol's *The Government Inspector,* a role that with its opportunities for ludicrous comedy and inspired fantasy Frith must have been born to play. The Citizens' Chairman Dr O.H. Mavor, better known as the playwright James Bridie, wrote thanking him for his 'brilliant performance', a sincere compliment, as Bridie was quite capable of writing castigating letters to actors whose work displeased him.

1945, too brought him into professional contact for the first time with Rachel Kempson, the 'bouncy English girl' he had liked so

R.A.D.A. After her Stratford season of 1933, she had gone to the Liverpool Playhouse and there become engaged to an actor in the company called Michael Redgrave, who had, up until then, been a schoolmaster.

Frith had visited Liverpool for the threefold purpose of seeing Rachel Kempson, meeting her fiancé, and trying to obtain an engagement from Willie Armstrong. In the third of these he had been unsuccessful. Michael and Rachel were playing together in *Richard of Bordeaux,* and it was obvious to Frith from the start that as an actor Redgrave had 'all the graces', and he had admiration for his high intelligence and intellectual erudition. He saw a certain amount of them in London during the thirties, and as a man he found Redgrave charming but suspected that his lack of humour and inclination to censoriousness might make him tricky. He was 'an attractive chap, who could be sweet and forthcoming but you never quite knew. You always might do or say something not appropriate.'

In 1942 his suspicions were slightly justified. Redgrave was appearing in and directing Patrick Hamilton's *The Duke in Darkness.* It came back to his ears that Frith had been critical of performance and production and Redgrave dispatched a letter of reprimand:

'Don't please, my dear Frith, develop into one of those sour semi-intellectuals who like and dislike by extremes, and principally dislike. Van Gogh was right when he said that the principal thing was to like and that error of taste was unimportant.' Apart from the questionable attribution to Van Gogh sounding such complete drivel, the tone of the letter was undeniably priggish. However, by 1945 Frith was obviously forgiven enough to be cast as the Gestapo Man to Redgrave's Colonel Stjerbinsky in Franz Werfel's *Jacobowsky and the Colonel.* This play, not very good on the evidence of a later National Theatre Production, had been a great success on Broadway with Oscar Karlweis, Louis Calhern, and, as the girl, the French film star, Annabella. Into this part Redgrave put Rachel Kempson. At rehearsals it became evident that she was gravely miscast, and Redgrave, who was directing as well, bullied her unmercifully to the intense embarrassment of all. On opening at the Piccadilly in June, the poor girl received the most dreadful notices; James Agate in *The Sunday Times* saying, 'Miss Rachel Kempson drenched the South West Corner of France with the authentic perfume of Wimbledon.'

Frith and Redgrave had one long scene, where under interrogation Redgrave had to pretend to be uncomprehending and stupid. Sitting with his back to the audience, he nightly pulled faces trying to get Frith to corpse with laughter: surprising in an actor who ostensibly took his work so seriously. One night Frith turned the tables by saying a line unscripted and unexpected; but when they reached the wings Redgrave turned very pompous. There was clearly one rule for him, another for others. The play did not succeed, but Frith continued to find Redgrave a most interesting character, noticing how he always tried to square circles: wanting to be the film star with the largest number of fan letters, and, at the same time, the actor most respected by highbrow weeklies like the *New Statesman*. It was to be some time however, indeed two important productions later, before he realised just how many circles Redgrave was trying to square; an internal battle of opposites that made him both so tortured a man and so exciting an artist.

From the beginning he admired his outstanding gifts, 'he was a leading actor, no question of it'. In spite of his height – (six foot three in a lesser talent might have been a handicap) – he was at his best, thinks Frith, in character parts rather than romantic leading roles. There was always an academicism that came in the way of full-throated romantic acting: a good rather than a great Hamlet.

In comedy, surprisingly, Frith found him excellent. His Aguecheek in an indifferent Saint-Denis *Twelfth Night* had imaginative flair: all gangly spindleshanks, making constructive use of his great height; and he was amusingly over-intense as the lover in Henri Becque's *La Parisienne* with Sonia Dresdel. But he was positively superb in the title role of Thomas Job's *Uncle Harry*, and in Chekhov's *Uncle Vanya*, where a complex emotional inner life needed expressing with a character actor's technique.

*

Just before *Jacobowsky and the Colonel* went into rehearsal, Victory in Europe was declared and E.N.S.A. decided to send a series of prestigious entertainments to newly liberated France, and to the British and American troops in occupied Germany. The Old Vic Company led by Laurence Olivier and Ralph Richardson went first in July reopening the *Comédie Française* with *Richard III, Arms and the Man* and *Peer Gynt*.

By contrast, E.N.S.A. then sent out the most successful West End Comedy: Terence Rattigan's *While the Sun Shines*. This is an excellently constructed and inventive light comedy, about an Englishman, an American and a Free Frenchman. Set in Chambers in Albany, where Rattigan himself then lived, the Englishman, a young naval officer called Bobby, Earl of Harpenden; Joe Mulvaney of the U.S. Air Force, and Lieutenant Colbert of the Free French

Army, are all in love with the same girl, whose father, the Duke, was played – as Dukes very often were – by the superb light comedian Ronald Squire. This character was modelled on Rattigan's father, Frank, a *roué* and Stage-Door-Johnny, whose success with the girls was the envy of many younger men.

The play had been running at the Globe since Christmas Eve 1943; for the tour, Squire was extracted from the London cast, Frith was cast as Lieutenant Colbert, and as Lord Harpenden an actor who had been at war for six years, Robert Flemyng. Flemyng's war had been one of quite conspicuous bravery. Joining as a ranker, he had finished a full Colonel at thirty-three, won the Military Cross, been mentioned in dispatches, and given an military O.B.E. after the Battle of Monte Cassino. Today he will talk about the theatre and the technique of acting until the sun comes up, but, with the gallantry of the truly brave, refuses to discuss his wartime activities. A man of exceptional sweetness of nature and charm of manner, he had made a marked success as Kit Neilan in *French Without Tears* before the war and was to appear in nearly all Rattigan's plays, after it, creating Mark in *Who is Sylvia?* and many others.

They toured Brussels, Düsseldorf, Berlin, Hamburg and, in October, played the Marigny in Paris. They were appalled by the devastation of wrecked Berlin, 'worse than Monte Cassino', as Flemyng observed. The Company was billeted in a villa which had belonged to a high ranking Nazi and his family, who had evidently left in a hurry. Frith found the experience weird and unsettling for it seemed like being an uninvited guest in someone else's house: objects, toys, photographs and other personal possessions had been left so untouched that they could tangibly imagine what these parents and children must have been like in their cosy domesticity.

They travelled by bus, but getting from one occupied zone to another was a laborious and sometimes alarming experience. Colonel 'leave this to me!' Flemyng was much in evidence sorting out surly Americans and aggressive Russians with Empire-building bluster and charm. 'The trouble with you, Banbury,' he shouted in a hotel room, 'is that you don't understand the army!' Indeed Banbury did not and roared with laughter, which sent the Colonel into purplefaced fury.

The authority and responsibility which the army vested in Robert Flemyng had a deep and lasting effect. He became an assiduous worker for theatrical charities and a long-serving committee member of Equity. The Officer's sense of duty to his fellows remained strong but the Gentleman's modesty and self-deprecation perhaps held him back from the final egotistical thrust which would have shifted him from respected leading man to box-office draw. He was the original Edward Chamberlayne in Eliot's *The Cocktail Party,* James Callifer in Graham Greene's *The Potting Shed,* and particularly Rupert Forster in John Whiting's *Marching Song* directed by Frith. These roles give him an honourable place in post-war theatre.

Returning to England, Frith joined the London cast of *While the Sun Shines,* and repeated his Lieutenant Colbert at the Globe for six months. Flemyng had told his friend Hugh Beaumont, managing director of H.M. Tennent, who presented the play, how good he thought Frith in the part, and on seeing the performance, Beaumont agreed, writing to Frith: 'I am most grateful to you for your performance . . . which I may say was far the best portrayal of the part that we have had from all the various versions.

Frith also brought back from the continent a 'small, esoteric present' for Michael Redgrave. A book of rarefied French poetry perhaps? He telephoned, and Redgrave asked him to bring it round and stay for dinner. Frith had always imagined the Redgraves' marriage, with its three children and – after Michael's film successes – large house in Chiswick Mall, to be happy and relatively untroubled, although rumours of his bisexuality must have reached him.

Frith duly arrived with his esoteric present to find a small group already gathered including Rachel's brother, Nicholas Kempson. But no Michael. They waited; the small talk becoming tenser, but still no host appeared. Eventually, at a late hour, they went into a frazzled dinner at which Rachel tried to keep up conversation through obvious embarrassment. Frith left the absent Michael his present and left, feeling sorry for Rachel and realising all was not well. But when he received no thanks, he understood Redgrave's awkwardness too, for thanks would have required an explanation of his absence, or an admission of bad behaviour. He suspected that Redgrave had difficulty facing sides of his character of which he was ashamed; and he was right.

But Redgrave was also capable of behaving very kindly. At this time Max Adrian was sent to prison for a short while for 'cottaging': importuning in the gentlemen's lavatory at Victoria Station. Redgrave was wonderful in this crisis: visiting him in prison, and helping him financially on his release. For a man who was himself vulnerable to similar suspicions, his actions must be seen as courageous.

*

Frith's acting career had reached a plateau. As a 'character juvenile' – the term used in *Spotlight,* the actors' directory – he was in regular work; he was sociable and knew most people in a still parochial West End; he was regularly seen at theatre parties. He was thought of as a reputable talent and even more so in comedy. Dorothy Primrose remembered him as 'very camp but great fun at those parties. I, shy Miss Prim, was rather intimidated by him as he seemed to know everybody – but nothing prepared me for the authority he was to exhibit as a director.'

What changed Frith Banbury from a successful light-weight into a man of real stature and influence in post-war British Theatre? The Senior director for H.M. Tennent, the most prestigious and powerful management in theatre history, the Champion of new writers, courageous manager, synonymous with West-End excellence in the opinion of many, the chief representative in the theatre of all that was middle-class and reactionary in the view of some a decade later?

It all happened during the run of T.W. Robertson's *Caste* at the Lyric Hammersmith in 1946 which transferred to the Duke of York's. In this he was playing captain Hawtree (monocle and moustache), a part originally offered to Paul Scofield, and playing it well and in good taste, 'staying nicely inside the picture and declining to jump out of it for the sake of an easy laugh', as Ivor Brown said in the *Observer*. And the opportunity to change from actor to director presented itself in the shape of a play written in pencil in a school exercise-book.

Afterwards, apart from once to test himself, Frith never acted again; but before we follow him on his directional adventures, we need to look at the West End in its immediate post-war existence and see what kind of theatre he was to be part of.

The West End 1940s

The two most important institutions in the West End, The Old Vic Company and H.M. Tennent Ltd, had both, in a sense, benefited from the war and, in particular, the founding of C.E.M.A. which by then had become the Arts Council.

The Old Vic Theatre in the Waterloo Road had been bombed and the company was housed at the New (now the Coward) Theatre. It was funded largely by the Arts Council, and, as its work was classed as educational, exempt from Entertainment Tax.

Here was seen charismatic acting and ensemble playing of a very high order. Run by the triumvirate of Ralph Richardson, Laurence Olivier and the director John Burrell, the performances of those years are still talked about: Richardson's Peer Gynt and Falstaff, Olivier's Richard III, Hotspur, Oedipus and Puff, and the supporting parts were cast, to put it mildly, from strength: Sybil Thorndike, Lewis Casson, Athene Seyler, Nicholas Hannen, Margaret Leighton, Joyce Redman and George Relph.

H.M. Tennent Ltd had been founded in 1936 by the composer and impresario Harry Tennent, and since his death in 1941, the managing director had been his brilliant young assistant Hugh Beaumont, who most had assumed, was also his boyfriend.

Tennents consisted of two sister companies: H.M. Tennent Ltd, a commercial, profit-making management, and Tennent Productions (called until 1947 Tennent Plays) which, as its work was considered educational, later amended to 'partly educational', was exempt from Entertainment Tax.

Entertainment Tax had originally been levied as one of the extra taxes raised to finance the First World War, and was a means whereby some of the profits from a number of popular successes like *Chu Chin Chow*, could be paid to the treasury rather than to the actor-managers. It was actually one of a number of stringent measures brought in to hinder war-profiteering. Surprisingly, nearly all the theatrical establishment seem to have supported it as a reasonable patriotic measure. That was not their opinion, however, when it was kept on after the war had ended. By 1942 it was being levied at 33.3% or, in other words, one third of all box-office income went to the treasury. There was a loophole, however, in this Finance Act of which, astonishingly, very few managers availed themselves, and only one, Hugh Beaumont, turned to his advantage. This was that if the plays were educational, and the company or institution presenting them was not established to make a profit (i.e. all profits had to be ploughed straight back into the company) the tax was waived.

The Old Vic had been exempt since 1934, as it presented the works of Shakespeare. In time, the Memorial Theatre Stratford-upon-Avon, the Open Air Theatre Regents Park, and Donald Wolfit's Company would follow suit. Beaumont realised that as long as he could persuade the Customs and Excise who administered this tax that the plays he mounted, either classical or new, were educational, he could both present as many as he was able, and avail himself of the tax-free management fee (ostensibly to cover running costs) which was £25 a week in 1942 and £40 a week by 1949.

The Customs and Excise would not recognise any company as educational unless it was recommended as such by the Arts Council, and in this Beaumont was lucky in that he had both personal empathy with and professional support from the Council's Chairman, Lord Keynes. Maynard Keynes liked his theatre both economically viable and glamorous; and Hugh Beaumont was both a very astute business man and a believer in expensive looking and star-studded productions. Keynes was homosexual too, in spite of his marriage to the dancer Lydia Lopokova, and was far more in tune with Hugh Beaumont than with his Council's succession of dour masculine Drama Directors such as Lewis Casson.

Beaumont's first non-profit making company, Tennent Plays, had been founded in 1942 to present John Gielgud in *Macbeth* and for five years it put on a series of classical plays as well as Priestley's *They Came to a City,* and Wilder's *The Skin of Our Teeth.* In 1947, when it looked as if the Inland Revenue might begin to question that company's operations, he simply wound it up and started another, Tennent Productions, which functioned in exactly the same way.

Ruthless and devious he could certainly be, but Beaumont was also much more altruistic than he is often given credit for. He would arrange for the non-profit making Tennent Productions to present sure-fire commercial successes like N.C. Hunter's *Waters of the Moon* with Edith Evans and Sybil Thorndike so that its profits could only be used to finance much less profitable work. For instance, he chose Tennent Productions to present Hunter's *A Day By the Sea* with Thorndike, Gielgud and Richardson, and Ackland's *A Dead Secret* with Paul Scofield, partly so he could give a production of John Whiting's *Marching Song,* a play which he thought needed to be seen. He was the leading light too in founding the theatre club which circumvented the Lord Chamberlain's ban on Robert Andersen's *Tea and Sympathy,* Tennessee Williams's *Cat on a Hot Tin Roof,* and Arthur Miller's *A View From the Bridge.* From the profit-making company, he took very little money for himself, and shamefully underpaid his small staff in their cramped and musty offices above the Globe (now the Gielgud) Theatre, although for long periods – for instance during the run of *My Fair Lady* in the 1950s – these profits must have been very considerable.

According to his biographer, Richard Huggett, Beaumont had said, 'The war has been the making of me . . . And to think that I owe it all to Hitler,' and certainly on V.E. Day there were twelve Tennent plays in the West End, and that was not counting the tours, repertory companies and concert parties working under Beaumont's aegis.

By using his non-profit making company so skilfully, Beaumont raised the standards in the West End. As running costs were low and all profits could be fed back into the productions, many noncommercial plays found themselves in the West End clocking up respectable, sometimes long runs, whose equivalent today would only be able to play a short season at Hampstead, the Bush, or the Royal Court.

By the mid 1940s, he had virtual monopoly of the West End, prompting a question as to why no other impresarios availed themselves of this loophole to tax-exemption. The answer is that Beaumont saw it first and moved fast; by the end of the war he had gained so much ground that there was simply no room for others to get the toe-hold that he had. He was easily the most powerful man in British Theatre, but his success made him many enemies, who by trying to link his two perceived weak spots, his homosexuality and his reliance on his non-profit making company, were to sling a lot of mud and cause much trouble.

Hugh Beaumont, known by his childhood nickname of 'Binkie', had been born Hughes Griffith Morgan in 1908, the son of a Cardiff solicitor. After his mother's remarriage he took his stepfather's name of Beaumont. This Beaumont was a rich timber-merchant. The family was thus provincial middle-class, which was obviously not nearly interesting enough for Binkie who liked to pretend a background of illegitimacy and great poverty. He worked front of house at the Playhouse, Cardiff, becoming assistant to the manager Harry Woodcock, who obviously fancied him. While there he was befriended both by Sir Gerald du Maurier and C. Aubrey Smith, whose touring production of *The Creaking Chair* brought him to London as the Company Manager at the Comedy Theatre, where he was made much of by Smith's co-star, Tallulah Bankhead. He was business manager at The Barnes Theatre and later became assistant to Harry Tennent, who found plays and booked tours for Moss Empires and Howard and Wyndham. H.M. Tennent Ltd, was always, technically, the latter's subsidiary. After Harry Tennent's sudden death from a heart attack in 1941, the board of Howard and Wyndham did not seem anxious to appoint Binkie as his successor. After talking to his staff, Binkie persuaded them all to write letters of resignation if he was not appointed, and armed with these he walked into the boardroom, talked to the board and emerged sole managing director. His trump card, the letters, he never needed to produce.

Frith, who knew and worked with Binkie closely for many years, remembers a man of contradictions: 'There has never been anybody like him except perhaps Diaghilev. Bit of a genius really, and devious; very kind in many ways; quite ruthless in others.' He stresses Binkie's sense of moral duty to the theatre and remembers how he considered it a dereliction of that duty when Celia Johnson could not begin rehearsals for *Flowering Cherry* because of her children's school holidays. He enjoyed deviousness so much that he was rather upset if he could not employ it. He liked to get his way in a Machiavellian manner 'rather like a Henry James character'.

The dichotomy of his homosexuality and need to be part of the Establishment dictated his taste. There was a strong component of middle-class morality in him. He knew what the public wanted and was anxious that nothing should offend 'Aunt Edna', the mythical thin-skinned typical theatre goer invented by him and Terence Rattigan. But the fact that he was a practising homosexual meant that he functioned outside the law and, if caught, could have been imprisoned. He liked to be surrounded by Respectability, because it was a defence against being found out. Moral rectitude in others was important and he took up censorious attitudes over people of both sexes whose lives he felt were in danger of being touched by scandal. This attitude had a considerable influence on the conduct of the West End Theatre and its fear of taking risks. A middle-class audience was enforcing its own sanctions, and paradoxically, it needed those with more conventional sexual proclivities to break them down. Which is indeed what happened in due course – after the reign of Binkie Beaumont.

Everyone I have spoken to who worked for him, considers Binkie's judgement to have been almost faultless. Furthermore, once hired, his employees were left alone to make and act on their own decisions. He knew how to delegate. He came to the first read-through; sometimes the first run-through on the Saturday morning at the end of the first week if there was the possibility of a cast change (the Tennent's contract reserved the right to replace without pay up until that point), and then he disappeared until the first dress-rehearsal. Then, what he said was completely trusted by actors, directors and writers; and he said it bluntly but diplomatically.

Frith cites an incident in 1971 when he and the designer Michael Annals took the set of *Captain Brassbound's Conversion,* readjusted after a budget cut, for inspection. They both knew it was not quite right but could not put their finger on the problem. Binkie, however, spotted it at once and saw exactly how to solve it. Coming down in the lift afterwards, Annals made the point that there was no one else – not even at Olivier's National Theatre – who could comment on a set in a way that made both director and designer feel like saying, 'why didn't we think of that before?'

For all his ruthlessness he knew how to give people time and make them feel important. Marjorie Sisley, Frith's secretary during his long collaboration with Tennents, said that Binkie had a gift shared by the record producer Walter Legge for addressing people with absolute blink-ered directness as if they were the only person who mattered for that moment. When he had found out what he needed, or felt that he had been agreeable for long enough, that intense concentration was instantly switched elsewhere. She also adds, 'and he *never* wasted money'.

He did not read books and was not well educated. His artistic educa-tion had been gleaned from friends like John Gielgud. Frith says, 'Theatre people today are fifty times more educated and culturally efficient than Binkie ever was, but haven't got that something extra – that sense of theatre'.

Much of Tennent Productions' most interesting work took place at or transferred from the Lyric Theatre Hammersmith where, from 1945, it was one quarter of the enterprise known as The Company of Four. The other three had originally been Glyndebourne, (whose admin-istrator Rudolf Bing had dreamt up the scheme), The Arts Theatre, Cambridge, represented by its director Norman Higgins, and the Theatre Royal, Bristol, represented by Tyrone Guthrie in his capacity as head of the Old Vic Company. Tennents provided the administra-tor – the much loved director and manager Murray Macdonald, and the administrative offices were above the Apollo Theatre. Glyndebourne and Guthrie soon withdrew, followed by Cambridge, so that by 1950 Tennents were left with the full responsibility.

Everything fell into patterns of four: four weeks rehearsal (a luxury instead of the usual two or three); four weeks on tour with a week each at Cambridge, Cardiff, Bristol and Brighton, (whose manager J. Baxter Somerville was technically the lessee of Hammersmith) and four weeks run at the Lyric before a possible West End transfer.

Murray Macdonald realised that the company would always remain the poor relation of the Tennents empire and thus unlikely to flourish, unless Binkie became somehow directly involved with the day to day running of Hammersmith. So he resigned and suggested that his successor should be John Perry.

John Perry shared Binkie's life and house, and worked for the Firm, as Tennents was called by its employees. As a lover he had been inherited from John Gielgud. He and Binkie Beaumont were to stay together until the latter's death.

Perry was Anglo-Irish and a great friend of the writer Molly Keane, who sometimes wrote under the *nom de plume*, M.J. Farrell. The two had collaborated on a play, *Spring Meeting*, which Tennents had produced in 1937 with Margaret Rutherford, directed by Gielgud. Perry, then not a very sought after actor, had left Gielgud for Binkie early in the war causing a brief period of acrimony between the two, and had then begun to work for Tennents. Most of his war was spent as an A.D.C. to the Governor of Gibraltar (his senior A.D.C. being Anthony Quayle) where he was nicknamed 'The Wingless Victory' as he wore an R.A.F. uniform but was unable to fly. This was a clever posting as he was able to organise a number of wartime tours and concert parties most of which were sent out by Tennents in London. In this capacity he had worked very hard and had been considered most efficient. His appointment at Hammersmith was, to a certain extent, a reward for passing this wartime test with such flying colours.

The reports of Perry's worth both as manager and man are conflicting. He was upper-class and well educated, a social and cultural asset. Robert Morley thought he protected Binkie from dissatisfied directors and actors, and implied that he was tactfully able to handle some of Binkie's more unpleasant tasks: 'John Perry had to do all the staving off'. But another actor who knew him well says, 'John wasn't very bright. It took me a long time to realise that Binkie covered up for him'. Marjorie Sisley, who knew most of the inner secrets of the managers' offices of the 1950s, spots the essential difference between the two men as it emerged in the case of two actors, one at Hammersmith, one in the West End, over whose possible replacement there hung a question mark. The directors of both plays had asked the management to attend a rehearsal. At Hammersmith John Perry made a great to-do; the stage-management were instructed to set up a special rehearsal and all the company, including the unfortunate actor, knew full well what he was there for. But in the West End, Binkie informed no one when he would put in an appearance, and watched silent and unobserved from the gods. Marjorie adds discreetly that she is certain that Binkie had to get John Perry out of more than one scrape.

Frith, while admitting Perry's capacity for hard work, found him bossy and the two started off on the wrong professional foot. Perry quite early on set himself in opposition to Frith, and it is a credit to both that, in spite of this, they collaborated so successfully. It seems clear that Hugh Beaumont was aware of every tension, knew every move within his empire, said nothing unnecessarily, and always retained complete control. He let John Perry imagine he was having his own way, but as Frith says, 'Binkie was behind everything'. Neither was Perry above playing the system. He was in the habit of inviting Robert Flemyng and others out to 'non-profit making lunches' and during his time at Hammersmith quite a few non-profit making jollities seem to have taken place.

Everything I had heard about John Perry over the years led me to imagine someone very tricky both socially and professionally, so it was a great surprise, when I finally met him in the course of writing this book, to encounter a dear, gentle old man, charming and courteous, indeed almost courtly; seemingly uninterested in or unable to remember his past. But this man had inspired great love in two of the theatrical giants of this century: Gielgud and Beaumont, and was in charge – nominally at any rate – of one of the most potent and exciting artistic forces in post-war London.

*

This, then was the West End Theatre in which Frith was already active as an actor and was about to enter as a director. Perry had taken over as administrator of Hammersmith shortly after that production of *Caste* with Frith as Captain Hawtree, which had transferred to the Duke of York's in January 1947. During the run Frith had lunch with an old friend, the actress Gwynne Whitby, who had been Hugh Williams's first wife. She had heard that Sir Kenneth Barnes was in a spot of difficulty at R.A.D.A. because a director had dropped out of a production of Pinero's farce, *The Times*, after rehearsals had begun. She thought Frith would be a good replacement and suggested that she put his name forward.

Frith rightly maintains that directors know whether they are capable of directing during the first few rehearsals they ever take. It will be self-evident whether they have authority: that ability to motivate others and release their energy; and whether they are able to create something individual and true springing from strict fidelity to the text and the author's intentions.

He walked up the stairs at Gower Street and had a momentary fit of panic, his mind blanking out. What should he say? How on earth should he start?

Twenty-two students were sitting waiting. He asked them to play a scene that had already been prepared. Afterwards he stopped them and spoke, and found himself surprised at what was coming out of his mouth. The students were listening and looked interested. He was directing them.

*

The job of director is a fairly recent development in the theatre. Obviously there had always been someone who was in overall charge of a production: rehearsing actors, ordering entrances, exits and moves. Until the middle of the nineteenth century the responsibility seems generally to have been divided between the stage-manager, (called the 'Prompter' in the eighteenth century) who hired the supporting players and made arrangements for the sets and costumes, and the leading actor who gave the entrances and exits and organised the actors' moves around his own performance.

There were some exceptions to this. David Garrick and his company at Drury Lane in the mid-eighteenth century, with more money and rehearsal time at their disposal, were apparently capable of achieving a properly integrated ensemble production; Jonson's *Every Man In His Humour*, was a byword for excellent team work and careful attention to the smallest detail.

By the 1870s it was fairly common for someone to be credited as 'director' in the programme, although he was nearly always otherwise connected with the production: author, leading man or stage-manager. The first director to be employed independently was Lewis Wingfield, hired by Lily Langtry for her *As You Like It* in 1890, and 'director' was what he was called. The name did not stick, however, and the term 'producer' was more often used from – the 1900s onwards. Gordon Craig in *The Art of the Theatre* in 1905, where he argues for the increased importance of the position of director, still calls him the stage-manager.

Directors in the modern sense really sprang from the Duke of Saxe-Meiningen, who founded his own troupe in the 1870s, and whose ensemble productions greatly influenced Stanislavsky in Russia, Reinhardt in Germany, and even Frank Benson in England. But from the 1900s, theorists like Adolph Appia and Gordon Craig were expounding the belief that the director should be the prime creator in the theatre, should carry an overall conception of a play and explore the text with the cast as well as take rehearsals and block the moves.

Here I have used the term 'director' throughout, but for most of the plays he 'directed', Frith was called the Producer. The word director in its original sense, filtered back from America during the late 1950s, and was established by the early sixties, while the 'producer' became, as in America, the person who raised the money and set up the production.

It is a fair baptism of fire to have to cope with the technical demands and precision of a farce at first go, but *The Times* was a success, and quite simply, Frith knew what he had to do for the rest of his life. Sir Kenneth asked him to direct two further plays: Rodney Ackland's *After October,* which he chose himself, and *Cymbeline,* with Shaw's last act, which was chosen for him. In the summer Barnes invited him to become a permanent member of staff and to be in charge of the final show, but, by then, a real opportunity for directing professionally had arisen and he told Sir Kenneth that he felt he was beginning to feel too cosy and safe as the most popular master in the school at R.A;D.A., and felt he needed to go out and work with the grown-ups.

Most actors who become directors are told by earlier actor colleagues that their move over has come as no surprise. They always seemed to have an overall grasp of plays, and to be viewing productions as a whole, rather than just from the point of view of their own part. Such was the view that Michael Gough had of Frith and which was reinforced during the Oxford *School for Scandal* in 1945. A group of the cast and their director, Christopher Fry, were concerned about their fellow pacifist Wynyard Browne, who had been invalided out of the Non-Combatant Corps with a nervous breakdown. They telephoned him in Norwich, where he was living with his mother, and asked him to come over; but he was unable to face people with whom he had been associated in the past and who were engaged in activities he would have liked to be doing himself, and declined.

While recuperating, Wynyard Browne wrote a play, in pencil in a school exercise book and, without much confidence, showed it to Michael Gough who suggested showing it to Frith. He went up to London, read it to Frith aloud, and it became the turning point of both their lives.

Wynyard Browne: Quiet
Plays from a Quiet Man

The genesis of Wynyard Browne's plays was the difference in his parents' backgrounds and hence the diversity of his relatives. His father, the Reverend Barry Browne (the basis for the Reverend Martin Gregory in *The Holly and The Ivy*) was an Irish clergyman in the Church of England, incumbent for most of Wynyard's childhood of a Norfolk country parish, while his mother's family, the Malcolmsons, were English and grander: one aunt, who was to provide characters for three of his plays, was the formidable widow of the Dean of Battle.

Born in 1911, Wynyard went to Marlborough (the school in *A Question of Fact),* and Christ's College Cambridge where he was a contemporary of Frith's schoolfriend, Geoffrey Wright. It was at Cambridge that he and Frith, who was then at R.A.D.A., first met. At this stage of his early life, Wynyard Browne was studiously the aesthete, dying his hair, wearing artistic clothes, and generally making a statement to assert his originality. Geoffrey Wright did not take to him at all, finding him a 'cold fish'. If this was so it was obviously a defence to protect a sensitive and introspective nature, for no cold fish could have written plays which have such warmth of heart and compassionate tolerance.

During the thirties, after coming down from Cambridge, Browne moved in the egg-head homosexual circle of Auden, Isherwood, Guy Burgess and Antony Blunt, Wynyard himself being bisexual. Frith met them all from time to time and felt slightly daunted by their high intellectual pretensions.

Wynyard made his living from journalism, and wrote three novels, the first of which, *Queenie Molson,* was well received and reasonably successful. While most of his friends were gravitating towards Communism – and, in the case of Burgess and Blunt, treachery as well – Wynyard became an ardent pacifist and Conscientious Objector. His gentle and ironic temperament was ill-suited to the rough physical labour required by the Non-Combatant Corps, and his war, although largely spent in the company of Michael Gough and Christopher Fry, was not happy.

While stationed at Manchester one weekend in 1941, he saw that Frith, on tour with *Rise Above It,* was playing at the Royal Court Theatre, Liverpool. He went to see it. There was fog that night, and, as the performance ended, an air-raid. Frith came out of the stage-door to find the unannounced Wynyard waiting. They found somewhere to have supper, and, back at the Stork Hotel, established a romantic friendship in which the sex was obviously of secondary importance. He visited again the following weekend; and then their paths diverged.

Wynyard eventually had a nervous breakdown, was invalided out of the Non-Combatant Corps, and sent to recuperate with his widowed mother, by then living in Norwich. It was while he was in Norwich that Frith, Michael Gough and Christopher Fry made contact with him and that contact was far from wasted, as during his convalescence Wynyard had written a play, in which he had little confidence, as his own self-esteem was currently so low. The play, completed in 1946, was called *Dark Summer.* He asked Michael Gough to read it, and, as we have seen, Gough suggested that Frith might have the better overall judgement of what made a good play. Frith's name was also brought up by the second person to whom he talked.

Before the war, the agents for Wynyard's novels had been the distinguished firm of Curtis Brown. Working there was an ex-actor called Archibald Batty, a marvellous old Pro. and much liked. Batty too suggested that Frith, as a friend, had views worth listening to; and shyly, Wynyard took his school exercise book, in which *Dark Summer* was written in pencil longhand, to read to Frith.

Immediately, Frith knew that he wanted to direct it, and he took a six month option with £100 of his own savings. Wynyard could hardly believe this favourable reaction, so shaky was his confidence still.

Frith took the play to Tennents, for whom he had worked in *While the Sun Shines.* At this stage, he wisely seems not to have proposed himself as the director as he had, as yet, directed nothing professionally. Binkie Beaumont liked it and said that the main company H.M. Tennent Ltd, would do it in the West End if one of three actresses could be persuaded to play the leading role: Flora Robson, Peggy Ashcroft or Valerie Taylor. Persuaded is the right word, for this leading role is a German-Jewish refugee, Gisela, who has to be extremely ugly. That eliminated Flora Robson, who felt herself to be a plain woman, for as Frith points out, it is enjoyable for an actress to play being ugly if she can put on a funny make-up and make a feature of it in an Ugly Duchess character performance; but it is another matter if she does not need make-up at all. For whatever reasons the other two actresses rejected it as well, and, after six months, the script was returned to Frith.

Wynyard then begged him not to waste his money by renewing his option, but, by now the play had become a cause, and Frith was single-minded in his determination to see it produced. The option was renewed a second time and, when Frith was acting in *Caste,* Tennents, without giving a reason, suddenly changed their minds and said that Tennent Productions would mount it at Hammersmith – if somebody reasonably well-known could be found to play Gisela. Joan Miller, who had made a success in a play called *Pick-Up Girl,* was engaged. So anxious was John Perry that this part should be well cast that he seems to have had little interest in who directed. Wynyard Browne wrote from Norwich: 'I am delighted about Joan Miller – How nice that someone is enthusiastic for a change. I've often said if I could write a few plays as good as Rodney Ackland's I should die happy; and it's with Rodney Ackland that you compare me. You don't say anything about you producing except that J Perry said he thought it an easy piece to produce. I hope v. much that if Tennents do it you will produce.'

The action of *Dark Summer* is set in the living-room of Mrs Hadow's house in an English Provincial City not unlike Norwich where the play was written. The time is the summer and autumn immediately after the war. The household consists of Mrs Hadow (Jean Cadell), a respectable middle-class widow of sixty, who lives with her son Stephen (Dan Cunningham), a man of twenty-eight, blinded during the war and awaiting a fourth operation which is hoped will restore his sight; Miss Loder (Nora Nicholson), an elderly spinster in reduced circumstances, taken in by Mrs Hadow after being bombed out, and who supplements her meagre rent by housework; and, sent as a cook by an agency, Gisela (Joan Miller), a German-Jewish refugee of thirty-five, who, before the war, was a Research Chemist in Vienna, and whose status with the Hadows is more that of an equal than a servant. While serving in wartime Cairo, Stephen has become engaged to Judy van Haan (Annabel Maule), a girl of smart-bohemian upbringing.

The play is built on the conflict of the four women over the one man. Stephen's blindness persists for the summer section of the play (Acts I and II), hence the title; and this blindness is clearly a metaphor for Wynyard's own state of mind during his Norwich convalescence. Stephen's confidence is severely shaken but not destroyed; his manner temporarily rather than temperamentally neurotic.

The premise is simple. In his blindness Stephen has developed a deep emotional bond with the unattractive Gisela, because of her fine mind and understanding spirit, but has fallen out of love with Judy who, with the aesthetic and sexual pleasure of looking at her denied to him, seems immature and shallow. Gisela knows that he has hoarded sleeping pills, planning suicide should his operation fail. In a powerful yet simple scene, she dissuades him:

GISELA. In Vienna I had many, many friends who killed themselves . . . They had lost everything, their business, their money, their friends. They were Jews. Everyone hated them. They had to leave their homes and many of them were old people. They were too old to start life again in a new country. It is quite different for you Stephen everyone loves you and you are young. You have your life before you.

She admits she too, has tried to kill herself, while working for an old woman in London.

. . . And one Sunday I go to a concert, the Philharmonica, and I was standing in the queue and outside the theatre was the photograph of a Jewish comedian who was coming next week and some children had written on the wall, you know how they do, 'Down with the Jews, Dirty Yid'. I was staring at it all the time I was waiting for the concert and suddenly I was so unhappy, I could not go to the concert. All that afternoon I was so unhappy and in the evening, when the old woman had gone to church, I tried to kill myself . . .

and

I go down to the kitchen and I begin to block up the windows and all the time I am thinking 'the Nazis are doing this to me, the Nazis are doing this.' And suddenly I see it was true. I was doing their work for them. And I see something more. Why are we against the Nazis, Stephen? Why must we always be against such people everywhere? Because they destroy, always they destroy. They are the forces of death, Stephen. And if we do not wish to be like them, always we must respect life. All life, Stephen, even our own. So I open the windows and cook the old woman's supper instead. (Act II Scene 2.)

She then declares her love, without sentiment and movingly. They kiss, and he asks her to stay with him if the operation fails. She promises, but says if it succeeds he must ask her again. As he goes it is obvious, and for obvious reasons, she hopes it will fail.

The operation is successful, however, and the Third Act encounter between Stephen and Gisela is excellently set up. After he teases and flirts with Miss Loder he and his mother sit down to a special supper cooked by Gisela but fetched by Mrs Hadow. When Gisela enters timidly and, at first, unobserved, she has changed into a 'foreign and rather odd looking' red velvet dress in an effort to make herself appealing. Stephen carries off the moment, but gives himself away by asking her to marry him far too abruptly. She asks to speak to Stephen alone, and says that she knows she is a disappointment and tells him to go to Judy. He does, and Mrs Hadow and Gisela are alone. Gisela tells Mrs Hadow of Stephen's sleeping tablets, and Mrs Hadow realises Gisela has saved her son's life. She leaves her alone to await Stephen's return.

When they come back, Judy tries to thank Gisela for what she has done, only to be told that she did not do it for her, but for Stephen. She tells them she is leaving the next day, for now the Ministry of Labour has cleared her work permit she has obtained a job as a Research Chemist in London. They say goodnight and Stephen and Judy leave to celebrate.

Dark Summer is an immensely promising first play and was so judged by the critics: but it is still a 'prentice effort, an adumbration of what Wynyard Browne was able to fill in fuller with more experience. He is already a perceptive playwright of relationships. If the plot is somewhat contrived, he draws his characters with understanding and humour and his writing is always sensitive. He writes true – with irony blocking sentimentality. He never begs sympathy for his characters. He writes them with warmth and asks us to be tolerant and understanding, but, because he never *requests* our emotional engagement, he often receives it. He is never a sensationalist.

Every character is written from their own point of view. Mrs Hadow, who could so easily be an over-possessive and interfering mother comes across behaving like most women of her generation and class; perhaps misguided, but wanting the best for her son's happiness, unwilling to trust his future to a girl like Judy, whom she regards as flighty. Is she so wrong? And Judy, whom can make the chaotic life of her gambling mother so readily amusing, really tells those anecdotes to make herself seem more interesting. Gisela thinks that when Judy has suffered, she will have the potential for understanding, and because we have seen her intelligence and vulnerability, we hope so too. One dreads to think what a lesser playwright of the 1940s would have made of this character.

Miss Loder is an entirely successful creation: comic and absurd, unpleasant and pitiful. Desperate to ding on to her dignity, in her social demotion she has retained none; while Gisela, the intellectual and spiritual aristocrat, has fitted into a life of intellectual deprivation with commendable dignity. Miss Loader thinks she has self-knowledge and, surprisingly, she is aware of how others view her, yet she does not think well of people, and attributes to Gisela the kind of scheming and self-interested behaviour of which she herself would be guilty. Yet her future uncertainty and her feeling of being adrift captures our sympathy.

The part of Stephen, Frith feels, was the play's weakness, and perhaps he does not quite have the three dimensions of the other characters, but, for me he is credible. The catalyst fought over by the four women; a basically ordinary and decent young man suffering extraordinary restrictions. Perhaps the fault was with the actor.

Gisela is a wonderful role because, from the start, we are aware of her intelligence and humanity. Her dichotomy is the complete security of her belief in freedom and the worth of life, and her insecurity in her worth as a woman. She may be tasteless in the gaudy dress she puts on to appear more attractive, yet her philosophy and her courage are in the very finest taste.

Although the subject matter is basically autobiographical in all Wynyard's plays, his own voice in the writing is quiet. He never proselytised because he knew that truth never constrains. Yet there are glimpses of his own views. The mixture of enjoyment and resentment at being the only man in a family of smothering women was not unknown to him, and his views on religion were Gisela's: humanist and anti-clerical.

The production was troublesome, and for Frith that trouble stemmed from the leading lady, Joan Miller. *The Evening News* described her as a 'former television announcer who was recently in *Pick Up Girl* and figured in a law suit over her contract with the New Lindsey Club'. Her husband was Peter Cotes, elder brother of the Boulting twins, and formerly the director of the New Lindsey Club. Wynyard Browne did not care for Peter Cotes, writing to Frith: 'the spectre of Peter Cotes well haunts me – a wraith of stale smoke from the Criterion Brasserie 15 years ago'.

Peter Cotes had just had a bad experience with Tennents. *Deep Are The Roots,* an American play by Arnaud D'Usseau and James Gow, with a racial theme, was being brought over from Broadway and three of the black American actors and a white girl, Betsy Drake, were to repeat their performances in London. Peter Cotes was engaged to redirect. After a few days of rehearsals the Americans went *en bloc* to Binkie Beaumont and asked to return to New York. They said the cause of their misery was Peter Cotes's direction. Beaumont, who could have held them all to their contracts, sacked Cotes and the production was taken on by the Tennent's Casting Director, Daphne Rye. This left Peter Cotes very bitter indeed, says Frith 'much more so than anybody else I have known in similar circumstances, and it rebounded on me because Miss Miller started to take direction from Peter Cotes at home.' Was Cotes deliberately causing trouble? Did he want to show Tennents that he was a far better director than a tyro like Frith Banbury? Or did Joan Miller genuinely find Frith no good? Whatever his motive, his actions resound as unprofessional. Neither Miller nor Cotes had a ray of humour, and like all the humourless they lacked a sense of proportion. In the last scene, Cotes invented a piece of business for his wife in which she pulled a cloth from a table and dragged it across the stage. This in a very delicate scene where direction and playing have to diffuse any possible melodrama in the situation. Frith vetoed the business: Joan Miller refused to remove it: and the management became involved. John Perry was angry that the production was causing problems but fully supported Frith's judgement. Worse was to come, however.

They opened at Hammersmith in October 1947, then played Bournemouth, did a series of one to three night stands in Holland and returned for a week at Brighton before the West End opening at the St Martin's in December. All the while there were rehearsals. But at Brighton, taking advantage of Frith's absence in London, Joan Miller called the full company, and the likes of Jean Cadell and Nora Nicholson arrived to find Peter Cotes in the stalls intending to direct them. 'This,' as Frith aptly observes, 'was bad'. So electric was the atmosphere by then – Joan Miller increasingly bolshie and refusing to do anything she was asked – that Frith was not alone in fearing that Cotes would appear and make a public scene at the First Night in London.

He did not, but Frith must still have been in a state, as he remembers the notices as merely promising. They were a great deal more than that. They were of a kind for which every new writer and director must pray:

'For two and a half hours last night, we were buffeted and rocked by an emotional storm of a play which has some of the best acting seen in London for years,' wrote David Lewin in *The Daily Express*. Philip

Hope-Wallace in *The Manchester Guardian,* ' . . . a serious and affecting drama of the kind growing rare on our stage. Not politics nor yet psycho-neurosis is its theme: but personal relationships . . . Well directed by Frith Banbury.' 'The dialogue keeps an uncommon edge and truth. The acting and Frith Banbury's production match it,' said Ivor Brown in the *Observer,* and to top it all, Harold Hobson in *The Sunday Times:* ' . . . halfway through the play the wonder happens, and the glory comes. After the fiancée has left, Gisela (Jewish, ugly, ageing and fat) makes Stephen a long declaration of love. It is a fresh, it is a unique experience; and I defy anyone to listen to it unmoved.'

Frith, who thought Jean Cadell and Nora Nicholson quite wonderful, felt that if only Joan Miller had had a sense of proportion she could have been very good, 'as it was she was quite good'. After a few weeks at the St Martin's, she relinquished the part because of her bad back and was replaced by Selma Vaz Dias. It is only fair to say, though, that the run did not survive this change of cast.

Peter Cotes continued to harbour a grudge against Tennents. He considered the theatrical establishment was a homosexual mafia from which he was excluded – virile theatre being his *forte.* He was later to write letters to trade papers venting this opinion. His bitterness and homophobia led him to try and cause trouble at a very high level.

This traumatic first production paid its dividends, however. Nothing was to seem so bad in the future, and Frith, thinking how he might have better handled Miss Miller, gained his famous expertise in dealing with difficult leading actresses.

Wynyard wrote to him before the First Night: 'Whatever they say I was entirely satisfied with your production. Your method, your manner may have irritated them; and that might justify a little fuss; but not all this. Ladies who go on the stage should be tougher. They should have thicker skins and their emotions more under control. Don't *worry* about it.'

The London run of *Dark Summer* closed after nine weeks and the play went on a fourteen week tour. The tour was re-directed by Joan Yeaxlee, who had been in charge of the summer season at Llandrindod Wells and who, more significantly, had just married Wynyard Browne. Frith was by then at the Guildford Rep. directing Priestley's *Ever Since Paradise.* Gisela was played on tour by Rosalinde Fuller, and Stephen by a young actor just out of the Air Force called Richard Burton, and what blazing inner torment he must have brought to the blind boy.

Wynyard wrote: 'Rosalinde is the funniest lady. I am devoted to her. But the best stories about her would be wasted in writing. They must be told – and with a wealth of gesture! You won't have heard I imagine that the boy is leaving after Brighton (breaking his contract I suppose!) to make a film with Emlyn Williams. A pity because he is v. good indeed. His own story is very *Corn is Green*. His father was a miner a thief & a drunkard. The terror of Rhondda [sic]. Richard was brought up in poverty by his elder sister & then adopted at the age of fourteen by the local schoolmaster whose name was Burton etc. etc. All this explains a lot.'

It was now that Frith went to his mother with a proposition. He asked her to set him up so he could present and direct plays of his own choice in his own way. Mrs Banbury, by now satisfied that Frith was making good in the theatre, gave him £10,000, a very considerable sum of money. Her largesse separated Frith from the lot of most young directors, and gave him a reputation as a Maecenas, which he has never lost.

His first action was to pay Wynyard Browne £1,000; one half non-returnable, the other in advance of royalties, for his next four plays. They both then set up a company, whose aim was foremost to present Wynyard's plays with Frith as the director. They were later to be joined by a third partner, Emmanuel Wax.

Frith was still in demand as an actor. He was offered Cloten in *Cymbeline* and Lysander in *A Midsummer Night's Dream* at Stratford in 1948, but he now wanted to manage and direct. Single-minded as always, he realised combining these with acting would only dissipate his energies.

While Wynyard was working on his second play, the literary agent Margery Vosper (sister of Frank) sent him a comedy by Basil Thomas, *Shooting Star,* which extracted laughs – at times almost farcical – out of the unlikely subject of the transfer system in Association Football. Wynyard was not all that keen on it but kindly wrote, 'You're a very good play-doctor & can, as we know, work wonders.' Wisely Frith did not carry all the investment himself, and theatre 'angels', being suspicious, as always, of new managements, most of the backing came from friends and colleagues: Roger Livesey and his wife Ursula Jeans; Marjorie Fielding and the agent Jack Hunter.

Basil Thomas was the cousin of Derek Salberg, whose family owned the Alexandra Theatre, Birmingham. He had already written the books for two musicals, and the lyrics for numbers like *Wind Around My Heart,* for Beatrice Lillie. He and play-doctor Banbury did a considerable amount of work on the original script, and the result is really not bad at all: certainly better than its reception warranted.

Shooting Star opened at the Grand Wolverhampton and toured the provinces. Howard and Wyndham, the owners of most of the major provincial theatres, either because they were unsure of the subject matter, or because they did not rate highly this new management, did not give it prestigious dates. They were right. In spite of good local press, the exploitation of a young player by a villainous team manager was not a theme that interested the middle-aged and middle-class audiences of the regions. It opened in London at the Playhouse, that charming theatre to which it is difficult to entice people. Frith remembers the reviews as excellent, and indeed they were, the kind of good reviews that dampen the spirits: 'For goodness sake,' said *The Sunday Dispatch,* 'don't be put off Basil Thomas's comedy because you're not interested in dirty work connected with footballers' transfers or in football. It's original, topical and funny.' Praise that must have kept people away in droves.

Buoyed up by the press, and thinking he had a great hit, Frith went down to the theatre the following morning to find that not one single ticket had been bought for any performance. Buying and selling footballers was clearly box-office poison. The actors arrived for the Second Night, delighted with themselves and expecting a long run, and were astonished at the news. The theatre had been booked for six weeks, so the play limped along with heavily papered houses, before closing with large losses for all concerned. It was, says Frith, 'A strange, instructive beginning to my career as a manager'.

The *Shooting Star* experience was instructive in that it brought home to Frith the difficulties of being both manager and director, so when Wynyard Browne delivered his second play *The Holly and The Ivy,* which arrived, needing little further work, and which Frith loved at once, he took it – wanting to abnegate managerial responsibilities and concentrate on directing only – to H.M. Tennent. Rather to his surprise, instead of a reply from Binkie, he was summoned to the Globe Theatre for an interview with John Perry. Here he was informed that Tennents loved the play too – indeed who could not? – and wanted to present it in the West End, under their commercial banner, but, quite categorically, without Frith as director. Frith, who owned the rights, asked why not. Because he 'had not done a good job' on *Dark Summer.* Did that mean Tennents considered the production poor? No, but Tennents considered he had not done a good job. Frith realised that Perry was still angry at what he hoped would be an easy trouble-free little play causing the management so many headaches. Wynyard Browne then went into action and, going above Perry's head, he saw Binkie Beaumont. Binkie said John only meant that Frith could not direct if the play was presented by H.M. Tennent Ltd in the West End. At Hammersmith, he would be quite happy for Frith to take it on. John Perry had meant nothing of the sort and was very unhappy indeed. Angry at being overridden he stayed well clear of *The Holly and The Ivy* Company until after it had opened.

With *The Holly and The Ivy,* Wynyard Browne came into his own. The humour and understanding already visible in *Dark Summer* are now elevated into real integrity and, at times, wisdom. Neither does he resort to the occasional dramatic contrivances of the earlier play, the plot here becomes much more of a pretext to observe the relationships of a group of people. He is a playwright of relationships, and looks on at his characters' doings with charity. Mood, action and character are now brought together as a whole, and the result is poetry. If he was compared to Chekhov it was surely only because they both share this style of poetic naturalism. They share too the gentle humour: poor lives being dealt with in a comic way. Obviously Browne does not have Chekhov's depth and range, but he has the irony which stops sentimentality. He is a minimalist of great charm.

The play deals with a quite specific social order: an Irish vicar of a Norfolk parish and his children and relations who are gathering to celebrate Christmas, the strange time of the year when everything is turned upside down. When the Lord of Misrule rules. The mood of the play is caught exactly by the playwright himself in the Preface:

'*The Holly and The Ivy* is, above all, a play of mood. It was suggested by the sight of a snow-covered tree outside a window on a lowering December afternoon and by the thought of those faded, melancholy Georgian vicarages, scattered all over Norfolk, in every village and country town, centres of a decaying Christian tradition, where the cross-currents of family feeling have an especial poignancy at Christmas time.

"The holly bears a savour as bitter as any gall," says the carol and these words might describe the sudden pang which most people have felt at some period of their lives during the festivities of Christmas, a cold breath of the irony which lurks at the heart of a great festival of religious rejoicing in a sceptical age.

It is this irony of Christmas which disturbs and blows away the myths of habit, so that the characters, during the course of the play, come to see each other for the first time as they really are; and the reality seems to them at first as strange and new as the familiar Norfolk landscape outside their windows after a night when snow has fallen.'

The whole play is set in the living room of one of these Georgian Norfolk vicarages. Tanya Moiseiwitsch (whom Wynyard and Joan wanted Frith to marry!) designed a set which looks completely right. A large tree, black and foreboding against a lowering sky, is seen through the window. In the First Act, it is Christmas Eve, the first since the death of Mrs Gregory. This act really only provides mood and atmosphere, and introduces the characters in their variety.

Jenny Gregory (Jane Baxter) has to decide whether to marry her fiancé David Paterson, (Andrew Crawford) or stay and look after her father the Reverend Martin Gregory, (Herbert Lomas) who is quirky, erudite, unable to listen, and full of Irish charm. His son Mick (Bryan Forbes), on National Service, has wrangled leave from the army. The other guests are: Aunt Lydia, Gregory's sister-in-law (Margaret Halstan) – based on Wynyard's aunt, the wife of the Dean of Battle – grand, gushing and the widow, after a brief marriage, of a King's Messenger, an experience which has made her sentimental about romance; and Aunt Bridget (Maureen Delany), Gregory's sister: a cross Irish lady living in reduced circumstances in West Hampstead, very sensitive about being poor, and quick to take offence.

Colonel Richard Wyndham (Patrick Waddington), a cousin of the late Mrs Gregory, a worldly-wise bachelor and ex-soldier, was meant to drive down with his goddaughter Margaret (Daphne Arthur), the younger Gregory sister who is a fashion correspondent in London; but he makes her excuses as she is apparently 'not feeling very well. Touch of 'flu, I think.' However she does appear later, obviously under strain and looking ill. She helps herself to whisky and is caught by Richard who tells her firmly that this is not the place to start her drinking.

In the Second Act, after dinner that evening, Gregory, noticing Margaret's lowness of spirits and pallor, repeatedly presses whisky on her. Finally she snaps: 'Didn't you hear me say "no thankyou"?' Richard saves this awkward moment by tactfully taking the glass himself. There is an uneasy silence after which Jenny says quietly, dropped as it were from far-away, 'how bitter the holly smells,' the atmosphere broken by Aunt Lydia's 'Holly? I didn't know it had a smell'. A real moment of mood and mood-change. After Gregory has gone to his study to work on his Christmas sermon, the aunts attack Margaret for her selfishness in leaving all the care of her father to Jenny. They tell her that in the event of Jenny's marrying she would have to consider returning home.

In a scene for the two sisters, Margaret discovers that Jenny does indeed wish to marry. Jenny asks why Margaret has changed so. What has happened to her? 'Oh why must you always crackle like ice?' Then Margaret comes clean: she has had an affair with an airman who was horribly killed, and by him had an illegitimate child, Simon. Jenny is sympathetic and excited, 'I long to see him'. But Simon has died of meningitis the year before. That is why Margaret has to anaesthetise the feelings she cannot handle. The tension here is very well sustained by the revelations being strung out. She did not come home before because she 'Couldn't stand the pretence . . . Father thinks of me as someone I no longer am. I *am* what has happened to me.' Jenny realises that Margaret's return is impossible and that she will have to stay, foregoing her own marriage.

Richard and Margaret talk about her alcoholism. He tells her that, paradoxically, she will only really be happy when she can remove the blocks that prevent her from coming home. She feels at ease with her drinking friends in London, and uncomfortable with her family, yet it is her drinking cronies that are not really her. She stays out and drinks because she cannot face returning to the loneliness of her flat while she is still sober enough to think.

MARGARET. I've always wondered why my parents ever chose you to be a godfather. You don't even believe in God . . . or do you?
RICHARD. I don't like the smell of hassocks, if that's what you mean.

Unable to bear the atmosphere Mick and Margaret escape by going to the pictures. Gregory explains his sermon about the origins of Christmas. 'It was the season of general licence when everything was topsy-turvy. The slaves were masters and the masters slaves.' The long quiet evening begins. The Aunts, Bridget and Lydia try to persuade Gregory to retire for Jenny's sake as well as his own. He questions Jenny, who is embarrassed, but he stresses that it is out of the question as he needs to work for another four years to pay for Mick at Cambridge, because a university is almost the only place left where truth is valued for its own sake.

BRIDGET. That's highfalutin' talk. What does the truth, as you call it, matter to Michael?

GREGORY *(suddenly angry)*. It matters to any man born, Bridget. I'll not have you saying that about Michael or anyone else. We're all born and we've all to die; and the truth matters to all of us – the truth about what we are and what we're for – the truth about human destiny.

Then Mick and Margaret return drunk. Margaret passes out and is carried upstairs by her godfather.

GREGORY (to *Mick*). You've not been near a cinema. Why don't you tell the truth?
MICK. The truth? *(Then suddenly bitter.)* You can't be told the truth, that's the trouble . . . that's the whole trouble . . .

It is Christmas morning in the third act. The sunshine is brilliant and the tree is seen snow-covered and sunlit against a blue sky. Last evening's traumatic happening has metaphorically cleared the air. Gregory asks Mick what he meant by saying he could not be told the truth.

MICK. Well – I meant – exactly what I said. You can't be told the truth. At least not by us. Not by Jenny and Margaret and me. The real facts about us would upset you too much. So we lie to you. Or, at least, if we don't lie, we conceal the truth from you. The whole situation in this house is built on lies and concealment.

Mick tells him about Margaret's drinking, Jenny's wish to be married, and Margaret's refusal to come home when Jenny asked her, 'because she couldn't face settling down here to a life of false pretences.' Mick tells him the whole truth about Margaret and leaves the room upset. Margaret comes downstairs, Gregory apologises for having failed her. 'That's what distresses me. That you *had* to manage alone . . . Michael tells me you've all of you always been afraid to speak freely before me.'

They then learn to talk, to communicate. Margaret has a long speech, to begin with fumblingly but later more smoothly articulating her emotions.

GREGORY. D'ye know Margaret, I think you'd be far more comfortable in the world, if you weren't so religious.
MARGARET. I'm not religious. That's the trouble.
GREGORY. But you are, you are. That is religion. What you've just been saying.

MARGARET. You don't seem to understand. I don't believe in anything.

GREGORY. Ach no, it's not belief that's religion. That's not the primary thing at all. There's something else has to be there before that, long before that – something that's the root of all religions in the world – a need. This feeling ye have – if you stick to it, if you go through with it, if ye're honest about it – this need to make sense of the world; that's the prime essential of all religion.

Although their ideas and beliefs are so different, there is no gulf between them because their minds are alike. They work in the same way. *'We can talk!* I can't get used to it.' It is not her idea of the world that has changed, but her idea of him.

Gregory putting on his gum boots to walk to church and take matins remembers an incident in Margaret's childhood, 'You asked me what a judge was. And I was tellin' you. And when I'd finished, there you sat on me knee, starin' at me and frownin' – and do you know what you said? "And who judges the judge?"' It was this moment that Robert Morley remembered all his life. He described Herbert Lomas putting on his boots and saying the last line as an example of great acting.

GREGORY. This talk we've had Margaret, I know the truth has been in that – if not in the words, then between the words . . . or between us. *(The Church Bells break into full peal.)*

The point of the scene, and of the play is that if people of goodwill and with open minds can talk to each other, however fundamental their disagreements about the purpose of life may be – they can connect. From now on Margaret can communicate with her father and thus her return home will be possible.

The Holly and the Ivy is a very English play, full of charm, humour and understanding. A period piece, true, and dealing in understatement, but it is somehow exciting because of its truth and poetry. A lovely play.

When it was being performed by nearly every repertory company in the country, Wynyard went to see a production at the Oxford Playhouse and came back fuming. The play in general and the father-daughter scene in particular had been heavily sentimentalised. It was played as if Margaret had been converted to Christian thinking and, having seen the error of her ways, would from now on, lead a moral rather than an immoral life. After the performance, Wynyard had a question and answer session with the audience. Sweetly and tactfully he told them that what they had wit-nessed was a sentimentalising of his play and a playing of the *scène à faire* in a manner which was against his design. Sweetness and tact he had, but he was also ironic and could be quite sharp. The audience was most indignant and person after person made it quite clear they preferred the tale of the Prodigal Daughter which they had just seen to what the author seemed to want. So he learnt a lesson which was, as he told Frith; 'Between them actors and audiences want to sweeten things up, so it's up to us dramatists to put more acid in to start with. This is the lesson I've learnt from *The Holly and the Ivy.*'

Over the casting, Wynyard had only one request, indeed it was more of an instruction: this was that Aunt Bridget, based on his own Irish aunt in Maida Vale, should be played by the great character actress from the Abbey Theatre, Maureen Delany. She had been the original Bessie Burgess in O'Casey's Easter Rising play, *The Plough and the Stars,* and had recently become internationally known as the brothel-keeper in Carol Reed's film *Odd Man Out.* An unsentimental actress and an unsen-timental woman, she was motherly (calling everyone 'dotie', the Irish for darling), and had a blunt wit. During the run of *The Holly and the Ivy,* one of the younger members of the cast married an Irish starlet. The company were invited to the reception. Maureen Delany took one look at the bride's family, a bunch of raffish Dubliners and loudly pronounced: 'She's nothing but a whore from the stews of Dublin!' Frith really loved her, and approved of her on stage and off. She worked for him again three times, and for two of these the role was re-written into Irish.

The other aunt, Lydia, was played by Margaret Halstan, a leading lady of the pre-First War Theatre, who had stories of being chased round the Dome at His Majesty's by Herbert Tree. These were told only in the strictest privacy, for she was something of a *grande dame* off stage. A most improbable friendship developed between her and Maureen Delany, who fussed over her comfort and made sure everyone accorded Miss Halstan the status they both considered she deserved. She continued acting into very old age and was still walking on nightly as the Queen of Transylvania, ('Charming! Charming!') in *My Fair Lady* when in her late eighties.

There was much talk of Ralph Richardson, who was keenly inter-ested, playing Gregory, and indeed, he was to play him later in the film, but Frith, knowing that an actor of Richardson's enormous personality would unbalance the delicate ensemble of his pro-duction, resolutely held out for Herbert Lomas known, because of his large size, as 'Tiny'. He was by then ageing and deaf, but his performance as the Irish parson was the performance of his career. Robert Morley was not alone in thinking that, at moments, it reached greatness.

Jane Baxter, sweet-natured English rose, played Jenny, and Daphne Arthur, intense and neurotic, Margaret, and as Mick, a slight young man, who later left acting for directing films: Bryan Forbes. Frith had a high opinion of his talents, but although he was rehearsing well, his performance was on too small a scale. Frith, wanting to boost his morale, took him out to lunch. Bryan Forbes sat at the table, white-faced. Frith said, 'I've asked you out to lunch to tell you I think you're going to be very good, but everything has to be four times larger.' Forbes let out a great gasp of relief, 'I thought you were going to give me the sack.' Frith was astonished but it reminded him of the basic insecurity of all actors: the director asks me to lunch, ergo either he wants to seduce me or to sack me.

The only role for which an actor did not immediately suggest himself was Richard Wyndham. Discussing the casting before rehearsals, Frith thought that it could be a wonderful part for an actor of real weight, yet sensitivity, with the ability to suggest Richard's past as officer and gentleman. There was one actor who had all these qualities: Cathleen Nesbitt's husband, C.B. (Cecil) Ramage. He had met his wife at the O.U.D.S., playing Antony to her Cleopatra, and, after a short career as a barrister, had gone on stage professionally; but he had also become alcoholic, and Tennents had decided that he was no longer employable. Cathleen Nesbitt, hearing of this faint chance of her husband's rehabilitation, went to Binkie Beaumont and assured him, as so many wives of alcoholics have done, that he was now reformed and sober. So he was cast.

The rehearsals were productive and untroubled. The complete absence of the management, in the person of John Perry, was noticed but not unduly worried over. One day however, Cecil Ramage sent a message saying that he would not be in that morning as he had a 'cold'. Frith says, 'I should have seen the red light but didn't choose to.'

The management stayed away from the opening in Cardiff at the end of February 1950. In spite of that it was a wonderful First Night with an appreciative audience and excellent local press. On the Tuesday – the day following the opening, and exhilarated by their notices, Frith and Cecil Ramage had lunch together. Cecil thanked Frith for taking the risk of giving him the job and said he was so happy with the play and the company, and that he thought Herbert Lomas quite wonderful: and Frith, on his side, was relieved, and confident that Cecil was no longer going to be a worry.

The following day, Wednesday, Frith returned to London, planning to come back for the Saturday matinee, but late that night the stage-manager telephoned with grave news. Cecil Ramage had been 'absolutely plastered' during the performance. He had dropped Daphne Arthur (who, ironically, was the one meant to be drunk) as he was carrying her upstairs, and had really ruined the evening. Miss Halstan had had hysterics at fall of curtain, Mr Lomas had retreated into complete deafness and the company was in turmoil. What was to be done?

Frith had two immediate thoughts. The first was that there was no point involving the management, who seemed to have no interest in the play whatsoever; the second, more practical, was that Ramage *had* to be kept sober until the end of Friday because on Friday, there would be no understudy if Ramage was unable to go on. One of the cast, Andrew Crawford, who played David Paterson, had leave of absence to complete a film, and David Langton, who was understudying both Cecil Ramage and Andrew Crawford, had to go on for Crawford. On Thursday Frith sped hotfoot back to Cardiff where Cecil was playing the two performances in an alcoholic haze.

At a hastily assembled late-night meeting, Jane Baxter and Daphne Arthur volunteered to act as Cecil's minders during Friday. Jane Baxter sat with him all morning, and, in the afternoon, Daphne Arthur took him to the cinema. During the film he said, 'Excuse me, I wish to visit the gentlemen's lavatory,' and disappeared for good.

Daphne rushed back to the hotel and shouted at Frith, 'I can't find him, I can't find him!' Together they ran upstairs and banged on Cecil's door and, sure enough, were answered by a strange gurgling. But the door was locked, and a chambermaid with a master key had to be found. On entering they saw Cecil, lying on the bed, dead to the world, surrounded by empty bottles. They shook him. He opened one eye and beamed, 'Frith!' (as if surprised and delighted to see him there.) 'You look worried.' He was plied with coffee to no visible avail, and Frith had to grey his hair and go on with the book that evening. This was scary, to put it mildly, as one scene had been reversed – the end at the beginning – and had not been typed out. The management were nowhere.

The next morning, 'To this distinguished chap, and oh so nice! I had to say "Cecil, that's it."' It was the end of Ramage's career. He lived a long life in a Separate-Tables Hotel on the SouthCoast, paid for by Cathleen Nesbitt, where his alcoholic binges were understood.

Frith telephoned Tennents. All John Perry said was, 'Get X', naming a completely unsuitable actor, but Frith insisted on his second choice, Patrick Waddington, and furthermore, told Perry, as representative of Tennents, that the offer needed to come from them. It was, in fact, Binkie Beaumont who telephoned Patrick Waddington, then holidaying on the Isle of Wight, and he came straight to Cardiff, rehearsing on tour, while David Langton played Richard.

Notwithstanding these dramas, the box-office takings at The Prince of Wales Theatre Cardiff for the week were £621 15s 8d, a large amount, and Binkie Beaumont and John Perry turned up at the opening night of the next date, Cambridge. This was another success. From the start it was clear the play was going to work. Binkie was obviously surprised it was so good – and delighted. It was, Frith thinks, a much better production than *Dark Summer,* helped considerably by Tanya Moiseiwitsch's set. It must have been now that Binkie recognised Frith's worth as a director and marked him out for promotion and collaboration. John Perry stood behind Binkie looking sheepish. 'He,' says Frith, 'rather had egg on his face for giving no support and for underrating the production.'

Beaumont had now made up his own mind about Frith's talent as a director and obviously never listened to Perry's opinion on that matter again. They arrived at Hammersmith on 28 March and transferred to the Duchess on 10 May, running for a year and a half – 412 performances. The reviews were nearly unanimous in praise. The *Daily Express* talked of the 'excited bravos and the stamping of feet' which met the final curtain. 'Herbert Lomas perfectly realises the author's conception. Here is a noble man whom everyone loves, and who loves them without understanding that their lives are being broken under his roof.' Ivor Brown in the *Observer* thought it the best play of middle-class domesticity since Priestley's *The Linden Tree.* Only the *Daily Worker* (the rumblings of unrest, like the fishwives marching to Versailles) said; 'If it is true that tradition is the backbone of the British way of life, I have come to the conclusion that that is what is wrong with the British Theatre too.' Strangely, it never did wonderful business, but it was possible then to keep a play running on reasonable rather than spectacularly good houses, but at its conclusion, Beaumont sent out two tours and it became staple fare for the reps. The film rights were sold to British Lion – the author's share being £1,000.

The famous came too. On the First Night, the *Daily Express* asked, 'Who was that tall man in front of me who laughed so much?' Answer, 'John Gielgud'.

Noel Coward wrote to Frith praising his, 'subtle and delicate direction, every movement seemed true and unforced . . . the whole play is done with taste and discretion. It was such a comforting and gratifying evening in the theatre.'

But the best letter came from Robert Morley. 'A beautifully acted oddly moving play, oddly because there doesn't seem to be, on the surface, anything very new either said or done and yet I have seldom if indeed ever so completely forgotten I was in a theatre.'

Frith was now a director of consequence, viewed by Beaumont in quite a new light. He was offered the direction of H.M. Tennent's official contribution to the 1951 Festival of Britain: N.C. Hunter's *Waters of the Moon* with the two Dames, Edith Evans and Sybil Thorndike. He had arrived.

Wynyard was contracted to Frith for another three plays, but he wrote slowly, for which Frith was unprepared. It was nearly three years after the opening of *The Holly and the Ivy* that the next play, *A Question of Fact* was delivered. By that time Frith had directed Dido Milroy's *Always Afternoon*, Rodney Ackland's adaptation of Hugh Walpole's *The Old Ladies*, Ackland's own *The Pink Room,* and a revival of John Galsworthy's *The Silver Box.* He had had a big flop with Neville Croft's *All the Year Round,* as well as the landmark successes of N.C. Hunter's *Waters of the Moon* and, both in the West End and on Broadway, Terence Rattigan's *The Deep Blue Sea.* By 1953 he was one of the most sought-after of West End directors, and after *The Holly and the Ivy,* Wynyard's reputation as a playwright was worldwide, at least in English speaking countries. So for this next collaboration they were no longer newcomers to their respective crafts, but two successful and established men. Indeed the gaps between Wynyard Browne's plays allowed Frith's career to flourish in a way that, had they followed one upon another speedily, would not have been possible.

A Question of Fact moves on from the naturalistic poetry of *The Holly and the Ivy* to a consideration of the power of imagination itself. The theme of its use and abuse is harnessed to a striking premise: an adopted child discovering that his real father was a murderer.

Wynyard, in his preface, sets out both theme and message:

> In Act One we see Paul Gardiner's imagination (and to a lesser extent the other characters) working, as it were, in a vacuum with only a single,

disturbing clue. In Act Two we see the imagination confronted by the facts, objectively reported in a newspaper; and in Act Three we watch the final confrontation of the imagination with truth. The message of the play (and to those who like a play to have a message, I admit, for once, that the play actually has one) is that only by imagination can we grasp the truth about our fellow men but that, if it is not to mislead us, imagination must be used with love and not with fear.

Paul and Rachel Gardiner (Paul Scofield and Pamela Brown), return from their honeymoon, during which something has obviously come between them. Before their marriage, Paul, who was adopted, has asked his mother about his real parents. After a row, in which he questions her motives for adopting him, she reveals that his natural father was hanged for murder. Paul's imagination, which makes him an inspired teacher in a public school, runs riot in a destructive way. He feels he has to leave his post in spite of the good opinion of his colleagues and a chance of promotion in which he could fulfil himself, and proposes to resign at the end of term. Researching the case in London, under the pretext of writing a book, he finds out that his father – Ron Smith – was described as a psychopath at his trial and, choosing to believe that criminal insanity is hereditary, he informs Rachel that they cannot have children.

Against Paul, the imaginative man – using this gift constructively, as one of the few classics masters who can bridge the gulf of centuries with their pupils, and destructively as the son of a man who he builds up to be a squalid monster – there is seen the power of imagination, or lack of it, in the other characters.

Rachel's mother (Mary Hinton) is a basically decent if conventional woman, but she makes cliched assumptions about people, and has a fundamental lack of understanding. Rachel is nothing out of the ordinary, and has no special equipment for dealing with the situation except – perhaps the one needful thing – love. Her old Nannie (Maureen Delany) is full of fantasies, with the absurd imaginings of the ill-educated and limited. Her father, (Henry Hewitt) along with the old schoolmaster, Arthur Lamb, (Harold Scott) represents the liberal civilised side of the English Establishment, but he has forgotten his access to that civilised enlightenment along with his Greek. Lamb is to retire, and wants Paul to take over his beloved library:

LAMB. You're the only man on the staff here with enough true humanity to make a good librarian. When some dirty little junior boy comes along – you know, one of those frost-bitten chilblainey boys with bad circulation – children of elderly parents, I often think – and wants, say, an engineering text-book ... It needs a man who can see that here may be the beginnings of some great mechanical or scientific achievement. In our job we must be friends to life – even in its most unprepossessing forms ... When some fat, pasty faced fellow wants nothing but erotic poetry – give it to him, give it to him! A good librarian ought to be able to see that here may be – oh, not only a scholar in the making but perhaps a great specialist in nervous disorders – or – or a bishop. You have that imagination, my boy. You can see beyond your nose.

Paul builds up a picture of his real mother as an impoverished, defenceless, little old woman. He finds out that she works in a Department Store and imagines the elderly assistant with bad feet and no hope. By now, feeling responsible for her welfare, he contacts her, and both he and Rachel are nonplussed when she proposes herself for a night's stay.

The arrival of Grace Smith at the end of the Second Act is the surprise of the play, because she is the complete reversal of all that the build-up has led us to expect: a very successful business woman; a buyer for a chain of shops; brisk; no-nonsense; self-possessed, and with exact intuition. Her entrance is set up quite superbly. Rachel's mother wants to leave. 'She's probably some frightful, scheming lady's maid. They used to be fiendish some of them.' But it is too late.

Mrs Smith comes in. She is an extremely smart, middle-aged business woman, very self-possessed, obviously prosperous and successful. Her slightly common accent is camouflaged by real savoir-faire and humour.

All of that description could be applied to the actress who played her: a real star of the past: Gladys Cooper. The effect of Grace Smith's entrance, already theatrical enough, must have been heightened still more by the charisma of the player. (Act II Scene 2.)

She tells Paul that he is like his father, which throws him into the expected fanciful turmoil. Then she explains her husband's charm and *his* power of invention which led him into being a conman – and his insecurity which led him to kill, in a moment of panic, a girl who threatened to reveal his past to his wife. He could never believe he was loved as Grace Smith loved him. Everything we hear about Ron has been seen in Paul:

What you have in common with Ron *is* something good – or it can be. It's all a question of how you use it. Ron became what he was because he was *more* talented than other boys of his kind, not less. He was gifted like you are. But his gift destroyed him. All along the line, imagination was his downfall. Don't imaginative boys here, at this school, pose and pretend and put on acts? Of course they do. But it doesn't matter. They're safe here till it's all over. But where was he at fourteen? A page-boy in a West End hotel . . . Out in the world, you know, that sort of adolescent posing and pretending doesn't take long to become delinquency, false pretences – crime. (Act III.)

But Paul has the means and opportunity to use this gift of imagination to enhance others – if not, 'This resignation of yours will be your murder.' Mrs Smith goes to bed knowing that Paul's greatest test is to come: to repair love shattered, that misuse of his gift has wrought on his marriage.

The play was again presented by Tennent Productions. As the rights were owned by a profit-making company: Frith Banbury Ltd, Frith had to accept, as always with this arrangement, the standard directing fee of £200 for the production, but a far higher box-office percentage than would have been accorded any director financially unconnected with the author: 1.5% of the Box-Office Gross until recoup., and thereafter 2%.

The overall budget was £2,000; over £500 less than that for *The Deep Blue Sea* the previous year – but that had been presented by H.M. Tennents Ltd. Out of this budget £140 was set aside for advertising; a low proportion by today's necessities; and the weekly salaries were as follows:

Gladys Cooper: £100
Pamela Brown: £80
Paul Scofield: £75
Mary Hinton: £40
Harold Scott: £40
Henry Hewitt: £40
Maureen Delany: £30

One hopes poor Maureen Delany was unaware she was earning less than anyone else.

The top salary for Tennent Productions was officially £75; for H.M. Tennent Ltd, £100. This remained in force for some years. So Scofield was on the official top salary, with Pamela Brown on more, and Gladys Cooper on the most H.M. Tennents Ltd ever gave, at that date, her star-status acknowledged. She was probably, too, like most of the biggest names, on a percentage of the Box Office Gross.

Frith and Wynyard were very lucky in their cast, not only the excellence of the three principles, but in the strength of playing from the supporting actors.

'I cannot see you getting that sort of cast in the theatre now. By that I mean you wouldn't get the supporting actors. They would only do parts of that length on the box for much more money, without having to go and do them eight times a week. We, in the theatre now, do have a terrible problem.

Paul Scofield was marvellous, his imagination so strong and playing on his own ambiguous personality. Pam Brown brought to a part that perhaps didn't have all the character that it might have had, enormous character.'

Scofield, then thirty-one, had just finished a season for Gielgud at the Lyric Hammersmith playing Witwoud in *The Way of the World*, Pierre in Otway's *Venice Preserv'd,* and the title role in *Richard II.* Apart from Edith Evans, there was no actor with whom Frith ever worked that he admired more. Their working relationship was to be developed in their next collaboration, *A Dead Secret.*

Pamela Brown, a superb actress greatly admired by Agate, never quite reached the heights predicted for her: she suffered extreme ill health for most of her career and died too young. Often in pain, at rehearsals she could seem remote and withdrawn from the rest of the company, which was a sadness, as by nature she was accessible and very funny.

Grace Smith must have been, in theatrical parlance, a gift of a part for Gladys Cooper. After she had accepted it she had walked into Binkie Beaumont's office and said: 'Well! Wonderful Play! Wonderful Part! There's only one thing to do with it – Learn it!' When she had left, Binkie turned to Frith and said, 'That means she *is* going to learn it.'

This was quite a relief as Gladys Cooper was not over fond of the rehearsals of plays, and in particular, of the learning of lines. She had just been in Noel Coward's *Relative Values,* and there had been rows. Coward, as was his custom, had wanted everyone to know their lines by the first rehearsal. Miss Cooper wanted the play cut. Noel Coward refused to cut until she had learnt. She refused to learn lines which might be cut, and this war went on for the twenty week tour, at the end of which she was still drying. On the First Night in London she had accepted the inevitable and had given a superlatively assured performance, but she and The Master were on very bad terms. Indeed assurance is the quality one most associates with her. On stage she always looked as if she knew exactly what she was doing, even in old age when, if inside information was correct, this was often far from the case.

Paul Scofield assessed her exactly when he called her an athlete. She loved swimming – Edith Evans had even called her beauty 'the real thing, straight out of the bath' – on stage she suggested complete fitness, and health of body, mind and spirit; relaxation and moment-by-moment enjoyment. She was in psychological jargon 'Centred'. For all the talk of her casualness of approach her attitude seems that of the absolute professional. She had no time for Arty Talk, and some considered her a philistine, but acting had originally been a means of putting her legendary beauty to sensible use and she had learnt how to do it with thoroughness. And with the minimum of fuss.

Frith found her the most consistent of leading actresses; her performance hardly varying from night to night, and Scofield remembers how she was always 'there' on stage, how sensitive to variations of pace or unexpected change.

Gladys Cooper's son-in-law, Robert Morley, thought Frith was very good with her, and that she had liked working with him, 'as far as she liked any director'. She also told Robert that as she did not appear in the First Act and in the First Scene of the Second, she had never bothered to read them, and had no idea what took place. According to Sheridan Morley, his grandmother's biographer, she had gone up to Pamela Brown at the first interval of the dress rehearsal and said, 'That was lovely, dear; I'd always wondered what the First Act was about, perhaps I should have read it.' Can it really have been true that she had not read the play until her entrance four and a half pages before the end of Act II? Or was it a pose to fit her brisk, no-nonsense view of herself? Either way she was the last example of the du Maurier era of theatre, and a most remarkable personality.

Paul Scofield remembers *A Question of Fact* as 'A gentle domestic play with the dear old theme of lost and found mother and son – it had charm and humour and for me was chiefly memorable for the opportunity to work with Gladys Cooper, whose power as an actress was often blurred by her previous reputation as a golden girl and consequently somewhat under-estimated. The women in that play were incredibly strong, the magic Pamela Brown played my wife and an exquisite actress, Mary Hinton, her mother. I think the play was memorable for me because in it I worked with these artists – but the play itself had integrity without real power – a cosiness perhaps, but beguiling in its sincerity.'

Both Gladys Cooper and Paul Scofield, unusually for leading actors, wanted to go on a long tour. For fifteen weeks they played every major English city as well as Dublin.

At the final run-through before the opening at Oxford, Binkie Beaumont decided, quite correctly, that the play was twenty minutes too long. Instead of letting the author and director know this simple opinion he started, as was his inclination, a chain of intrigue. Dido Milroy, who was supervising the clothes, was taken out to dinner by Binkie who started a convoluted scheme in which Dido was meant to make Binkie's intentions clear to Wynyard and Frith. So when, two nights later, Wynyard blithely announced that twenty minutes needed cutting, Binkie's face fell. He had been pre-preempted in his machinations, and it looked as if all the fun of being an impresario had temporarily flown out of the window.

On the First Night in London on December 10, 1953, Gladys Cooper absent mindedly forgot to take out the polo mint she was sucking before her entrance and, on her first line, spat it across the stage. If the audience were surprised she was quite unperturbed.

The run, at 332 performances, was as respectable as the reviews: 'Let it be said at once that this is an exceedingly good play,' said Derek Granger in the *Financial Times,* setting the tone for most of the critics. 'If it is not quite that major work which many theatre goers (with justification) hope that Mr Browne will soon complete, it is still by far and away the most interesting and absorbing new play of the season.'

West End plays with messages, however, had one rigorous opponent in the young critic of the *Daily Sketch,* Kenneth Tynan. It was not until the following year he found his real base of power at the *Observer,* but he was already articulating an opinion shared by other young intellectuals concerned with the theatre that, if drama's duty was to have a pronounced social purpose, serious plays in the West End, by dealing with a middle-class and thus restricted social *milieu,* were failing lamentably. In an article called, surprisingly, *Commonsense and Cucumber* he singled out Wynyard as an example. But he picked the wrong man. To suggest that Wynyard wrote *boulevard* plays where cucumber sandwiches were eaten was silly; but Wynyard's irony is quite without savagery, and, because of that, the charge of 'cosiness' made by Paul Scofield is not an unjust one. Cosiness makes an audience feel safe. Although it may have its understanding deepened, it will not be challenged – Tynan wanted a middle-class audience to feel uncomfortable when confronted with 'real' problems. A play set in a public school is most accessible to an audience who shares that experience. Tynan wanted an audience disturbed and shaken up. Wynyard Browne's plays do not do that. The point should surely be: is the writer using an enclosed world or a particular social order as a microcosm for a universal macrocosm? In Chekhov's case he obviously is; in Wynyard Browne's sometimes yes, sometimes no. The difficulty of communication between the generations is shared by all classes, and so is imagination, but he sometimes writes about problems which are particular to the middle class, for example the loss of dignity which comes from declining financial security.

The fault in Tynan's article was that he became personal, resorting to juvenile one-liners for amusing put-downs: 'I had been promised a skeleton and I got Gladys Cooper.' His left-wing views were offended by the private, rather than state, patronage afforded to Wynyard.

He might never have become a full time dramatist at all had it not been for the enterprise of a private patron, who was sufficiently impressed by his first play *Dark Summer* to put the author under contract until he turned out another. The result was *The Holly and the Ivy,* another success; and now we have *A Question of Fact.* All these were directed by the patron himself, Frith Banbury.

Tynan would have been surprised to learn that both patron and author were socialist pacifists.

In 1959, when Wynyard delivered his next play *The Ring of Truth, Look Back in Anger* was three years old and the English Stage Company at the Royal Court was flourishing. This was the new relevant theatre, and Frith and Wynyard, along with Rattigan, Ackland, and Hunter, had been left out in the cold – and that is why the best comedy of the decade is unremembered.

In *The Ring of Truth,* Wynyard used an incident from his own marriage: the loss of Joan's engagement ring, as the start for a comedy, at times farcical, in which the rational and the intuitive mind collide. The scientist husband and artist wife, both desperately trying to understand the other's reactions, produce the conflict which is the pivot of the play. A mildly corrupt insurance man, two officious policemen, and an assortment of difficult friends, relations and servants, all exclusively concerned with their own welfare, spin events out of control until the rational man is driven to panic through superstition, and the intuitive woman to discard all feelings which are not backed up by hard facts. The plot construction is a joy. The more chaotic the misunderstandings and cross purposes, the tighter his craftsman's control. The characters at all times retain reality and keep our sympathy; and the sustained mayhem that ends the second act, with the marriage shattering under the laughter, is very impressive indeed.

When Emma Gore, a successful textile designer (Margaret Johnston), loses her engagement ring, she intuitively feels it will be followed by disaster. Her husband Tom, a mathematician with an industrial firm (David Tomlinson), dismisses her fears: a ring is only a symbol which can become the focus of an emotional association.

Staying with the Gores, rather to Tom's displeasure, is an old schoolfriend of Emma's, Ambrosine Wyman (Martha Downs). This much married lady has lived for a long time in America, where she has picked up a great deal of psycho-babble. Renting a cottage in the woods is Clifford Small (Tom Bell), a very 1950s young intellectual writer whom the Welfare State has educated with theories but not prepared with practicalities. He is an example of the irrational man: and the irrational woman is splendidly represented by Tom's mother, Mrs Gore senior (Irene Browne), a real Edwardian *Grande Dame,* who lives in a flat over the garage, concerned only for her own comfort and attended by a neurotic companion, Miss Privett, whom we never see.

Then there are the servants: Nannie (Wynne Clarke) looks after the Gore's three-year-old, precocious (and, mercifully, offstage) daughter, Cressida. She is full of dubious theories of child psychology, picked up from articles in *The Nursery World,* which are used to expose the incompetence of all parents – Tom and Emma in particular. Joe, (Anthony Sagar) a North-Country window cleaner, now the Gore's cook-handyman; and Mrs Prizborski, the cleaning woman (Carmel McSharry) a fat jelly of a local girl, who, when her vanity is offended, 'stings passively like a jellyfish'. She is married to a paranoid Pole, (Alexander Kardan) who is quite convinced the Polish are hated by all.

Then there is the Insurance Inspector, Mr Filby (Arthur Lowe), so anxious that his firm should not be seen avoiding paying out that he manufactures a false claim, and – the triumph of the play – the two policemen. P.C. Wimbush (Brian Wilde) young, officious, suspicious, loutishly trying to assert a non-existent authority; and the appalling Sergeant Borall (John Slater) self-important, insensitive, stupid and formidable.

There are also two cameo roles: Tom's boss Sir John Pritchard (Lionel Gamlin) and his terrified wife, Mary (Constance Lorne), both slaves to the whims of their temperamental French cook, Madame Pommard.

Here are two scenes with the police. The first, the interview between Sergeant Borall and Tom's mother, old Mrs Gore, is great fun:

MRS G. You think I took the ring don't you?

SERG. I didn't say that madam.

MRS G. No, but that's what you think! Oh, you're just like Dr Fawcett, you think I'm jealous of my son's marriage. You think I stole the ring as a – sort of symbol – just like in those stupid plays on the wireless . . . Oh, it's too disgusting! What's happening in the world? When I was young, we were taught to regard the police as our friends . . . In London they simply helped one across the street or whatever it was. They were charming . . . My father always carried a police whistle on his watch chain. If he wanted a constable he simply whistled . . . No one ever dreamt of suspecting one of anything . . . not ladies and gentlemen.

And, in the second, Nannie 'Miss Threllwell to you' is enraged when P.C. Wimbush, suspecting Cressida, searches the nursery:

NANNIE *(venomously)*. Great brute!

P.C. This woman attempted to obstruct me in the course of my duties.

NANNIE. Huh! Funny sort of duties!

SERG. Now that's enough, Miss Threllwell! The constable and I are here to make enquiries into the loss of a ring –

NANNIE. Well, is that any reason why he should smash Jennifer's face in?

SERG *(agitated)*. Smash her face in? Good God! What is this, Wimbush?

P.C. Only a doll.

NANNIE. Only a doll! Don't you realise children love their dollies? She's sobbin' her heart out up there – 'Jennifer's nose is all gone, nannie. Jennifer's nose is all gone'.

And she gives in her notice.

Enough to set a mark on her for life – to see her favourite dolly crushed to death by the jackboot of the law, set on her by her own mother and father . . . laugh that off, Mr Small, it's worse than Communism.

The play avoids being a farce, for if in farce all the characters are basically amoral and self-seeking, here Tom and Emma are decidedly not so. Also the action as well as the characters always remains *probable*. The feel is that of a light comedy. The loss of a ring, in itself, may seem an unimportant premise, but the ring is a symbol of much greater issues: marriage, security, remembrance and love, which, when removed, produce such shock waves of insecurity and suspicion, that even those tenuously connected with it, are affected.

Bernard Levin, reviewing the First Night in *The Daily Express* has the play's measure exactly:

Mr Browne's caricature is so delicate, his observation and his ear so acute, that we begin to accept his characters as real . . . The marvel of Mr Browne's construction is that everything is perfectly to scale . . . What is more the dialogue is on a remarkably adult level. Even at its funniest (which is very funny) the writing is always tough yet supple and at its most serious – the superbly played scene in which David Tomlinson, as the husband, suddenly realises that his marriage is threatened – it reminds us that wise and true things can be said even in a framework of laughter.

The anti-authoritarianism of the portrayal of the two policemen looks forward to Joe Orton's Inspector Truscott in *Loot* seven years later – and having two policemen gives Browne more scope to ridicule officiousness and stupidity with greater variety than Orton was able to do with only one.

John Slater, who played Borall brilliantly, thought the part not funny but frightening; and the play is, indeed, the story of the havoc wrought when a stupid man has power. We feel the Gores have set going a rigid and insensitive machine in their house which could grind their lives to powder.

Why then did this play fade away after only a moderate run? The reviews were very good, and appreciated the play's stature. Even *The Daily Worker* gave it a rave review; the lone voice of dissent was, predictably, Tynan in the *Observer*. 'Worried by nuclear tests?' he wrote tersely, 'Juvenile crime, swastikas? Feel safe at the Savoy.'

And here, perhaps, is the answer. Some years after the drawing room comedy had – according to theatre historians – been rendered obsolete, the last great drawing-room comedy was written. *The Ring of Truth*, was certainly the last major drawing-room play, French windows to the garden and all – but it is also a bridge between that *genre* and the blacker, harder comedy of the sixties. It is very anti-authoritarian, and given that destruction is seen to be caused by a system which allows the wrong people to hold authority, the writer's viewpoint can hardly be dismissed as right-wing.

Drawing-room comedies would fill West End theatres for many years to come, but nobody would claim them as important examples of new writing. *The Ring of Truth* has been lost between the comedies of Rattigan and the rise of Orton. 1959 was the wrong year for it to have been written if it was to be remembered. Browne looks backwards to an earlier and gentler comic spirit which was being swept away. It was too soon after *Look Back in Anger*.

I believe that *The Ring of Truth* is the best English comedy to have been written in the twenty-three years between *Blithe Spirit* in 1941 and *Entertaining Mr Sloane* in 1964.

Frith felt he needed all his energies for directing, so the management this time was Robert Morley and his agent and friend, Robin Fox. They lost £2,000 mainly because it was an expensive cast, but Frith was blamed for, as Morley put it, 'Messing it up by getting the wrong people. An awful girl – what was she called? Married to the agent.' (Margaret Johnston was married to Al Parker.) 'It wasn't Frith's best production . . . Well, it may have been better than I thought, but I was the money.'

Nobody seems to have thought much of Margaret Johnston as the wife, Emma, except for Frith. An arresting and original actress, perhaps she was not at her best in light comedy. Dido Milroy, who organised the clothes again, was also instructed to give her lessons in deportment, sophistication and style, which cannot have greatly boosted her confidence.

David Tomlinson, however, was considered exceptionally good as the husband, Tom. It is a marvellous part; journeying from elaborately eloquent sanity to sustained mania. All the other roles were luxuriously cast: Arthur Lowe as the Insurance Man, Carmel McSharry as Mrs Prizborski, the hefty Wynne Clarke as Nannie, and most of all, as David Tomlinson's mother, Irene Browne, who could play upper-class grandness second to none, and who also caught the character's feyness.

Wynyard still owed Frith one more play, but he was becoming restless. He wanted to move away from domestic drama. He was also aware that younger dramatists considered him old fashioned. He had the extraordinary and unrealistic idea that in future all his work should be directed by Charles Marowitz, presumably because he thought that he represented the contemporary more than did Frith.

His final play, *A Choice of Heroes* is an epic drama about revolutionaries in Russia of the 1880s. It has a strong, well-constructed plot, but it reads like a translation from a foreign language. Without the direct memories of past experience, this most autobiographical of writers floundered. Perhaps the truth is that when he had no more family and associates left to pillory and to understand, Wynyard Browne was written out.

The play was never put on, and the story of the efforts to produce it is not a happy one. Frith did not like it in its first state, was unable to make Wynyard see what he felt was wrong, and there was a temporary falling out.

Olivier, Gielgud and Scofield rejected the leading role, Souvorin, and so did twelve others: Peter O'Toole, Peter Finch, Alec Clunes, Claude Dauphin, Mogens Wieth, Harry Andrews, Andrew Cruickshank, Marius Goring, Leo McKern, Laurence Naismith, Micheál MacLíammóir and George Devine.

Then, in 1963, Michael Redgrave suddenly seemed interested. Wynyard, who had known him at Cambridge, went to Chichester where he was playing *Uncle Vanya* to discuss it, and returned convinced that he was going to be both leading man and director, with Frith as co-presenter only.

In early 1964, Wynyard went into hospital. His heavy smoking had led to emphysema. Word came, while he was there, that Redgrave had decided not to do it. Frith thought this final rejection broke him. Perhaps he realised he had no more to write.

The next morning a nurse brought him breakfast. He sat up to eat it, and fell forward dead. A heart attack. He was fifty-two.

None of his plays except *The Holly and the Ivy* had made any real money, and he died poor. Because Joan had briefly been an actress, the Actors' Charitable Trust made contributions towards the upbringing of their small daughter, Clarissa.

He had written four performed plays. Two of them are among the best to have been written in English since the war; that neither *The Holly and the Ivy* nor *The Ring of Truth* have had major revivals is a serious omission in the British Theatre.

On Wynyard Browne, let Frith have the last word: 'He was gentle and sweet, but very ironic. Quiet plays from a quiet man.'

Part Three

A Producer in the Fifties

The West End 1950s

Hugh Beaumont was the first theatrical manager to treat his actors in the way that a solicitor or an agent treats a client: a different approach and manner for each. In so doing he spoke every language but his own. He understood their separate requirements and was as expert talking dresses to Dame Edith Evans as he was giving Robert Morley a life free of trouble by providing delicious food backstage between the two Saturday performances and letting him off the occasional matinee to go to the races.

That was his secret with people. His secret in business was that he never wasted money, unlike Peter Bridge, whom many regarded as his possible successor as the presenter of all-star, glossy revivals. Bridge squandered money and his career was short. Beaumont's thrift was sometimes so extreme as to be embarrassing.

In 1954, Morley wrote for himself, *Hippo Dancing*, an adaptation from the French of André Roussin. He decided that a French leading lady was required. With his partner and friend Robin Fox, he went to Paris and selected an actress with the reassuring name of Colette Proust. She spoke English quite fluently in her own selected vocabulary, but during the first week of rehearsal it was plain that she was quite at sea speaking foreign dialogue. Beaumont appeared at the dreaded first run-through without books, this time on the Saturday morning of the second week of a four week rehearsal period, and complained that he was unable to understand a word she said. Afterwards Morley was taken aside, and the dialogue, as he remembered it, went as follows:

'Get rid of her.'

'How, Binkie?'

'Give her a fiver.'

'We can't, she's rehearsed for a fortnight.'

'Well I'm not going to give her a fortune.'

And he did not. Five pounds and the boat-train fare back to Paris concluded that episode.

At the beginning of the fifties, the personnel in the two Tennent offices – one above the Globe, the other above the Apollo – numbered six, plus

John Perry at Hammersmith, and a lawyer and accountant who were not on the premises. The office was run by Elsie Beyer, a former nurse who seems to have been generally unloved. She was seconded to an Old Vic Tour of Australia with the Oliviers, where she upset the company, was less than efficient and was finally sent home in disgrace, much to Binkie and John Perry's disappointment, who were trying to get rid of her themselves.

The Press Officer was Vivienne Byerley. Tennents had a strange embargo on all personal publicity, and she was known as 'No News Is Good News'. When John Gielgud was arrested for importuning men, Emlyn Williams suggested that the best way of keeping it quiet was to hand the information to Miss Byerley.

Kitty Black, known as 'Noire', because of her Francophilia (she translated Camus, Sartre, and Anouilh for the Firm for little renumeration) has written her own revealing account of her years at Tennents, under the title *Upper Circle*. Others were struck by her extreme capacity for hard work: she sat up all night typing the manuscript for the television version of *The Old Ladies,* to save secretarial expenses. To her fell the unenviable lot of dealing with young actors seeking employment. Through her many first chances were given, but she was also capable of being very tough when rejecting, once receiving an anonymous post-card with WE ALL LOATHE YOU written across it. She did not work happily with John Perry, who, although not alone in finding her bossy and tactless, was the only person prepared to tell her so to her face. This he did, when suggesting they part company. The resignation was good fortune for her as she moved on to a successful spell as a literary agent. She had already been superseded in her dealings with actors by the appointment of an official Casting Director – the first in the British Theatre – Daphne Rye, an attractive woman of intelligence and talent, whose life was at its happiest and most successful during her time at Tennents.

Beaumont's technique of cossetting his actors was one reason why he had the choice of the very best; the other – and this went for his directors and designers too – was his backstage triumvirate of technicians who were, at that time, unmatched in their fields: Ian Dow, the Production Manager; Lily Taylor, the Wardrobe Mistress; and Joe Davis, the Chief Engineer.

Dow, a reserved and sometimes testy Scotsman, subjugated his personality to his work. Although not always the easiest of men in his personal dealings, professionally, no one was able to fault him, and all he was associated with seem to have given him their complete professional trust. Apart from his technical expertise, admired by the stage staff, he was never fazed, never panicked.

Every surmountable problem was solved. He was forthright and talked level with the grandest of directors, the most temperamental of designers. At the point he retired to run a small hotel in Norfolk with his wife, he was looked to as the *doyen* by nearly every Production Manager working in the British Theatre.

In the wardrobe, Lily Taylor was one of the finest exponents of her craft: the cutting and the making of costumes. She had exceptional organising ability, and the Tennent costume department was better run and more meticulously notated than any other at that date. She had taste and the knowledge, so strangely absent in some Wardrobe Mistresses, of making an actor look good and feel confident on stage. Actresses like Diana Wynyard, Vivien Leigh and Coral Browne who wore their clothes with sophistication, knew she spoke the same language, and she was much admired as well, by Ginette Spanier, *directrice* of Balmain, who provided dresses for some of the leading ladies whom the management particularly wished to please.

Joe Davis has a place in theatrical history. He and Richard Pilbrow between them, invented an entirely new position on the production team: the Lighting Designer. Lighting had, until then, been worked out by the director and the Stage Manager, with the Electrician hanging lamps and explaining what was possible or not. Some light on the actors' faces, providing a few credible sources of illumination and, with luck, a bit of mood and atmosphere was the extent of most directors' hopes. Either Pilbrow, who quickly founded his own company, or Davis, lit nearly every West End show in the fifties and in so doing created an art form. They took advantage of the considerable progress made both in electronics and in the quality of stage lanterns in the years after the war. This advance in lighting was the reason for the whole change in the fabrication and application of make-up (from grease-paint to pancake) and it had a vast influence on stage design and methods of set construction. Ironically it was the Tennents lighting designer who helped make obsolete paint and canvas, the staple materials for the box-sets in front of which so many plays they presented were acted. He was lucky too that the convention of all lamps being invisible was disappearing. Although it was not yet acceptable for whole gantries and batteries of lights to be seen by the audience as we find now; front of house lighting (that is, lamps attached to the front of the dress circle), for long a feature of the Broadway Theatres, was being increasingly used. It was because of lighting, as much as anything else, that the picture-frame stage became only one of many ways of staging a play. To this Davis's work made a significant contribution.

When he became older, Davis gained the reputation for lighting the stars very kindly, indeed Marlene Dietrich would use no one else. He was also expert on the slow build – for instance over the whole of the first scene of *Waters of the Moon,* so that the lights did not reach full intensity until Edith Evans, or in the revival, Ingrid Bergman, had made their entrances. The last play he lit was the 1984 revival of *The Aspern Papers,* suitably – because he had lit nearly all his productions – directed by Frith. The quality of light he achieved was quite extraordinary. It was Venetian light, unique because it is a combination of direct light, and light reflected by the rippling surface of murky water. Griffith James, the Company Stage Manager, said that at the technical rehearsals, Davis, by now a sick man, had spent literally hours experimenting with ways to achieve this effect.

This, then, was the team behind some of the most memorable and sumptuous West End plays of the years immediately preceding the New Wave.

Frith and Wynyard were joined as partners in the firm of Frith Banbury Ltd, by a reluctant solicitor called Emmanuel Wax. His life's dream was to write, an ambition he never accomplished. Practising as a lawyer before the war, on demob from the army he decided theatrical management might be his forte. He knew Michael Gough, and it was at his suggestion, for the second time, that a partner came Frith's way.

In 1948, the new management had set up its headquarters at 33 Haymarket, next door to the now defunct tobacconists, Freibourg and Treyer (purveyors of snuff to H.R.H. the Duke of Cambridge). Frith took an office on the first floor, and 'Jimmy' Wax, as he was known, who needed to continue as a solicitor for pecuniary reasons, one adjacent. In order to fulfil his literary aspirations vicariously, Wax also became a Writers' Agent – and a very successful one too: Christopher Fry and later Harold Pinter were among his clients. Banbury and Wax found that their temperaments complemented the other. Frith, with his single-minded enthusiasms wanted to find concrete reasons for doing what excited him, while Jimmy Wax was more cautious. He tried to see the dangers; the reasons why it was unwise to proceed. If Frith wanted an actor for a particular part badly enough, he was apt to agree to unreasonable and uneconomic terms: Jimmy Wax imposed restraint: the artistic mind and the legal. He knew all there was to know about the drawing up of contracts, and because it is unusual – in England at any rate – for an impresario to be a lawyer as well, he gave the management credibility and *kudos.*

His other great contribution was to bring in to run the office, a girl who had been working for him as a temporary secretary. Marjorie Sisley had previously worked in the Contracts Department of the Rank Organisation when it was at its height, and later in the publishing department of Keith Prowse, the ticket agency. She knew Jimmy Wax socially which is how, on leaving Prowse, she came to be helping him out. It was said of Marjorie that if she had to telephone an actor to say he had been unlucky in an audition, she somehow boosted his confidence so much that at the end of the conversation he felt as if he had been successful. Hers was a very different manner to that of some of the ladies at H.M. Tennent: actors were treated with a courtesy and consideration not found at most of the other London Managements. It was due, in equal parts, to Frith having been an actor – knowing what rejection was like – and to Marjorie Sisley's natural good manners and genuine interest. Her comments on scripts too were thought invaluable.

At the beginning, Marjorie was shared by Frith and Jimmy Wax, but soon, when Jimmy obtained his own secretary, she worked solely for Frith. Later the office arrangements split: Jimmy Wax moving to Cadogan Lane, and Frith to his house in St James's Terrace, on the north side of Regents Park. Marjorie was not so happy with the move. On either side the houses had been bombed, and structurally number 4 was in a precarious state. Frith always seemed to arrange for the workmen to re-build the fallen ceilings while he was away. So Marjorie sometimes found herself both running an important impresario's office and making ten cups of tea four times a day. She called St James's Terrace 'Heartbreak House'. But it was this house that Frith loved, as he has never loved anything else inanimate; and it was from there that he set up his best work. Any amount of trouble and expense was worthwhile to keep it going and when it was demolished in the early 1980s, he looked, at times, as if he felt his life was over.

Another who figured very largely in both Frith's professional and private life for many years was Dido Milroy. She was on salary with Frith Banbury Ltd as play reader (a service she also provided for Al Parker), but her influence extended far further. Frith consulted her on all matters artistic, and trusted her judgement implicitly. She was a strong personality, not suffering fools gladly, and had considerable intelligence. She inspired great devotion from many, antagonism in a few. There was, said Marjorie Sisley, whom she always treated like the secretary, 'a great zest about her'. Short and plump, it was that zest which made her so attractive to men, as did her style and allure. Her work on anchoring *Waters of the*

Moon to reality and giving it place can be read in Appendix 2; she made substantial contributions to the finished versions of many other plays. Often her amendments and re-writing had to be passed off as Frith's own, for fear of causing resentment from the playwrights. She 'arranged the clothes' – the designer being responsible for *décor* only – for a number of Frith Banbury Ltd's productions; for this she had a great gift, including *Shooting Star, The Pink Room, A Question of Fact,* and her own *Always Afternoon,* adapted from a short story by Shelagh Fraser, which had a short run in 1951. She remained vital to Frith's life and work until her third marriage to the American poet, W.S. Merwin. With him she collaborated on a poetic drama about Witchcraft in the Restoration, *Darkling Child* in 1956, which reads like overblown Christopher Fry. It was unsuccessful, but is of interest as being the only modern poetic play Frith ever worked on. Her taste, her sense of the visual, and insistence that character and place needed to have recognisable social definition, was a great influence on the first phase of Frith's career as a director; just as her successor, Christopher Taylor's way of breaking down a text under the scrutiny of an economist's mind, and his rigorous demand for a moment-by-moment emotional truth, was to become a priority later on.

'Things always seem so much easier, when you do plays with that nice Mr Beaumont,' Frith's mother had said to him after one First Night, and they undoubtedly were; but for the first decade of their association, Frith, as far as making money for his own company was concerned, did not have a great deal of bargaining power with Tennents. All co-productions were with their non-profit-making branch: Tennent Productions. This meant that even if those plays, as was sometimes the case, had been commissioned by Frith Banbury Ltd, his company was neither able to invest nor draw any profit from them. One way round this was to pay a higher director's royalty on top of the flat fee of £200 for director's services – but very carefully organised so as not to alert the Arts Council and the Customs and Excise Department. There was prestige in the association, but not a great deal of renumeration. It was not until 1957, and *Flowering Cherry,* when both the play and the two big names of Ralph Richardson and Celia Johnson were taken as a package to Beaumont, that Frith was able to insist on a coproduction with H.M. Tennents Ltd, and thus have a full share in the profits. Some of the later plays they presented jointly lost money, however.

1957 was, ironically, the year that Entertainment Tax was finally repealed. Beaumont claimed publicly that the levy was the bane of his life, but it had in reality given him a virtual monopoly of the West End, through the operations of his non-profit-making companies. Its demise meant the beginning of the end for Tennents, who had fought so long and hard against it.

The events leading to its abolition had begun three years earlier in 1954, when Woodrow Wyatt and five other M.P.s brought before Parliament *The Theatrical Companies Bill,* which sought to redefine the way in which non profit-making companies were run. There was no doubt as to the intended result of the bill: to break the monopoly held on the West End by H.M. Tennent. Nor, to most people, was there any doubt who was really behind it.

Peter Cotes's disappointment and bitterness at the affront he considered he had received from Hugh Beaumont and H.M. Tennents in 1947 remained undimmed. Not only did he see his enemy retaining great power over the Commercial Theatre but he saw him managing to do so by what seemed to him slippery methods. As the enemy was cleverly never quite on the wrong side of the law, the law itself was obviously too vague and should be changed. Also, he and his allies noted with displeasure, a great many homosexuals seemed to be working in all spheres of the London Theatre, which was, of course, because Beaumont was homosexual himself – and only gave jobs to boys of similar persuasion – not to the masculine Cotes and his virile friends. Binkie Beaumont had been magnified into a gay Al Capone.

These people, who had no cause to love Tennents, thought the way to break them was through the law which, in its present form, allowed Beaumont as managing director of H.M. Tennent to be a director of Tennent Productions. This was the gist of Wyatt's proposed bill: 'No director or principal officer of a non-profit-making company *may be employed by, or have a financial interest* in a profit-making company.'

Frith acted fast. On March 15, three days after the bill had been published, he wrote to Wyatt not mincing his words about what he knew was the bill's hoped intention.

I am fearful that in your zeal to break the monopoly of Tennents in the London Theatre, you may succeed in throwing away the baby with the bath water. Would you spare the time to hear the other side of the question? . . . it is quite possible, even probable, that our theatre might, if this bill goes through as it is, be delivered from the hands of Mr Beaumont only to fall into the hands of people far less scrupulous and with far less artistic discrimination. [That is commercial managers only seeking financial gain. He concludes:] The net result might well be quite different from what was intended.

The day after receiving this letter, Wyatt called on him at 33 Haymarket. He questioned Frith closely as to Beaumont's professional integrity, repeated Cotes's accusations mentioning him by name, and asked him point-blank whether there was any truth in his information that Beaumont employed only homosexuals. Frith replied honestly: no, it was quite untrue. The majority on the Tennents' pay-roll, both in the office and on the stage-management teams, were heterosexual; and a high proportion of them heterosexual women. Homosexuals may find themselves more socially comfortable in the company of other homosexuals, but if this influenced Beaumont's judgement in any way, he only employed people who he knew were *exceptionally* good at their jobs. Added to that, most of the actors whose names were then on posters for Tennent plays were known to be married. Wyatt appeared satisfied.

After he had left, Frith followed up his arguments in a letter to Wyatt, and he also put them publicly by writing to the Editor of *The Sunday Times*.

He points out the confusion of terminology over the word 'director' in the theatre. If it is taken to mean 'director of the play', were the bill to become law, the entire income of the profit-making firm of Frith Banbury Ltd would be cut off because it came from non-profit-making theatre. If Old Times Furnishing Co. (profitmaking) has a contract with Tennent productions (non-profit-making) then why not Frith Banbury Ltd?

The bill also proposed that no non-profit-making company should pay for any services given by a profit-making company, which as Frith made clear would have meant the end of the theatre, as non-profit-making companies would be unable to hire theatres from the profit-making companies that owned them.

The bill did not become law, but it made plain how unsatisfactory was the taxing of entertainment and to what confusion and bad blood it led. A tax that caused so much trouble was clearly not worth keeping, and it was repealed three years later. The subsidised theatre increased in importance; the founding of the National Theatre in 1963 really toppled Tennents from their unassailable position – then, in 1979, both subsidised and unsubsidised were crippled again by a new punitive levy on theatre seats: Value Added Tax. Governments never seem to be helpful to the theatre for very long.

We can only speculate what would have happened had the bill become law. It would probably have made the theatre even more commercial minded – profit-making at all costs – to the marked detriment of artistic standards. Frith, I think, did help save it from that.

Peter Cotes and his kind had a victory of sorts too, although, surely, not quite in the way they intended. They had nudged Government's consciousness in the direction of removing the tax, and thus freed their enemy, Hugh Beaumont, of many headaches, as well as weakening his power. Tennents were to remain a force to be reckoned with for another twenty years, but never again was one man to have both such artistic influence and such managerial power over the entire British Theatre.

This vendetta against Binkie Beaumont brings up the vexed question: how much truth is there in the belief, still current in certain quarters, that the West End Theatre of the 1950s was dominated by a homosexual Mafia? Though everyone interviewed for this book – both hetero and homosexual – professed it to be rubbish, why was it so widely believed to be true? Were those at the top apt to give preferential treatment to other homosexuals? No one has ever claimed that heterosexuals were excluded because of their orientation but if, for example, two actors of the same aptitude, one gay one straight, were up for the same job, was it usually the gay one who was employed? The answer is: not necessarily so. But because this book is focused on the life and career of a homosexual man, and because many of his friends and associates were also homosexual, it may seem as if the theatre of the time was a gay paradise. If given, this is a false impression. Looking at the cast lists of Frith's productions, naturally one sees the names of some homosexual actors – and actresses too, but there are far more heterosexual ones. But the proportion is about the average balance found between the two in what is (appropriately here) known as the Straight Theatre – musicals and ballet perhaps having a higher, but not that much higher, percentage of homosexuals. Frith claims the whole rumour to be 'Codswallop. Some actors are. Some aren't. That's all there is to be said. I frequently don't know when I cast – often never know – I just go for the most suitable person.' In his case, I think this was true; but what of the other managers of power?

Nearly all can be completely discounted. Sir Bronson Albery and his son Donald would have been very displeased to have been tarred with that brush, as would Peter Saunders; and the enormous Henry Sherek was anything but gay – just happy when he had eaten well. So it is back to Binkie Beaumont again, and one fact must here be stressed: Beaumont was in a stable homosexual marriage and after the 1930s,, appears to have had only one affair outside his relationship with Perry, and that was not with an actor. This had come about because during the 1950s, Perry fell in love with a young American who later became an impresario in Britain, and Beaumont found a boyfriend of his own. But in spite of this, their relationship endured. Beaumont was a 'respectable' homosexual: he lived with his business partner. He was, however, very censorious about the sexual morals of others, and not only promiscuous homosexuals. Even women who were considering divorce came in for censure. If there is hypocrisy it is surely forgivable. Homosexuality was illegal and he needed to protect his own position and, above all, ensure that no hint of scandal or unpleasantness was ever connected with the firm of H.M. Tennent. Binkie disapproved if *anyone's* private life interfered with their work.

His stage staff largely consisted of heterosexual men like Joe Davis and Ian Dow, and it was Tennents who first realised that women often make the best stage-managers.

Most of his office staff were women, and one of them (not Kitty Black), was known to enjoy sex with young actors – Richard Burton landed his first job with the Firm that way. And so it is ironic that the only rewards for sexual favours at H.M. Tennent appear to have been given to heterosexuals.

Naturally there were many who rationalised their own disappointments by blaming Binkie's, or Terence Rattigan's, or indeed Frith's, sexual orientation, while all the time congratulating themselves that it was they who were normal. Robert Morley said, 'Binkie never rocked the boat by installing homosexuals in the cast. In the house yes – John Perry, Alan Webb, but not in the theatre. It is not true that the West End was governed by homosexuals, although it didn't help that Binkie was in charge.' Even in the house, though, the guest list consisted of actresses and their husbands, women friends, and heterosexual men. If some of Binkie and John Perry's friends were fellow homosexuals, it is, surely, not to be wondered at.

Frith, although he saw Binkie socially in London, preferred to keep their relationship primarily professional. He thought it wiser for their work if he did not become too close. Although invited to Knotts Fosse, Beaumont and Perry's house near Cambridge, the invitations were not accepted, and once on the telephone, when Beaumont attempted to pry into some aspect of his love-life, Frith refused to be drawn and the gambit was not repeated.

Of course, to the next generation, who prided themselves on their lack of pretensions and working-class clear-sight, the world of H.M. Tennent's must have seemed very effete. An affected world, where the most powerful manager, Beaumont, the most successful playwright, Rattigan and an actor-knight, Gielgud, were known to be homosexual. In 1959, a John Deane Potter, doubtless prompted by certain disappointed people in the theatre, wrote an article for the *Daily Express,* attacking the 'unpleasant free-masonry' of the West End, and propagating the *canard* that homosexual managers cast homosexual actors ('evil men . . . should be driven from their positions of theatrical power'). The article thankfully, led to nothing further, except a reply from John Osborne in an article for the same paper, saying that the idea of driving any homosexual from the theatre was 'detestable'. He then rather spoilt his defence by ascribing to homosexual artists, 'unreal chintzy plays, gorgeous decor and a glamorous selection of theatrical lords and ladies glittering over all'. What he was objecting to, surely, was middle-class rather than homosexual theatre, and it was a mistake to associate the two.

Glamour is, after all, often associated with effeminacy; realism and grit with virility. Such stereotypes are nonsensical. The Royal Court harboured as many – or as few – homosexuals as did any other theatre.

N.C. Hunter:
Plays That Actors Liked To Speak

On an autumn day in 1950, two events took place, one in London and one in North Wales. In London, Dame Edith Evans had been feeling unwanted, which was the usual state of her spirits when unemployed. She had been sent a play by Tennents for which she had no enthusiasm, and, having nothing better to occupy her time, walked from her Set in Albany to the offices at the Globe Theatre to return the script.

In Denbighshire, Norman Hunter, in deepest melancholy, went for a long solitary walk and came to a decision: he would give up his useless ambition of being a playwright, and return to schoolmastering.

At the Globe, Dame Edith, shown straight into Binkie Beaumont's office as befitted her status, handed back the play. Was there anything else she could read? Beaumont replied there was not. Her eyes, of unequal latitude, went to a pile of rejected scripts on the desk. She took the top one. Was there anything for her in that? Beaumont demurred; but she could read it, if she wished; he would be interested in her opinion. Dame Edith walked back to Albany with *Waters of the Moon* under her arm. Had Binkie, devious as ever, left it on the top on purpose?

On his walk, Norman Hunter admitted later, he had reviewed his life. He was forty-two, married to a devoted Belgian woman, Germaine, and was the author of several novels and nine plays, only one of which, *All Rights Reserved*, in 1935 had been of any success. They had earned him little money. But, during his wartime service with the Dragoon Guards, Norman Hunter had a Road To Damascus. In his back-pack, through the discomforts and the horrors, he had carried one book: *The Complete Works of Anton Chekhov*. Writers who love Chekhov's short stories are always rewarded; but those who become obsessed with his plays are not quite so lucky; any comparison with the depth, humour and absolute truth of the original makes their work look thin; thinner than perhaps it is. Norman Hunter was a man obsessed, and *Waters of the Moon* was homage to his Master.

That evening, having read the play at one sitting, Dame Edith telephoned Binkie Beaumont at his house in Lord North Street. If he was willing to present it, she would like to play Helen Lancaster. He was, and telephoned Hunter, whose fortunes were thus reversed.

Beaumont had no illusions about the stature of *Waters of the Moon*. He knew that in order for it to have body and substance it needed to be given the full Tennent works: luxury casting, a high budget, and magnificent staging. He decided, too to give it the further *cachet* of being the official H.M. Tennent contribution to the Festival of Britain, and, for its presentation, he arranged the Haymarket Theatre.

He did not, at this stage, appoint a director but, with Dame Edith in the lead, approached Dame Sybil Thorndike for the secondary role of Mrs Whyte. Dame Sybil's husband, Sir Lewis Casson, and her son John, tried to dissuade her from entering into what was likely to be a long run in a supporting part. But Mrs Whyte surprises everyone by her ability to play the piano, and Dame Sybil, thinking it would be great fun to play Chopin and Schumann on stage, said yes. It was to be the first and last time that the two Dames worked together. Wendy Hiller was next, accepting the sex-starved drudge, Evelyn Daly, for the promise of working with them.

It was with these three already on contract that Beaumont asked Frith Banbury to direct. The production of *The Holly and the Ivy* had been a revelation to him, and his attitude towards Frith was now one of great respect, quite uninfluenced by John Perry's doubts. This offer to direct the showcase of the grandest London management for the Festival that was meant to usher in the postwar era – The New Elizabethan Age – was unquestionably the greatest opportunity that Frith had yet been given in his career. He read the play and was rather dismayed.

Apart from reading like a synthetic piece of *faux-Chekhov*, the action seemed to him to take place in limbo. Hunter had given himself no opportunity to provide any atmosphere. The *locale* was described as 'a small hotel in the West Country', with one exterior scene, for which it was envisaged that a drop-curtain should come down in the old fashioned pantomime way (Act Two Scene One). Hunter did not seem in the least disturbed by these misgivings. 'He was so in love with Chekhov, whom he had discovered rather late in life, that he didn't think more was necessary. I, however, did. I felt that the play as a play was thin, and needed every help it could get.' To this end Frith asked Dido Milroy to make out a *mise en scène,* a history of a country house which, being made into a hotel, had certain associations for the various people who lived in it and which Hunter, thinking all the suggestions were Frith's own, eventually incorporated into the script. (See Appendix II.) These additions made a considerable difference to the atmosphere and amount of mood generated.

Frith took the notes on the play's world-background to Dame Edith at Albany. He also wanted to analyse Helen with her by the Stanislavskian disciplines of motivation and objective. If he was hoping that she would be impressed with his thoroughness, he had another think coming. According to her secretary at that time, Jean Batters, she listened to him politely and took in nothing at all. By intuition she already knew all she needed about Helen Lancaster.

The first piece of casting for which Frith was responsible was Kathleen Harrison as the kindly *nouveau riche,* Mrs Ashworth. He then added his old colleague Harold Scott as the duck-shooting Colonel Selby; Cyril Raymond as Helen's tolerant husband, Robert Lancaster; Nan Munro as the hotel proprietress, Mrs Daly; and as the Austrian refugee Julius Winterhalter a genuine Austrian refugee, Leo Bieber. As the young people: Owen Holder played John Daly, and Patricia McCarron Helen's daughter, Tonetta Landi.

N.C. Hunter describes the play as a comedy: in the Chekhovian sense of comic reactions to potentially tragic situations. The trouble is that his comic reactions when they occur, as in Act Two Scene Two, are just not funny or inventive enough.

The main text is preceded by a quotation from Hazlitt: 'To what piece of insignificance may not human life dwindle! To what fine agonising threads will it not cling.'

The cornerstone of this play, as Dido Milroy saw at once, is humiliation. Humiliation for the Dalys who own the house and hate it because it represents their bad fortune; and humiliation for its resident guests, who were once richer or freer, and now feel they have no choice but to live there.

Three days after Christmas into this group's shabby but ordered lives come the Lancasters, a family of rich cosmopolitans whose car has skidded into a snow-filled ditch, who shake up the routine, give them differently hopes or resentments, and disappear again when the snow has thawed, leaving behind the same circumstances but altered perceptions.

The play has echoes of *The Cherry Orchard:* the Lancasters bringing the energy and glamour of another world into a set provincial society, and in the last act, Helen / Ranyevskaya returning to London / Paris, the echoes are very loud indeed. There is also an almost direct quote here from *Uncle Vanya*:

The Colonel, Mrs Whyte and Mrs Ashworth stand watching them go. The noise of the car fades away. There is a long pause.
MRS WHYTE. There. They've gone. *(There is another pause.)*
COLONEL *(thinking).* Today's Wednesday. They came on Saturday. Three days and a bit.

There are still further Chekhovian resonances. Evelyn Daly, an English Sonya or Varya; Anya for Tonetta; and John Daly like Chekhov himself with a weak chest. Hunter's affection for his characters is obvious and he understands them too, but he has little irony and no natural gift for poetry. When he heightens his language it becomes excogitated and self-conscious.

The best scene of the play; where there is suddenly action and the truth is told, is the New Year's Eve Party (Act Two Scene Two). Evelyn Daly drinks too much of the champagne salvaged from the Lancaster's car: ' . . . Playing with people's hopes and dreams. You shouldn't do it Mrs Lancaster.'

HELEN *(laughing).* My dear girl – what nonsense!
EVELYN. You're strong, it doesn't matter to you. But most of us spend all our time trying not to hope for what is quite unattainable, trying to be content with what we have. *(Near tears.)* It's not kind to make us dream of the waters of the moon, of all kinds of happiness that are out of reach. Why do you come here to disturb us all?

The moment when the grumpy and down-putting Mrs Whyte turns off the wireless to which the young are dancing and starts to play the piano, is one of genuine theatre. She also knows life's great lesson:

EVELYN. Perhaps I could be pretty too if I didn't always feel so tired, so bad tempered, if I didn't have to work so hard every day, every day . . . my face is beginning to get quite lined and I'm not yet thirty. Don't you think life is unfair to some people?
MRS WHYTE *(no longer playing).* It's stupid to talk like that. Life isn't fair or unfair, or tragic or comic or anything else. Life is life – that's all. One must accept it.

But Mrs Whyte finds that acceptance difficult.

Mrs Whyte is the best drawn character because her language is never heightened and she is a recognisable type: the gentlewoman for whom a sudden change of fortune (the death of her son, and her husband leaving less than she expected) has forced her old age into reduced circumstances.

Tonetta Landi rings true as well: the self-absorbed, pampered girl who for the first time is made to stop and think about others, to be genuinely concerned for them, unlike her mother Helen, who is pure Ranyevskaya: elegant, warm-hearted, impulsive, volatile, and ultimately shallow. She is even half-French to give her a 'foreignness'. Only two of the characters have truly learnt anything: through falling for Helen Lancaster's charm and superficial knowledge of Austria, Winterhalter learns the worth of Evelyn Daly's love; and, through her confrontation with genteel poverty, Tonetta Landi learns compassion and social conscience.

'N.C. Hunter wrote plays that actors liked to speak,' said Marjorie Sisley. He did. There was never any problem finding 'names' to be in his plays. His characters are possibly not very original, but are very actable; each having a good scene with most other people in the play in turn, as well as a good solo moment. In *Waters of the Moon* the principals even have a soliloquy or its equivalent, a device which Chekhov had dropped after *Uncle Vanya*.

Why then has *Waters of the Moon,* had two major revivals – one in the West End and one on television – when many more stimulating plays of greater profundity have been forgotten? Indeed, with *The Deep Blue Sea, Separate Tables* and *The Chalk Garden,* it must be the best known pre-Royal Court play of the 1950s. The answer, I think, lies in the play's self-sufficiency – that very lack of detailed background of which Frith complained. None of N.C. Hunter's plays are connected much to an outside world, and thus they have dated very little. Living so far from the capital, he writes a pure kind of English quite free of contemporary jargon and slang. The action could quite easily be updated a decade without any difference being made. And the best parts he wrote were for the middle-aged or old.

The management were still not completely sure of Frith's ability to handle four very distinguished actresses all at once. They rehearsed on stage at the Haymarket, where a shadowy figure could be seen gliding about the upper circle. A spy was on the prowl. Years later Toby Rowland admitted that it had been him – on Binkie's orders. A few days later he had gone. Binkie was satisfied.

Spies notwithstanding, Frith 'thoroughly enjoyed the rehears-als. Edith was a great actress: Sybil a great woman. Sybil allowed the audience to control her – "Oh, the dears they're laughing, let's pull a funny face" – Edith wouldn't allow an audience to do that. She manipulated it.'

Dame Sybil Thorndike brought with her onto the stage her own spiritual force and moral fearlessness. All who acted with her speak of the look of absolute trust she could give a fellow actor on stage, thereby steadying and centring, just as she herself was steady and centred. When she overacted, and she could, it was because she had entered into a conspiracy of fun with the audience – even as Medea, Hecuba, or Lady Macbeth.

Dame Edith was very different. She was the absolute prototype dedicated artist who never compromised the truth. She had that quality, common to all great actors, of being able to delude herself completely on stage. The characters she played inhabited her true Dionysiac possession. She hardly changed her make-up from role to role, yet in photographs her face and body look quite different and always exactly right. Much has been said and written about her ability to assume beauty – her own face was idiosyncratic and irregular – and of her ability to communicate the spirit of youth when she was long past that state herself. Her mastery over mind and emotion and the control it gave her over herself and others was almost that of an Eastern mystic. She distilled feelings to their essence and projected them with clarity and focus. All great artists – one thinks of Maria Callas – seem to have a freak concentration on stage; an intensity which is not inward looking but is sensitive to its surroundings. Her own individual gifts: her sexiness, the much imitated voice cascading up and down scales, her mastery of style and high comedy, all brought something quite unique to her work. She never chose the obvious, yet she always seemed to choose the truth. Her mixture of complete physical relaxation and the authority that comes from knowing exactly what she was doing ranks her as one of the very greatest British actresses of any age. For many people – again like Callas in opera – she spoilt any part she assayed, in the sense that they could never see anyone else playing it.

Dame Edith could flounder at rehearsal before she saw the way, 'Edith always talked when she was nervous,' said Wendy Hiller. The first time that this happened, Miss Hiller caught Dame Sybil's eye, and they both looked at their watches and timed her. The discussion with Frith, which, to Miss Hiller, seemed at cross-purposes, lasted seventeen minutes. Afterwards, at lunch, she asked,

'Is Edith always like this?'

'Well,' said Dame Sybil, 'if one realises that Edith is only interested in Edith; if one *accepts* that fact, one can be quite fond of her.'

The discussions, at cross-purposes or not, must have been necessary, for Dame Edith's performance lifted the play from the mundane into something rare. Frith thought her playing of the final act, when the Lancasters abruptly leave, remarkable:

'Edith did it in a way more valid and less sentimental than what Hunter had thought of. He wanted it slightly "Ranyevsky" – lingering over her departure but, instead of making a meal of the scene, she threw it away, and made it more effective by playing it as if she had left the whole play: left the *ambience* of the play: left the people. She was leading her own life, and had forgotten about them – almost. She withdrew her spirit from the play. She was on to her new life, you see.'

There are many photographs of that act and it is interesting to note how Dame Edith uses the veil of her hat: up for the short direct conversation with Mrs Whyte (see frontispiece) and down for the remainder of the scene. The veil is constructed so that her eyes are quite visible, yet there is a curtain between her and her present surroundings.

Reece Pemberton the designer, had placed the set on two revolves, which meant that the Third Act could be played out of doors, (as well as the first scene of the Second), except that by then, all the snow was seen to have melted in the night: the branches of the trees no longer weighed down, and a vista of Dartmoor suddenly visible. In the Second Act exterior, the only colour had been a red coat thrown over a garden bench. But, at the final dress rehearsal, a snowman was suddenly added to the set of this first exterior scene. Dame Edith, whose immersion in a role was so deep that she was known to be pushed off-balance by an actor wearing a different tie, was not told.

On her entrance she shied like an over sensitive horse, and was obviously thrown throughout the whole scene. In the interval, Frith found her desolate and in tears. 'That horrid snowman,' she wailed, *'please* take him away!' Frith went to Reece Pemberton, who on hearing the request, promptly burst into tears too:

'I love my snowman. If he goes I shall be very angry.' Frith searched for Binkie Beaumont to arbitrate. Binkie thought for only a split second:

'The dame's tears,' he said, 'are more important than the designer's tears. Get rid of it.'

The First Night was on April 19th, 1951, and the notices for the play were fairly tepid, most critics wondering why such superlative acting was being lavished on such a slight piece. Harold Hobson summed up their feeling in *The Sunday Times*.

Tennent Productions have taken our Titian and our Rubens, set them in a palace, furnished them with exquisite paints and brushes (for the play is staged enchantingly) and put them to designing Christmas Cards. They do it so beautifully that our breath is taken away and the protest dies on our lips.

They were the kind of reviews that Norman Hunter received all his life, yet no actor, however great, can make something out of nothing. He did provide a good skeleton to put the flesh on. If he was sneered at by highbrows, he was at least a good actors' writer.

Few productions have provided more theatrical anecdotes, because people fondly hoped that a rivalry between the two Dames would produce fireworks. The two best known ones have been so overtold, largely I suspect, because Frith dined out on them for a long time afterwards, and they were heard by many.

One stemmed from the staging of the beginning of Act Two, Scene Two: the New Year's Eve Party (see photograph), Helen is reading Winterhalter's hand Downstage Right. The game of bridge is Upstage Centre behind the sofa; an increasingly drunk Evelyn stands by the piano, Upstage Right of the sofa; and on the sofa – in unquestionably the dominant position – sits Mrs Whyte, disapproving and slightly tipsy, with only the half-asleep Colonel Selby, in her line of sight. All her reactions therefore, and they are many, would look like direct communication with the audience. Even though the scene should be Dame Edith's, it was not an opportunity for scene stealing that Dame Sybil felt inclined to pass over.

One day, Frith, who had been absent from performances for a time, was telephoned by Charles La Trobe, the Stage-Manager with the news that Dame Edith had been in tears after the last two performances.

'Oh, why?', asked Frith, knowing quite well why.

'It's because of Dame Sybil's overacting.'

So he went to the next Saturday matinee, after which he wrote two notes. One to Dame Sybil; 'Why ruin a lovely performance by pulling too many faces?' and one to Dame Edith; 'Please understand that Sybil's overplaying is due to enthusiasm and *joie de vivre*'.

Early the next week came their replies. 'Thank you dear Frithy,' wrote Dame Edith. 'I'm sure our good reputation for freshness is in great measure due to your vigilance and I cannot be too grateful to you. I will not discuss people's *motives* for overplaying because I have not yet arrived at your kindly Christian estimate. But I'm progressing. Much love, Edith.'

Then from Dame Sybil, who starts disingenuously, by thanking Frith for an earlier lunch given for her and her brother, Russell Thorndike, and goes on:

Thank you for your note, yes I was a bit highly coloured on Saturday, I had 2 grandchildren in front + very anxious they should know just what everything meant – consequently much underlining – but I took your sweet rebuking to heart + it's better again I think. Every night something goes a bit different: or one gives away oneself!! Good luck to your American show [*The Deep Blue Sea* on Broadway.] I hope you have another huge success. Yr. affect Sybil.

The other anecdote was over the clothes: To draw out the contrast between the well-heeled Lancasters and the dowdy residents, Dame Edith and Patricia McCarron had originally been dressed by Hardy Amies, while Dame Sybil wore a tatty old woolly. After a year, Binkie Beaumont, decided to splash out even more and re-dress the first two by Balmain, whose *directrice*, Ginette Spanier was a friend and ally of his. (This was not unusual in a long run. The actresses flew to Paris on Sunday, where they had fittings that afternoon and on Monday morning, and flew back for the Monday performance. Mme Spanier later brought over the dresses as part of her own personal luggage to escape customs' duty.)

Binkie, with Frith in tow, went into Dame Edith's dressing room, where a very long discussion about the new dresses ensued. When the Dame was satisfied they turned to go. On their way out she stopped them: 'And do give Sybil a new cardigan.'

Waters of the Moon ran for two years, breaking every previous record at the Haymarket and it later toured with Irene Browne replacing Dame Edith. Frith wrote to Dame Sybil thanking her for her beneficial influence on the company spirit. She replied:

My dear Frith, How very sweet+ *like you* – to write. I need not say how I enjoyed working with you, and I do hope I shall work again under yr. direction. No, it's not only me that's kept us all free of friction. I will mention *specially* Kathleen, Cyril and Nan – but all of us have been very happy together. I think it is partly too the atmosphere of the Haymarket. Yes, I'm sure I shall enjoy the tour. I believe Irene will be very good tho' of course Edith will be an incalculable loss – especially financially!!! Still she doesn't like the provinces + that's that! Much Love dear,+ good luck always. Yr. very aff. Sybil. Lewis sends love.

There was a successful revival of *Waters of the Moon* at the Chichester Festival Theatre and at the Haymarket in 1977 mounted as a vehicle for Ingrid Bergman. In this Dame Wendy Hiller played Mrs Whyte, a part that she says she found 'easy'. She also felt that Ingrid Bergman as Helen started with advantages not naturally possessed by Dame Edith: 'Edith came on with great flat feet in a mink. Ingrid was much more "right" – being foreign helped.'

Coda

Frith only directed Dame Edith Evans once again. In the early days of commercial television, Tennents formed their own company, called – unbelievably – BINKIEVISION. Its purpose was to promote Tennent plays in ninety-minute film versions. For its first two offerings Rodney Ackland adapted Wynyard Browne's *A Question of Fact,* and his own version of Hugh Walpole's *The Old Ladies.* Frith directed, with the technical assistance of Quentin Lawrence, and Dame Edith played Grace Smith in *A Question of Fact* ('bringing an extra dimension to her which was quite wonderful but which it didn't need') and Agatha Payne, the mad, greedy gypsy-like woman in *The Old Ladies,* a part which she had played on stage twenty years earlier. She was now much nearer the correct age.

They rehearsed for two weeks on the set and Rodney Ackland complained that it looked much too clean. He wanted plates with five-days-old food, empty bottles, and filthy saucers. Frith agreed and instructed the set-dresser to dirty it up. Little did he know that Dame Edith had been listening to the conversation and 'I found myself summoned to her dressing room and she said:

"I don't like this idea of *that* Rodney Ackland. It's only *his* idea that this is a dirty woman. She's *not* a dirty woman and I've never played her as a dirty woman!"

'I thought "Oh yes you have, and what's more, it will be very worrying if you don't".'

'She then went on the set and played her as a dirty woman, no doubt delighted with herself that she hadn't.'

*

Hunter's next success, *A Day By the Sea,* another piece of imitation Chekhov, opened at the Haymarket in 1953, again with a prestigious cast: John Gielgud both directed and played the frustrated diplomat, Julian Anson, with Sybil Thorndike, Lewis Casson,

Ralph Richardson, Irene Worth and Megs Jenkins. It ran well over a year for 388 performances.

Like Wynyard Browne, Norman Hunter was not a fast writer, and it was four years later that he completed his next work *A Touch of the Sun*. It is an immeasurably better play than either *Waters of the Moon* or *A Day By the Sea*, because he had found his own voice. One feels he is writing from direct emotional experience, and because the figure of Chekhov is not so obviously standing before him he does not try so hard to conjure up atmosphere. He was not naturally a poet, and the absence of heightened language is something of a relief. He has assimilated the lesson, rather than copying the teacher. Again the cornerstone is humiliation: a family split by riches and poverty, and the loss of confidence and self-esteem that poor relations feel when in the orbit of their richer counterparts. It is also well constructed and highly literate.

Binkie Beaumont asked Frith to direct, but from their correspondence it is clear that it took some wooing. He was not playing hard to get, but was, by the end of 1957 when the approach was made, famous and very busy. He had just directed and co-presented with H.M. Tennent, Robert Bolt's *Flowering Cherry*, which had not only introduced a major new playwright to the West End but was running to very good business at the Haymarket, and earlier in the year had directed Rodney Ackland's fascinating study in petty criminality, *A Dead Secret* at the Piccadilly, with Paul Scofield. The year before, 1956, he had directed *The Good Sailor*, an adaptation of Herman Melville's *Billy Budd* at the Lyric Hammersmith, followed by *The Diary of Anne Frank*. He also had *The Deep Blue Sea*, *The Pink Room*, *A Question of Fact* and *Marching Song* behind him. He was expecting a commissioned play: Wynyard Browne's *The Ring of Truth* and awaiting the delivery of his friend Christopher Taylor's *The Velvet Shotgun*.

As with *Waters*, he felt that the script needed work, and that one character was a cypher. It was only when Norman Hunter had agreed to changes and Michael Redgrave and Diana Wynyard were secured for the leading roles that Frith accepted the production.

Philip (Michael Redgrave) is an ascetic, stick-in-the-mud deputy-headmaster of a school for boys of 'slow development' in Leatherhead. He is poor and rather sententious. The character, one feels, is Hunter at his most self-critical. His wife Mary (Diana Wynyard) has known some Riviera life before her marriage as had Norman's Belgian wife, Germaine. Living with them are Philip's bankrupt father, Robert (Ronald Squire); a prodigal Edwardian *roué,* and their two children Johnny (Dinsdale Landen) and Caroline (Vanessa Redgrave), who have been educated on the state. The family are awaiting the arrival for lunch of Philip's brother Denis (Anthony Oliver) and Margaret, his Canadian heiress wife (Louise Allbritton). Denis has left England three years before; made a fortune, and married this rich girl. He is to manage the English subsidiary of Margaret's father's firm and they have bought a manor house where Robert is shortly to move. They also have a villa in the South of France to which they invite Philip and his family. An invitation which Philip accepts, even though it will mean borrowing £100 from Denis.

At the villa in Cannes, Philip feels out of place and disapproves of the fellow guests; Sir Joseph Vanderhoven, an *immigré* financier (Martin Miller) and Gerald Harcourt, a rich socialite (David Langton). Johnny and Caroline, on the other hand, are loving every minute of their stay. Margaret does not like Philip and thinks of his family as poor relations, although Sir Joseph is interested in Philip's disapproval of capitalism, and Gerald Harcourt has fallen for Mary.

Margaret gives a dance, at which Philip is a fly in the ointment, pompously patronising his younger brother, and too uptight to join in the dances. When Sir Joseph tries to make Caroline drink another glass of champagne, and Philip knocks the glass from his hand, and Gerald offers Johnny a job and Philip insults him, Margaret implies he must either apologise or leave. Philip apologises but decides to cut short the holiday four days early. Denis asks Mary; 'What is it? What's the matter with him? He seems to have changed so, Mary.'

> MARY. People do change under pressure, and that's how we always seem to be living nowadays – like people at too high an altitude . . . Here's a piece of unnecessary advice – don't ask us again. It was sweet of you to have us this time, but you can see for yourself it doesn't work.

Philip's behaviour in this act is credible and well-handled, and both rich and poor have their points of view put with fairness. The rich may be superficial but they are fundamentally decent. It is clear that both the brothers are reacting, in their different ways, to their father's profligacy. Philip has a great inferiority complex because he feels a failure for his inability to provide good things for his family.

Back in Leatherhead, we see Johnny's resentment at having been patronised at the villa, because of his grammar school education. All he claims to want is to make enough money so that his children can go to public school with proper jobs waiting. Robert is brought back by Denis in disgrace, having made a pass at the housemaid, stolen some lobster patties, and come downstairs when Margaret had some guests. Philip says that he and Denis are so far apart in wealth they had better just 'keep in contact', at which Denis, losing his temper, protests even Philip now thinks he married Margaret for her money – which he probably has. He seems very scared of her.

Mary returns from seeing Gerald in London under the pretence of seeing her sick sister. She confesses her affair to Philip, but says she has now rejected Gerald.

> MARY. There must be something that makes me so enjoy what's new, what's different. I've never been quite as single-minded as you. There's a way of looking at the world, an uncommitted attitude to living, that you may think despicable, but that I – I can accept easily enough. We're not meant to look out of the same window, surely. There are even sorts of luxury and idleness that – for a moment, anyway – seem to justify themselves, seem to be more reason for holding on to life and loving it . . .

Philip tells Mary that he feels he has become stale as a teacher:

> I'm a teacher, and I must teach or we don't eat . . . What nonsense people talk about liberty! There's only one free nation in the world – the nation of the rich – the rest of us are just an army of prisoners.

> I like to fancy myself an idealist, a despiser of materialism and so on. But if it's true, if it's not just an attitude, then why am I sometimes simply twisted with envy of people who've money and freedom? Why do I covet? Why do I hate? Why? . . . People shouldn't try to live beyond their spiritual means – they shouldn't attempt roles they haven't the moral character to sustain . . . *(Suddenly, violently.)* Oh, damn this school to hell.

He decides not to attend the first day of term assembly, but Mary makes him, 'To work half-heartedly would be to make our existence futile.'

She has learnt confidence from the Riviera and Gerald's interest. She has ceased to be a drudge. 'I won't be the wife of a cynic, or a man who surrenders when he's tired or dispirited – understand that!'

It is a strong ending with Mary taking charge: 'He must work, don't you see? – It's the only way. What happiness can there be for us unless this life is his choice and his satisfaction, and his fulfilment in the end? How else can we live? How else?'

In the original version, Frith thought Margaret, the Canadian heiress, to be no proper character at all – just two-dimensionally unpleasant, and he told Norman Hunter so. Hunter said that he disliked Margaret – which, as Frith pointed out was no reason to punish her. She had to be written from her own point of view and he entrusted this task, pretending the re-writing was his own, to Christopher Taylor – and a very good job he made of it. Her charm; her original wish to be liked quickly changing when her relations-in-law will not play her game are well drawn; and her transatlantic smart-talk of the fifties rings true.

Anyone who has ever felt themselves to be a poor relation will identify with the Lesters' various reactions on being beholden to others, and anyone who knew smart life in the South of France, at around this period, will testify to the credibility of the villa and its guests. We can also infer that, before the success of *Waters of the Moon,* Norman Hunter's own circumstances, as an impoverished schoolmaster, married to a wife who had known better, make this work, and the character of Philip in particular, partly autobiographical.

Since appearing with Frith in *Jacobowsky and the Colonel* twelve years earlier, Michael Redgrave had become one of the most celebrated classical actors in the country – second only to Olivier and Gielgud. If Philip Lester learns to face his life with honesty, Redgrave still could not. His male lover was installed in a flat near his family house, and alcohol was beginning to be mentioned in connection with his work. Over this matter, Frith spoke confidentially to Glen Byam Shaw who had directed Redgrave and Peggy Ashcroft in *Antony and Cleopatra* at Stratford, perhaps Redgrave's greatest Shakespearean role. Frith remembers:

It had been obvious to Glen. Alcoholism in an actor, at first, only shows itself to his colleagues. 'Why is that scene so slow tonight?' It can have a wonderful effect but it never keeps up. Sober up and the energy will go, so more is needed. Drink makes an actor do well in one scene, but it may be his undoing for the rest of the play. Probably Kean was like that, and certainly Wilfred Lawson was.

He had another insight into Redgrave's complexities when he went to discuss the part with him one morning. He arrived at about 11.15.

> We talked, and after a bit Michael got up and started pacing the room in a nervous manner, and eventually I said, 'Michael, is anything wrong? Can I help?' And, after a pause, he said, 'May I ask you something?' 'Yes, certainly.' 'My mother's coming at half past twelve. Do you think you would mind staying here for a bit?' I said, 'Not at all. Anyway I know her.'

Frith and Margaret Scudamore had appeared together in a Sunday night production.

> I was asked because Michael hoped she would behave herself in front of me. Margaret appeared at 12.30, pretty far gone with gin, and Michael was as tense as anything and said: 'Will you have a drink, mother?' and she said, 'Yes, gin and tonic'. She had a very rasping voice, and was formidable in parts like the Bishop's wife in *Robert's Wife* – Michael gave it to her. She took one sip and shouted, 'More gin!' She then started abusing him – telling him he wasn't any good, and was running his career wrongly. She was quite horrid to him. It had an awful effect: he was suffering to hell and beyond. She later died in a home – Coral Browne was marvellous to her – and Michael's father, Roy Redgrave was an alcoholic too.

For Philip Lester's daughter Caroline, Redgrave suggested his own twenty-one-year-old daughter. She had played in repertory at Frinton and at Cambridge, but Binkie and Frith were nervous, thinking that if they considered her unsuitable they would have an offended leading-man on their hands. 'So what a relief, how exciting it was when Vanessa Redgrave walked on stage and we saw that particular quality of vulnerability, power and beauty. She read three or four lines, and I said to Binkie, 'What a relief. We obviously won't get anybody better, and I can really truthfully say that. There won't be a charge of nepotism.'

It was her first West End appearance. She professed to identify with Caroline's insecurity staying with her rich relations, and at her wonder at the beauty and glamour of the South of France. She fell in love with Dinsdale Landen who played Johnny and he drove her about in his smart convertible sports car.

Robert was played by Ronald Squire, in his last stage appearance. Frith considered him a masterly comedian, and was proud to have directed him. For Margaret, he was able to cast the real thing: Louise Allbritton was a chic American actress who lived in London and moved in very smart circles, and, as Mary, Diana Wynyard – nee Dolly Cox of Croydon.

Unlike her schoolfriend Peggy Ashcroft, Diana Wynyard completely transcended her suburban origins. Her beauty was grave and strong; her elegance and style flawless; her acting, from Shakespeare to drawing-room comedy accomplished, and often underrated. She was christened by Michael Benthall of the Old Vic, and thereafter known to her friends, as 'Auntie Di', because she managed herself and others with such aplomb. In the theatre she was obviously in charge and fulfilled, but in her own life, her choice of men did not always make her so happy. She was to die of cancer while still in her fifties.

Diana Wynyard was dressed faultlessly *dans le théâtre et en ville* by an elderly Jewish lady in North London called Trude Zahler, and there she was sent for the simple but lovely white evening dress that the schoolmaster's wife wears in the Second Act. Margaret the socialite should obviously be more grandly and expensively dressed, and Louise Allbritton was dispatched to Paris and Balmain for *all* her clothes. This fact was kept from Miss Wynyard, and Louise Allbritton was told not to mention her trip. On the Monday of her return, Frith did not call Diana Wynyard to rehearsals, so she used the opportunity of a free morning to meet some friends from Paris at the airport. It was such bad luck, one is almost sorry for Louise Allbritton. Off the plane she came dressed in Balmain from top to toe, laden with Balmain boxes, stinking of Balmain scent and ran slap into Diana Wynyard. She feigned *insouciance,* 'I always go shopping in Paris', but a rat had been smelt. And Miss Wynyard was not best pleased.

A Touch of the Sun opened at the Saville on 31 January 1958, to respectful but not very enthusiastic notices – the exception being Hobson in *The Sunday Times* who was full of praise. It ran for three months before Redgrave, who received the *Evening Standard* Best Actor Award withdrew due to other commitments. It was still doing good enough business for Tennents to replace him with Michael Gwynn and transfer the play to the Princes (now the Shaftesbury). It ran in all for 202 performances.

Having briefly found his voice, N.C. Hunter seems to have lost it again almost at once. He floundered about trying to find a new style – of his subsequent plays only *The Tulip Tree* in 1962 has merit. But during the 1950s he represented to many much that was both right and wrong about the West End Theatre. His plays were beautifully staged and expensively mounted, they provided good acting parts, but only *A Touch of the Sun* perhaps lives up to its modest ambitions. He is a civilised writer but, unlike Wynyard Browne, has neither a very original nor an interesting mind, and no wit. Nevertheless, at one stage of his life he attracted a certain amount of resentment as do all those whose success outmatches their talent.

Waters of the Moon occasionally makes an appearance in rep. because some actresses of late middle-age wish to play Helen Lancaster, and the other plays are sometimes heard on the radio, where, because of their literate dialogue and evocative atmosphere they work well.

N.C. Hunter died in 1971 at sixty-two. He is remembered as a courteous and considerate man who thought himself fortunate that his work could be seen so sumptuously, and who could provide actable parts in plays of a respectable standard for the middle-aged and elderly.

His widow, Germaine, kept his room and most of their house in mid-Wales as it had been when he was alive. She spoke to him often through spiritual mediums and thereby derived much comfort. Norman proved tougher in death than in life. When, during the revival of *Waters of the Moon* in 1977, the management asked Germaine to accept a smaller author's royalty to keep down costs, she asked Norman, and Norman said no.

Terence Rattigan
and The Deep Blue Sea

'I hear Terry Rattigan's written a new play and Kenneth Morgan's to be played by Peggy Ashcroft.' So went an actors' joke of late 1951.

With only his second play, *French Without Tears* in 1936, Rattigan, Frith's contemporary at Oxford had become a very successful playwright. He and Frith had kept in touch fitfully during the thirties but were not close. Rattigan had co-written with Anthony Maurice a comedy satirising Hitler called *Follow My Leader*. It had been banned during Neville Chamberlain's abortive peace efforts at Munich when the government were anxious not to offend the Third Reich. After the outbreak of war, this ban had been lifted, and it was put on in December 1939: the Christmas of the phoney war.

In it a Goering and a Himmler figure – played by Francis L. Sullivan and Walter Hudd – dress up a little painter, played by Reginald Beckwith, as Hitler. The premise, neither amusing nor true, being that Hitler was a nobody manipulated by powerful figures. The Himmler character was called, none too subtly, Sliwowitz, and Frith was his henchman, Quetsch.

It was, not surprisingly, the only full-blooded flop that Rattigan ever had. In Cardiff, where it opened, the director was sacked, and, at the Apollo, it closed after ten days; a footnote to Rattigan's work, as it rarely seems to be mentioned by his biographers, and Frith is the only member of the cast still alive.

In the company was a young actor called Kenneth Morgan, who was both good looking and intelligent. Even though he was already the boyfriend of the actor David Evans, Rattigan fell deeply – indeed obsessively – in love, bombarding him with presents and excessive attention. Whether his passion was ever reciprocated nobody seems sure, but probably the affair was unconsummated. Morgan broke up with Evans and entered a relationship with another man. Nobody seems sure exactly why he killed himself but his death had the most traumatic effect on Terence Rattigan.

His grief effoliated into *The Deep Blue Sea*, a play undoubtedly founded on this homosexual suicide. Frith, flavour of the month after *Waters of the Moon,* was asked to direct and of one thing he is sure: that the existence somewhere of a homosexual version of the play, supposedly rejected in horror by Binkie Beaumont, is 'Absolute rubbish. I saw Terry every day for months on end and he never mentioned it – neither did Binkie. Hester and Freddie, the lover, were an amalgam of his thoughts and feelings, and he put a lot of himself, too, into Sir William, the understanding husband.'

It is not stretching a point to compare *The Deep Blue Sea* with Eastern European plays before the fall of communism. When writers had to express their dissatisfaction with the system through disguise and metaphor, their plays had far more power and impact than now when they can treat any subject straightforwardly. Likewise Rattigan, because he was living his love and grief through three heterosexual people out of their emotional depths, was able to produce one of his best, and certainly his profoundest play.

Hester Collyer (Peggy Ashcroft), an ordinary and conservative woman, has left her husband, a successful lawyer now a judge, for a young pilot. She and Sir William Collyer (Roland Culver) have everything in common but sex: 'You must understand that I am very inexperienced in matters of this kind,' he says; she and Freddie Page (Kenneth More) have nothing in common but sex. In her middle thirties she has discovered physical passion for the first time and with an appetite of which she is ashamed. When they kiss, the stage direction read, *'Hester instantly responds with an intensity of emotion that is almost ugly.'* To satisfy her urges she has given up her marriage and position to live with Freddie in a seedy flat in Westbourne Park. But after a while, Freddie cannot meet her demands, 'I can't be a ruddy Romeo all the time,' as he tells his friend Jackie Jackson; and Hester – denied the promise even of this – attempts suicide, a failed attempt with which the play begins. During the action we discover what drove her to this act, and whether she is likely to repeat it. 'Anyway,' she tells her husband, 'when you're between any kind of devil and the deep blue sea, the deep blue sea sometimes looks very inviting. It did last night.' When he asks her to return to him, she replies, 'I'm not any longer the same person.' She has discovered sex.

Freddie, often unemployed since the war and confused over demands he cannot meet is drinking heavily. His immaturity and intellectual limitations make him quite unequal to understanding Hester's plight, so when he leaves her she sets up a second suicide and is saved by Mr Miller (Peter Illing) from a neighbouring flat. A doctor, struck off the register after a term of imprisonment for an undisclosed offence – which we guess from Mrs Elton (Barbara Leake) the landlady, 'It takes all sorts to make a world, after all – doesn't it,' to have been homosexual. Through facing life in adversity, he is now a bookie's clerk, and working voluntarily in a hospital for infantile paralysis, he helps Hester find her purpose. He sees talent in one of her paintings. She lights the gas fire, but the flame is a metaphor for her hope and her future.

Rattigan had already promised Hester to Margaret Leighton. But Frith thought she would be far too beautiful and unusual (for the same reason Vivien Leigh was miscast in the film). Hester is, in Freddie's description, 'A clergyman's daughter, living in Oxford, marries the first man who asks her and falls in love with the first man who gives her an eye'. 'I really think you're the most attractive girl I've ever met,' has been his opening gambit, and she falls for this cliched patter because no one has ever spoken to her like that before. To cast an actress renowned for her beauty makes a complete nonsense of the character. Hester must suggest a highly-sexed and sensitive woman under a pleasant but unremarkable exterior. To this end, he insisted – the first time he had laid down the law to management and author – that the part be played by Peggy Ashcroft. She was unavailable for six months, and for six months they waited for her. 'I've never been happier about anything.'

During the hiatus, Frith directed Neville Croft's *All the Year Round*, and worked with Binkie and Rattigan on the casting. Freddie was proving a problem. He is one of 'The Few': those young Battle of Britain pilots who were national heroes at twenty, but who at thirty were, if they had no aptitude for civilian life, washed up and directionless. The characterisation is excellent: the slang; the golf at Sunningdale; the cheery manner disguising mental dimness. His conversation consists only of his handicap, the speed he drove on the 'Great West.', and his plans to try out a new drinking club. Hester, talking of him to Sir William says, 'that R.A.F. slang used to irritate me slightly I remember. It's such an anachronism now, isn't it – as dated as gadzooks or odds my life.'

COLLYER. He does it for effect I suppose.
HESTER. No, he does it because his life stopped in nineteen-forty. He loved nineteen-forty. Freddie's never been really happy since he left the R.A.F.

It was the slang that Rattigan, who had himself been in the airforce, knew first-hand.

Freddie's dare-devil physical courage contrasts well with his emotional cowardice and immaturity: 'My God, how I hate getting tangled up in other people's emotions. It's the one thing I've tried to avoid all my life.'

In 1951, one would have thought, it would not have been difficult to find someone who could *be* rather than *act* Freddie, a necessity when Freddies could be found in any Thames Valley pub, but, to begin with, such was not the case. Frith was inclined towards Jimmy Hanley, who fulfilled some of the requirements. Then Roland Culver, who had already been cast as Sir William, suggested a golfing chum of his, a relatively unknown actor called Kenneth More.

More gives an account of how he won the part in his autobiography, *More or Less.* How, at the first audition, having not seen the script he was told by Frith: 'You are playing a very sexy young man. The older woman is mad about him, not because of his looks or background, but just because he *is* sexy. Now go ahead and read.' After that, it was no wonder he read badly and no wonder Frith still wanted Jimmy Hanley.

Rattigan and Beaumont, however, obviously saw something to which Frith was blind: Kenneth More not only looked exactly right for Freddie Page, but in manner, and to some degree in experience, *was* Freddie Page. He was given the play to read and a second audition was arranged.

Having been given two enormous glasses of whisky by Rattigan he read well, and on completion turned to the author and asked 'Howzat?' Like a cricketer, or like Freddie. His suitability for the part is exemplified by the language of his summary of the evening: 'I knew I was home. The part was mine, Frith now backed me to the hilt, and all through playing golf with Roland Culver!'

The completed cast read the play six weeks before rehearsals started, Tennent's invaluable custom when presenting a new play, so that further work could be done on the text. Terence Rattigan attended and then, presumably thinking the play needed no improvement, departed for ten days to New York. But, during his absence Frith and Peggy Ashcroft knuckled down to some serious thinking of their own.

It seemed to them that there were areas that needed attention, and here Peggy Ashcroft was to prove invaluable; being quick to detect falseness and cut through theatricality. At this stage, Hester was more a generalisation, a concept rather than an individual human being. Frith, with Peggy Ashcroft's guidance, pinpointed aspects of the character which needed fleshing out, and sections of the script that needed re-writing. 'Through her,' says Frith, 'the play was re-worked to its benefit.'

On Rattigan's return, Frith, with suggested changes in hand, went to dinner at Chester Square. The author listened politely seemingly giving no reaction. During the meal there was a telephone call for Frith. It was Peggy Ashcroft:

'How are you getting on?'

'All right – I think.'

At the end of the evening, Rattigan escorted Frith to the front door still urbane and non-committal, but the moment it had closed he was on the telephone to Binkie Beaumont saying that between them, Frith Banbury and Peggy Ashcroft were ruining his play. The response did not satisfy the playwright who then went round to Binkie's house in Lord North Street, where he found that Binkie had already gone to bed. But Rattigan made him get up and they sat up all night talking. The next morning Frith was summoned to the Globe Office. There he found Rattigan all smiles. He quite agreed with the suggested changes and all the re-writes would be on their way. Frith never found out what it was that Binkie had said to him.

The overall budget was quite a lavish one: £2,500, and rehearsals began at the beginning of February 1952. At an early stage, Peggy Ashcroft stopped what she was doing and said: 'I'm not enjoying this: I feel as if I'm walking about with no clothes on.'

'That means that you're going to be smashing,' thought Frith, 'for what you're saying is "I've got to tell a truth about it, but it's a truth I don't like telling",' and it is his conviction that by some extremely clever acting from her, and afterwards Celia Johnson, certain inadequacies in the part were covered up.

In later years, Dame Peggy was to say that, as a woman, she had little in common with Hester Collyer. But it is the belief of Frith and others to whom I have talked, that the parallels between Hester's comparatively late discovery of physical passion, and the circumstances of Dame Peggy's own life at the time, were not dissimilar. She was married to an eminent Q.C., Jeremy Hutchinson, and one of her two earlier marriages had been sexless. She was, by all accounts, a most passionate and amorous woman, whose enjoyment of sex with many lovers also shocked her sense of respectability. There is conflict between Hester's conventional manner and her relish of sex. Maybe Ashcroft truly found no common denominator between herself and the character, or maybe, like Hester, she had difficulty acknowledging it.

The reviews, after the opening night at the Duchess Theatre on March 6, 1952, were universally encomiastic. Absolute raves which no, play or production in the West End can ever have surpassed. I select just three.

'The production by Frith Banbury and the playing of a faultless little company are beyond praise,' wrote Alan Dent in *The News Chronicle,* 'But this is no good reason (as so often it is made) for not expressing that praise. So let me offer the largest possible bouquet to Peggy Ashcroft for a performance of acute and even agonising sensibility.'

Harold Hobson in *The Sunday Times,* vividly recreates his night's experience:

> . . . to concentrate more fiercely with this single point of experience (a woman's obsession with a man) Mr Rattigan preserves the unities of time and place. It is the best play he has written. In the two principle parts, those of Hester and the judge, Miss Ashcroft and Mr Roland Culver seem to me to touch the greatest heights of which acting of the quietest school is capable. There is not a moment when I was not enthralled. The grave beauty of Miss Ashcroft's voice, the sad loveliness of her face are unforgettable things: her story of how she fell in love with Freddie Page – and its last words, 'I knew there was no hope for me – no hope at all' – are almost too heartrending to be borne.

And T.C. Worsley in *The New Statesman and Nation* thought 'The producer Mr Frith Banbury deserves special praise for meeting without ducking the rawness of the emotional scenes.'

It ran for over a year; Celia Johnson taking over as Hester after three months. Two months later, Peggy Ashcroft returned for another three months, and then Googie Withers played for the remainder of the run.

Frith had now done the hat trick: three triumphs in a row, and, at forty, he was a director esteemed and in demand.

Coda – America

Early in the run, Margaret Sullavan, the American film star, came to a performance. She had not been on stage for eight years and had only made one film. She was looking for a vehicle in which to make a comeback: a good play to present her as a middle-aged woman. She still looked very young with her trademark fringe and bangs: a most attractive girl. She decided that *The Deep Blue Sea* was to be this vehicle; so, using her name and Rattigan's, Alfred De Liagre Jnr.

and John C. Wilson (Jack Wilson, Noel Coward's ex-boyfriend) prepared a Broadway Production. Frith was engaged to re-direct with the
English actor Alan Webb as Sir William Collyer and Herbert Berghof
as Miller. Kenneth More, whom Tennents were prepared to release to
make his American debut, refused to go to Broadway, and Jimmy Hanley
was brought back from Australia, where since losing the part of Freddie
Page, he had been playing in a farce. And that was the first problem – for
enjoying the easy work and the sun, Hanley had succumbed to a natural
propensity for over-indulgence and become immensely fat. In New York,
Frith met him at the airport, saw him wobble off the plane, and then had
to drive him straight to Miss Sullavan's apartment and present him as her
lover. She was plainly aghast and he was put on a strict diet.

Margaret Sullavan was a complex creature. Off stage she was charming, intelligent and interesting to talk to, but the minute she went through a stage-door or
on to a film set, some devil entered, and she behaved with unbelievable rudeness.

She was obviously full of insecurity. She wanted to play Hester correctly
and wanted to be good, but lacked the necessary stage experience and
technique to make this possible. At rehearsals, failing to make satisfactory
progress, she fell back into her well loved girlish mannerisms; what she
knew she could do. She wanted to sit on the floor like darling Maggie
Sullavan, the girl-next-door. Frith pointed out that women like Hester
sit up in chairs. She also tried to have all the furniture moved downstage,
plainly because she feared her personality would not travel the length
of the stage. Interestingly, all the cuts that had been made in London,
because Peggy Ashcroft could convey the feeling without the words, now
had to be restored, as Margaret Sullavan was unable to act subtext.

Frith's fault-finding was beginning to annoy her. It was his first experience
of Broadway with its custom for outsiders like agents and press-officers attending rehearsals, and he started to act the director directing: frankly, showing off.

'The trouble with you,' she said sharply one day, 'is that you're enjoying
yourself too much.'

When having her fitting at Bergdorf Goodman on Fifth Avenue, she
created a big scene: refusing to try on the neat and conventional dresses
that Hester would wear because she thought them 'dowdy'. She insisted
on chic, over-smart clothes which might have enhanced Miss Sullavan
but which Hester would not have dreamt of wearing. Finally she abused
the *vendeuse* and threw the dress at her.

They opened in New Haven at the start of a five week pre-Broadway
tour. The First Night did not go well, and she announced that she wanted

Frith replaced by Joshua Logan. The management telephoned Rattigan for his permission which was not given. He said bluntly that either Frith remain or there would be no Broadway opening. Thwarted in this, Miss Sullavan then turned nasty. The tour moved on to Washington D.C., where the notices were not good, and in her dressing room, like a joke B Movie Star, she screamed with rage and threw the props about.

News of these American tribulations reached London, where the company at the Duchess heard, inaccurately, that Frith had been sacked.

Before the First Night on Broadway at the Morosco, suitably in view of the off-stage fireworks, on November 5, she had a table brought on stage, on which were placed her presents to the cast. After the quarter of an hour call had been given, she was still distributing them. 'And that's for you, and they'll change it if it's the wrong colour . . .'

'Could one,' exclaims Frith, 'see Peggy Ashcroft do that?'

Poor Margaret Sullavan had not the power for the part. Sex is never mentioned, but it is a play about sex. As there was no sexual tension at all between Sullavan and Hanley, the play itself seemed completely pointless – and it was the play that was attacked in the reviews. John Chapman in *The New York News* summing up their spirit with the headline: 'Margaret Sullavan Weeps, Loves, in a Sudsy Drama, *Deep Blue Sea*', continuing, 'A soap opera about hopeless love . . . unworthy of the excellent acting bestowed upon it,' and the respected Brooks Atkinson in *The New York Times* said: 'Sullavan gives the performance of her career . . . *Deep Blue Sea* is too slick and thin to have any significance beyond the acted performance'.

Miss Sullavan's name had produced a large advance booking and, on that alone, it ran for four and a half months in New York.

Jimmy Hanley left as soon as he could, 'because Maggie Sullavan was such hell' [Frith] and Freddie was played by Kevin McCarthy (brother of Mary, the novelist and critic). On the day he came to read it, after a performance, Miss Sullavan was in a bad mood because the heating system at the Morosco had been making burping noises. Frith recounts: 'She took it out on Kevin, who was a well-known actor. I have never seen anybody so rude; I was quite ashamed for her.'

It was, understandably, a trying time for Frith. He is inclined to the stiff upper lip legacy from the Admiral when unhappy, but luckily for him, his old R.A.D.A. friend Leueen MacGrath, now living in New York with her husband the playwright George S. Kaufman, saw beyond that, and they both showed kindness and gave support. Luckily for him, too, the leading-lady's inadequacies made the writer seem at fault not the director, and Frith was accepted by New York Theatre Society, a world where success is everything. He made contacts which have served him well professionally since; and friends, like Milton Goldman, and Ruth Goodman Goetz who remained in his life thereafter.

After Broadway, there was a tour for the large public anxious to see Miss Sullavan. At Milwaukee, she announced she would not continue, and for the last date, Chicago, Uta Hagen (Herbert Berghof's wife) played Hester, who Frith thought superb, but, denied their star, no one came and it closed after two weeks.

When he returned to London, he discovered that Margaret Sullavan had written to Peggy Ashcroft, now again at the Duchess, and the gist of this letter was: 'Dear Miss Ashcroft: This is to tell you that you can play the part and I can't.'

Margaret Sullavan eventually killed herself. In 1960 she was touring *Sweet Love Remembered,* a new play by Ruth Goodman Goetz. It opened on a Monday in New Haven to a bad press. On Tuesday she asked to be released from her contract, a request which was refused. She could not cope. On Wednesday, instead of throwing a tantrum as she had in 1952, she took an overdose. She left her bedroom door open with the bed so arranged that she could be seen lying on it, histrionically, from the corridor: attention-seeking to the last.

*

Frith hoped he might be asked to direct the first production of *Separate Tables* in 1954, but that production went to Peter Glenville, which Marjorie Sisley thinks one of the two major disappointments of his career (the other being Bolt's *A Man for All Seasons* going to Noel Willman). The next time he directed a Rattigan play was in 1970, a revival of *The Winslow Boy.* Suitably, the lead was Kenneth More.

Frith Banbury at 22.

Frith Banbury at 32, as Joseph Surface in The School for Scandal *at the Oxford Playhouse*

Frith Banbury at 52.

Frith Banbury at 82.

Dark Summer. *Dan Cunningham, Annabel Maule, Nora Nicholson, Jean Cadell and Joan Miller.*

The Holly and the Ivy. *Daphne Arthur, Herbert Lomas, Cecil Ramage, Maureen Delany, Jane Baxter, Bryan Forbes and Margaret Halstan.*

A Question of Fact. *Mary Hinton, Henry Hewitt, Gladys Cooper, Pamela Brown and Paul Scofield.*

The Ring of Truth. *John Slater and Irene Browne.*

Waters of the Moon. *(The New Year's Eve Party.) Leo Bieber, Edtih Evans, Wendy Hiller, Patricia McCarron, Kathleen Harrison, Owen Holder, Cyril Raymond, Sybil Thorndike, Nan Munro and Harold Scott.*

A Touch of the Sun. *Diana Wynyard, Vanessa Redgrave and Michael Redgrave*

The Deep Blue Sea.
Peggy Ashcroft and Kenneth More

Hermione Baddeley as Christine Foskett
in The Pink Room

A Dead Secret. *Anthony Wilson, Madge Brindley, Gretchen Franklin, Dinsdale Landen, Harold Scott, Paul Scofield, Arthur Lowe and Megs Jenkins.*

Robert Flemyng as Rupert Forster in Marching Song.

Love's Labour's Lost. *Group includes: Paul Rogers (on ground left),*
Charles Gray and Ann Todd (centre), Eric Porter, John Neville and
Virginia McKenna (right)

Flowering Cherry.
Celia Johnson and
Ralph Richardson

The Tiger and the Horse. *Michael
and Vanessa Redgrave.*

Moon on a Rainbow Shawl.
Earle Hyman and Soraya Rafat.

Part Four

Rodney Ackland:
Either a Fog or the King Died

Both as man and writer Rodney Ackland was Frith Banbury's Cause in Life. But each time the interest in his work looked like escalating it proved to be a false start. For Frith, Ackland's talent was one of the most important of the century. He was a theatrical outsider, ahead of his time and often misunderstood – and, after the late 1950s dismissed by some to keep company with Emlyn Williams and Enid Bagnold – to a world of commercial glamour and moral convention which, in fact, for nearly thirty years he had stood back from and attacked. In the last decade there have been noteworthy revivals of his earlier plays, in the theatre and on television, and distinguished writers have promulgated his cause in journals; yet, by the main-stream theatre – the new theatrical establishment of the big subsidised companies – he has been avoided. Perhaps, as always, he will be forced to remain outside that establishment – to which he half yearned to belong, but from which he really needed to be detached; so he could reveal it with uncompromising lack of flattery.

During a Memorial Evening at the Orange Tree Theatre in Richmond when scenes from his plays were interspersed with reminiscences, Sir John Gielgud, in a taped interview, explained the poor attendance at the First Night of *The Old Ladies:* 'Either there was fog or the King died, or something,' and the biographer and critic Hilary Spurling – Ackland's champion for two decades – commented in her talk, that this was always Rodney's story: as with the characters in his plays, the time was never quite right, the moment never came.

'Rodney needed to surround himself with freaks,' said Joss Ackland, possibly a distant cousin; and Frith, too, has noted that ordinary sane people, when drawn into the orbit of his chaotic and strange existence, started to behave in an Acklandish way. Life around Rodney took on the guise of one of his plays. 'Life imitating Art, as it were.'

His world, as Hilary Spurling wrote in his obituary was 'generally urban, louche, unstable, emotionally precarious and morally far from reassuring'.

And, in a famous *Spectator* article of 1968, she speaks of the appeal of his characters,

> chronically hard up, out of work, subsisting with a forlorn gallantry, or more often a disdainful and rackety gaiety. There is something immensely engaging about these strangely affronted beings – for the most part failed or aspiring novelists, painters, poets, actresses, all nourished on the passionate conviction that a mistake has been made, that somehow their native talent must be recognised and rescued from the sordid surroundings which, by an oversight, have been temporarily foisted upon them.

This Ackland's-Eye view of the world is indeed very arresting. No one writes better about failure.

Joe Orton, writing about his own work said: 'It's always a fight for an original writer because any original writer will always force the world to see the world his way. The people who don't want to see the world your way will always be angry.' So with Ackland; an extremist himself, he produces extreme reactions from others. His characters hide their heads, ostrich-like, unable to face painful truths, and so too, perhaps, do some of his audience and readers.

He was born Norman Ackland Bernstein in 1908, the son of a Jewish businessman and Ada Rodney, a well-known performer on the Halls and Principal Boy in Pantomime who, in Frith's words, 'got the bird at the Lewisham Hippodrome'. There is a photograph of her dressed up as a basket of flowers. When Rodney was six, his father went bankrupt and, 'the house was sold, the servants dismissed, and from then on Rodney and his two sisters were brought up in straitened circumstances.' Mrs Bernstein sold stockings from door to door, an occupation to which she often returned when fortunes were low. His father's insolvency and a child's remembrance of past luxury were to be the causes of his own profligacy and irresponsibility over finance.

After training on a scholarship with Elsie Fogerty at the Central School, he became an actor in many provincial companies – his ceiling being reached in the title role of John van Druten's *Young Woodley* on tour. Acting, Rodney later claimed, was only a means to break into his first love, the cinema.

Komisarjevsky's production of *The Three Sisters* at Barnes in 1926, with Gielgud as Tusenbach, altered the young Ackland's theatrical perceptions, and, as for others, changed his life. Although unable to read Russian, Chekhov and indeed most turn-of-the-century Russian writers were the great influence under which he wrote his first play *Improper People*, produced at the Arts Theatre in 1929. He was twenty-one. It concerns a suicide pact between two lovers who cannot afford to marry. His aim being, 'to tell the truth about living without money in the suburbs – a subject on which I felt I could speak with authority'. It was found by one critic to be, 'nearly as boring as Chekhov'.

His next two plays *Marion-Ella* and *Dance With No Music* (both 1929) were written for the star of his *Young Woodley* tour, Leonora Corbett (although the film-star Madeleine Carroll in fact created the lead in the latter).

Marion-Ella concerns the unhappy plight of a girl who realises she is half of a divided personality, and *Dance With No Music* is about a sexy actress in a Seaside Repertory Company.

But it was his third play, *Strange Orchestra* (1931), which brought him both into the West End and into the consciousness of Frith. The action takes place in a Bloomsbury flat owned by Mrs Vera Lyndon – a Bohemian woman with an illegitimate child, a kind heart, and a number of dispossessed lodgers including a thief. She was based on an eccentric actress friend of Rodney's, Gwladys Evan Morris, who ran just such an establishment. It was she who created the role at the Embassy, Swiss Cottage.

Frith thought it the best play he had ever seen:

Having been brought up in a conventional English upper-middle-class household, I was entranced by this picture of free-living bohemians, to whose life-style I, still in my teens, had come to aspire. It was quite different from any other play I had seen in the theatre of the twenties or the early thirties – not, of course, in its style, but, more important, in its content. From then on I made the point of seeing, generally more than once, every Ackland play that was produced.

John Gielgud directed it in the West End the following year: his first production of a modern play. He found the characters engrossing: 'They are uncertain of their jobs, they quarrel, make love, indulge in scenes of hysteria, behave abominably to one another, perform deeds of unselfish heroism, and dance to the gramophone.'

He asked Mrs Patrick Campbell, who had by then offended so many people that she was barely employable, to play Vera Lyndon. To his surprise she accepted. At the first rehearsal she pretended to find the play incomprehensible, 'Who are all these extraordinary characters? Where do they live? Does Gladys Cooper know them?' But after rehearsing superbly for a fortnight she left – 'She's not quite a lady is she? I'm afraid you'll have to get Poor Dear Maud [Lady Tree] to play her' – and Laura Cowie took over.

The run was short but the play received an encomium from Agate in *The Sunday Times:* 'as much superior to the ordinary stuff of the theatre as tattered silk is to unbleached calico'. Praise which Rodney was often to quote in years to come.

Gielgud, too, writing in 1939, applauded the 'distinctive rhythm' of his plays, 'The moods and subtleties of his characters are woven together in a distinctive pattern. His vision is apt to be limited to his own particular type of atmosphere, but at least he deals with real people.' An assessment which remained valid.

Two years later, Frith 'could hardly believe his luck', when he was asked to be in a revival of *Strange Orchestra* at the 'Q' Theatre (at the end of Kew Bridge) directed by the author. It was his first professional association with Rodney, who was four years the elder, and his first meeting with this lovable but impossible man.

During the thirties and forties, Rodney wrote both original plays and a number of adaptations. The best of the former was *Birthday* (1934), about the hilariously appalling Moorehouse Rees family – a wonderful *exposé* of the middle-class selfishness and philistinism which he despised. This was directed by Basil Dean at the Cambridge, and Rodney acted in it himself, as he did in the overtly autobiographical *After October* (1936).

Many Acklandphiles consider *The Dark River* (1937, performed 1943) his masterpiece. Hilary Spurling has called it, 'perhaps the one indisputably great play of the past half-century in English'. Set in an old house in a Thames backwater where a group of assorted characters fail to face up to the impending European catastrophe – a world where the past battles with the future, it is certainly full of glories – of conflict, mood, and poetry, but for me it lacks some of the edge and clarity which is found in his other work, relies too heavily on coincidence, and has one character – the film director Reade – whom I find unconvincing. Peggy Ashcroft was much acclaimed as Catherine Lisle in the first production, which Rodney directed.

Apart from *After October,* with its appealing theme of young playwright disappointed, none of these plays was a commercial success. The middle-class audience had to view a picture of itself in a less than flattering light, and that did not ensure long runs. But he had one powerful admirer in James Agate: at least to begin with, then even he turned – and, as so often with Agate, for personal reasons.

Having given his usual praise to *After October,* Agate, who also liked good-looking young men, invited Rodney to lunch at the Savoy. Rodney, always a pathologically bad time-keeper, arrived an hour late, and, according to him, was never forgiven. Certainly a note of sourness appeared in Agate's reviews of Rodney's plays from then on. Rodney, in turn resented this fickleness, and began to bear a grudge which was to find its expression in the portrayal of the ugly, homosexual Agate as a bald, lesbian literary critic in *The Pink Room* a decade later.

Another of Rodney's resentments was that his adaptations received more attention than his original plays, and, in later years, were more frequently revived. The first of these was *Ballerina* (1933) from a novel by Lady Eleanor Smith, and the superbly macabre *The Old Ladies* (1935), from the novella by Hugh Walpole, in which the three old women were played – it is clear, faultlessly – by Edith Evans, Mary Jerrold, and Jean Cadell, with Gielgud directing. Evans and Gielgud were also in his adaptation of Dostoevsky's *Crime and Punishment* in 1945. There was *The White Guard,* from Bulgakov in 1938, *Before the Party,* from the short story by Somerset Maughan, and Ostrovsky's *The Diary of A Scoundrel (Too Clever By Half)* both in 1949.

His great love, the cinema, also claimed his prolific energies. During the forties, he wrote the script for Emeric Pressburger's *49th Parallel,* and was scriptwriter – and, for a day director – on *The Queen of Spades,* with Edith Evans and Anton Walbrook. He also directed *Thursday's Child* (1943) with Sally Ann Howes and Stewart Granger. He gave an entertaining account of the frustrations of his cinematic career in a memoir, *The Celluloid Mistress* (1954).

I cannot discover exactly when it was that Rodney became a Buddhist, but it was early on. There are allusions to it in *Strange Orchestra.* The author was obviously more than just interested in the subject by then, and Gielgud noticed he was vegetarian. Like many on a spiritual quest in the thirties he developed this interest in oriental religions through the writings of Rabindranath Tagore, which seem very accessible to the Western mind. Although a Hindu, Tagore's philosophy also contains the essence of Buddhist teaching:

'Man's individuality is not his highest truth: there is that in him which is immortal. If he were made to live in a world where his own self was the only factor to consider, then that would be the worst prison imaginable to him, for man's deepest joy is in growing greater and greater by more and more union with the All.'

This is the very opposite of Existentialism, where the Self is all we have and where good actions and bad are rationalised; and of Marxism, where the Spirit is denied, and everything can be found in the world of Matter. All Rodney's plays are, in a sense, a reply to the Existentialists – an antithesis of Sartre and Camus. The three great influences of his life – Chekhov, Dostoevsky and Buddha were to him quite compatible.

How successful a Buddhist was he? He had a certain unworldliness, even naiveté in some matters, but serenity through acceptance of his earthly lot he did not attain. Let us hope that disappointment at the world's neglect and, in later life, bitterness at the lack of appreciation accorded, were, at least, alleviated by Buddhism's guidelines over the unimportance of the recognition and approval of others.

He was a person of marked contrasts. Humour and understanding were in opposition to paranoia and prickliness; and efficiency and professionalism in the theatre were placed against fecklessness with money and an inability to organise his own life.

As a young man he was assumed to be primarily homosexual, although it was known he was sometimes attracted to women, as he was to his friend Emlyn Williams's wife, Molly ('Emlyn never knew!') with whom he had an affair at the Williams's house in a Thames backwater, which stayed in his mind for Ella Merriman's schoolhouse in *The Dark River*. But his first serious partner was the actor Eric Holmes, and the friendship continued after the affair concluded – Rodney arranging for him to play two small parts in *Crime and Punishment*. The most important of his affairs with men was with Arthur Boys, a successful Australian Interior Decorator (Nigel Childs in *Absolute Hell*). They used to walk down the street holding hands hoping to *épater les bourgeois*, until, climbing onto a local bus by himself Rodney was asked by an old lady, 'And how is your poor dear blind friend?' Boys assisted Rodney with writing the screen play for *The Queen of Spades*, but when they found that their names were in smaller letters than Alexander Pushkin's on the opening credits they sued the Production Company, World Screenplays – and won. They were awarded derisory damages with no costs, which, as Rodney had spent all his savings on the case, was rather a Pyrrhic victory. Indeed, he was always very litigious, so much so that Terence Rattigan suggested that his parting shot should be, 'sue you soon'. He was even suing *The Times* as late as 1975 over an item in The Diary which had displeased him.

His relationship with Arthur Boys was volatile too. Boys could calm Rodney's acute nerves at moments of crisis, and give a measure of support during theatrical tribulations, but at home their life was stormy; there were also some public rows; and, by the end of the forties, they had parted.

It was at a party in 1950, that Rodney met Mab Poole, and it was love at first sight. They married two years later and for twenty-two years, until her death from cancer of the throat in 1972, they never spent a single night apart.

Mab (or Mabbie), was the second daughter of the playwright Frederick Lonsdale. During the thirties she had married Mr Poole and lived a very pukka county life in the Shires. This existence did not suit her, and, in spite of the birth of a son Michael, the marriage was unhappy. During the war, she came to London and found a job with Alexander Korda at London Films. There, she worked alongside and became great friends with the redoubtable and enormous Moura Baroness Budberg, ex-mistress of both Gorky and H.G. Wells. Her work was mainly that of an uncredited script writer: her revisions and additions to Graham Greene's *The Third Man*, being considerable, if unattributed. During this time she met and fell in love with the famous American war correspondent, H.R. Knickerbocker, who was ready to leave his wife and children for her when he was killed in an air-crash over Amsterdam. 'She was a very special person,' says Frith. 'Shy – she covered her mouth with her hand when she spoke; a gentle charming person.' She and Rodney took absolute delight in each other's company, and their marriage was completely fulfilled and as happy as bliss. There is a delightful story of them both lying in bed reading – Rodney tearing out the pages of a book as he read, and handing them to Mab.

But to say their married life was one of vicissitudes would be an understatement. They led a fly-by-night existence, for Rodney was usually on the run from the Inland Revenue. They changed addresses a great deal. Over the years, Frith received letters from Rodney headed variously:

'Little Vienna', Ovingdean, Sussex.
Cambridge Court, Edgware Road.
A6 Albany.
Tredeague, St Austell, Cornwall.
25D, Ladbroke Gardens.
36A, Putney Hill.
Sanary, France.
27, Cathcart Road.
193, New Kings Road.

So we can see how their fortunes fluctuated.

They owned, Frith observes, 'no things'. Their possessions, luckily in view of their frequent moves, consisting only of a few treasured books and Rodney's scripts. Their only permanence was their love for one another.

At other times they seem to have lived in a flat off Belgrave Square – presumably after some advance – and, for a while, they were lodgers of the actress Mary Merrall in Carlton Hill, St John's Wood, where took place a typical example of life as an Ackland play.

Mary Merrall was the widow of the actor Franklin Dyall. An aristocratic looking and sounding woman, she was also a Communist. 'She combined,' says Frith, 'a predilection for Stalin with the silver teapot. One moment it was, "Is it one lump or two?", and the next, "Stalin is the Saviour of the World and only the Communist Party can make life bearable".'

After her husband's death, she went 'strange', and, at the age of sixty-three married a young Irish layabout and jailbird of twenty- seven who, after he had cleaned her out, started nicking things from the lodgers. Mabbie soon found that she had 'mislaid' a pair of earrings. So when there was nobody else in the house, she, Rodney and Frith crept into the boy's bedroom and stole them back again. Eventually the police were called:

'Oh, Franklin! Franklin!,' Miss Merrall wailed when he was safely back inside, 'Had you been alive this could never have happened!' which, as Rodney pointed out was a redundant observation as, had he been alive, she could never have married the yob in the first place.

Frith first started to know Rodney well when, in 1950, he directed a revival of *The Old Ladies* at the Lyric Theatre Hammersmith, and the professional *rapport* between them was instant. Rodney said that Frith thought of what was needed before he did, and he told me shortly before he died that his trust in Frith's judgement was absolute. He and Mabbie christened Frith 'Nanny Banbury', and Nanny Banbury was called upon regularly to sort out the imminent catastrophes, and rectify the continuing chaos of their lives – and sort them out he did.

If righting the neglect accorded to Rodney's plays was the greatest Cause of Frith's life, the Acklands' finances were his greatest charity. Not only did he for forty years try *incredibly* hard to interest powerful people in Rodney's plays, but he spent large sums of money frequently to extract him from penury. Bills were paid, rent arrears settled, advances given, which he must have known would not be repaid, and, latterly, plays commissioned that both of them, in their hearts, must have known would never be written.

Frith's files tell the stories: Rodney spins a yarn to the Inland Revenue saying – quite untruthfully – that he is an employee of Frith Banbury Productions. He then secures a loan against the same fib so that, on default, the moneylender sues Frith. Yet there is always something very endearing about Rodney's begging:

'Frith *dear,'* he wrote in an undated letter from St Austell:

'Will you be an angel yet again and save our name down here by changing a post-dated cheque with Mabbie against her quarter's income due in the middle of June?

'We'd been banking on having my money from the *Before the Party* script in time [for television, this must have been the mid fifties] but simply couldn't get it typed properly down here and it was consequently only delivered last Friday, 3 weeks after I'd finished it. Please do this if you can possibly manage it. Our landlord who lives in a mansion overlooking us is the *enemy.* An ex M.P. Tory, Undersecretary of State with the wartime government, loathes Russian plays and novels, and as Sheriff of Cornwall sat at the Assizes condemning people to be hanged. So you see what might be in store for us if we default with rent, electricity, phone, local tradesmen etc. etc.! Apart from these money worries it is *divine* here, in fact splendid. Could you possibly come down – so many things re plays I want to discuss. In haste for post. Love from both, Rodney.'

The production of *The Old Ladies* had two of the original cast of three: Mary Jerrold as the patient and sweet old lady; Lucy Amorest, who lives in expectation of a letter from her son and a cousin's legacy; and Jean Cadell as the timid, spinsterish and ill May Beringer, who owns the piece of amber greedily lusted after by the disturbingly unbalanced Agatha Payne – whose gypsy taste sees it as a thing of great beauty. When Edith Evans had played this part originally she had been terrifying – but, unfortunately, it was now taken by 'a silly fool of a woman, who had got too big for her boots when she was a star', Mary Clare. The purpose of the revival was to rehabilitate her to her former status.

From photographs she looks ludicrous: hammy and *grand guignol* in a play which creates its tension by keeping characters and events in believable proportion. *The Times* found her 'Grotesque. She presents the character much as an actor might present Long John Silver.' And like a bipedal Long John Silver in drag she looks. But the same critic, A.V. Cookman found the rest of the play 'beautifully rendered', and Frith's production 'absorbing'.

Absorbing too are Rodney's letters to Frith during rehearsals – astute and helpful: the exact moment in the last act that Agatha should creep downstairs and sit in the hall waiting, is *while* Lucy is praying for preservation against the dangers of the night. And there are some wonderfully vivid descriptions: Agatha should be 'a huge lumbering mass enveloped in oriental dressing-gowns and shawls, who drinks cocoa as though it were blood. An ogress seething in shapeless flesh and stewing in malignant juices of her own devising'.

'If plays of this type are to be more than shockers they must have some kinship with tragedy, and tragedy cannot exist apart from greatness though this may be warped or only potential.' For Rodney, 'Always the play came first – before the playwright's *amour propre.*'

Reece Pemberton's set looks wonderfully evocative – the three old women's bedrooms all visible at once on different levels and distances from the audience.

But the chief importance of the revival from Rodney's point of view was that he had found his director, and – eventually – his torch bearer. He presented Frith with the script of a play which had been circulating the managers' offices for some years with no success, but of which he was justly proud called; *The Pink Room* or *The Escapists*. It struck Frith as a very moral play.

It was Terence Rattigan who eventually provided the means for *The Pink Room* to be produced. Before rehearsals of *The Deep Blue Sea* started, Frith had shown him the script; his reaction was enthusiastic. Moreover his accountant had advised him to offload some of his considerable earnings for that year, and financing a play by an admired, if less fortunate colleague, must have seemed the most constructive of expenditures. Binkie Beaumont, who had rejected the play as being too uncertain commercially, was asked to provide the wherewithal of production: stage-management, rehearsal space, publicity, and organisation of pre-London try-out at Brighton, and with Rattigan footing the bill, this he seems to have done quite willingly. So the often repeated story that he had rejected the play as being 'an insult to the British people' seems improbable. In fact, he allowed the play to rehearse in Tennent theatres, and be performed at the Lyric Hammersmith under Tennent Productions' auspices, if not with their financial involvement. Because of Frith's enthusiasm and Rattigan's need to spend his money as soon as possible, *The Pink Room* went into rehearsal in May 1952, two months after the premiere of *The Deep Blue Sea*.

Summarising the plot presents a problem for, as Nicholas Dromgoole observed, the play has as many plots as it has characters. He continues: 'It is the skill with which these intertwine and interact on each other that creates his dramatic tension. The dialogue may seem inconsequential, disjointed, not getting anywhere, but in fact, not only does its humour delight and its content hold our interest, but gradually through it the characters reveal themselves to us so that we begin to accept and understand them as real people' – and he sums up the common denominator of these characters as 'the persistent way so many people cling to hopes without having the guts and determination to bring them to reality, so there is only in the end self deception'.

The Pink Room is the name of a West End drinking club where, against the background of the 1945 General Election and the announcement of its result three weeks later (time needed to count the votes of the Forces), a diverse collection of lost souls try to keep reality at bay – with drink anaesthetising their pain, and dulling their fears for the future. Jokes, quarrels, sex and fantasy ward off the horrors of self-knowledge. Presiding is the club's owner Christine Foskett, mocked by some of her *habitués*, generous, vulnerable and terrified of solitude.

The fecundity of invention that Ackland has for his gallery of characters, and the intricacy of construction as he weaves and intertwines their lives and absurdities, dazzles. One admires the mechanics and structure of the piece as one would the workings of a delicate and beautiful clock. The complexity of the play's form seems so effortless and his ability to juggle so many balls in the air at once denotes a truly masterly control of content. He can hit on more than one emotional level at once – like the very greatest of composers or writers. His world is both funny and bleak at the same instant, both glamorous and seedy. The characterisations are minutely and wonderfully observed – as anyone who has known the cigarette smoke and shallow sociability of drinking clubs can verify, and the central character, Hugh Marriner, a writer of early promise now in pieces, is a glorious, absurd, Ostrovsky figure. The moment of startling reality when Douglas Eden comes to tell Elizabeth Collier of her friend Herta's death in Ravensbruck – news she is incapable of taking in for its horror – makes us realise, as Francis King pointed out in *The Sunday Telegraph* in 1988, that the whole club is a concentration camp, the inmates bound together in a common doom. The curtain of the First Act in which the G.I.s wearing grotesque party masks, return in search of booze and, with compliance, gang-bang Christine, is both sophisticated and shocking.

The drunken artist, and ex-P.O.W., Michael Crowley, waving his pistol before de-wigging the arrogant lady critic; 'You'll none of you escape what you're trying to escape from,' is both preposterous and tense. Even Mrs Marriner, Hugh's mother, escapes from reality with her library books, and is panic-stricken when these are denied her.

Dromgoole speaks of Ackland's 'rare ability to present deep emotion on stage without trivialising or sentimentalising it, and the wit scattered in incandescent glory across his scenes without any heavily laboured "funny moment".' One notices, too, the superb way he can diffuse the grand moment: Hugh's vituperative speech to the critic Ruby Bottomley is mimicked and mocked by a vagrant from the street standing behind him and pulling faces.

The Pink Room is uncategorisable and its characters are far removed from the then accepted version of the British – that their reactions to the war and its immediate aftermath were full of humour, pluck and phlegmatic heroism. Indeed in its anti-heroic view of the Londoner coping with deprivation, it is ahead of its time, and because of this, for some years, managements had rejected it, even though it was delivered with a glowing testimonial from Tyrone Guthrie. He considered that it has 'considerable historic interest. And if people turn to it for historical evidence, they will, I think and hope, be rewarded,' and he describes the play as 'a symphony in the Chekhov manner – many voices, many themes, woven together in a loose but distinguished pattern'. Rodney Ackland had a jig-saw mind which enabled him to use complex construction with such confidence. Once, when bankrupt, he was dictating a scene from off the top of his head to Marjorie Sisley, when he suddenly telephoned Carey Street, giving them facts, figures, excuses and promises. That over, he calmly went back into the middle of the interrupted scene without pause.

Guthrie had said: 'All large communities had their Pink Rooms,' and the locale was loosely based on the French Club off St James's, founded for the recreation of the wartime Free French. The *patronne,* Olwen Vaughan was one of the Acklands' friends, who tried bravely to bring some order to their peripateticism and was thus rather more together than Christine Foskett. The fictional Pink Room also had elements of the more raffish Colony Rooms and a trace of the grander Gargoyle Club owned by David Tennant, whose ex-wife was Hermione Baddeley.

So the casting-interviews held at 33 Haymarket started with an obvious choice: Hermione Baddeley as Christine; and seldom can she have had a part to which she was so suited, for Christine is an instigator; someone who creates drama and events about her. She needs an actress of personality and warmth – and one of emotional courage who can act the scene of naked terror with which the play ends.

Hermione 'Totie' Baddeley had just been declared bankrupt: her young lover, Laurence Harvey, had proved to be a very expensive Kept Boy. On 28th May, 1952, *The Daily Mail* reported that she had 'arrived by bus at the London Bankruptcy Court yesterday for her public examination. She was in court for two minutes then the examination was adjourned and Miss Baddeley went off to rehearse a new play *The Pink Room*'.

During the rehearsals, and knowing Totie's propensity for the gin of an evening, Frith asked her understudy, Phyllis Montefiore (who was playing the small role of Fifi, the prostitute), to be her minder. Each day after rehearsal – Harvey being safely at Stratford – 'Monty' would take her home and test her lines, thereby learning them herself, and only when an entire scene was Dead Letter Perfect could the gin bottle be opened.

The rest of the large cast was being completed: David Yates (who later became the director, David Phethean) was Hugh Marriner; Heather Stannard, who had recently had a success in Fry's *Venus Observed* was Liz Collier; the distinguished and masculine Austin Trevor was the 'queer' film director, Maurice Hussey; Lally Bowers was the lady critic's girlfriend (called Maisie in the original version); Betty Marsden was the Treacle Queen Lettice Willis; Helen Cherry (Mrs Trevor Howard) was Hugh's disapproving wife Diana (a role Rodney was able to change into his disapproving boyfriend, Nigel, in *Absolute Hell*) – and both the aunts from *The Holly and the Ivy*, Margaret Halstan and Maureen Delany reappeared respectively, as Julia Schillitoe, the lady in reduced circumstances fast losing her marbles and Madge the mad religious maniac who appears hurling imprecations at the club members through the street window.

One part which was causing difficulty in casting was Sam Mitchum, the ingenuous Canadian airforceman who has an affair with Liz Collier. Then one day, following a letter of introduction from Philip Merivale's daughter Rosamund, who had seen him in a student production in Toronto, arrived a genuine sexy Canadian and innocent abroad, Christopher Taylor. He was later to become the most important friend and colleague of Frith's life. At this stage, although he thought him exactly suitable for the role, Frith engaged him merely as the understudy on account of his inexperience. When no more suitable candidate appeared, Taylor was promoted to playing the part although his contract stated – rather ominously he thought – that the management could dismiss him after five days' rehearsal. It was, in fact, a customary safeguard.

For a boy who had been to High School in Ottawa, University in Toronto (a first in Economics), and a job for two years as a Research Economist with the Tariff Board, the *milieu* of *The Pink Room* with its seedy cosmopolitanism, seemed – not surprisingly – very foreign. Sam was then the longest part after Christine, and intuitively, Christopher found him unconvincing.

He attended the first read-through at the Apollo with fear and trembling. Of the rest of the company he had heard only of Heather Stannard, whose *Venus Observed* success had filtered through to North America. He was greatly cheered, however, by Totie reading so badly – like a five-year-old child – that he thought: 'if that crone has got the lead then I'm going to be a very pleasant surprise!' During the coffee break he shyly introduced himself to a man who he thought was playing the policeman in the next act, 'I'm very glad to meet you Mr Taylor,' the man said. ' My name's Terence Rattigan.'

At the beginning of the play, Christine has to open the club and greet the plain upper-middle-class soldier, Donald Crutchley (Bryan Coleman), whom she lusts after. Frith asked Totie if she could throw herself at him with more vigour.

'Oh, my dear!' she replied, 'it's very difficult to do it first thing in the morning when one's been at it all night!'

The final run-through was in the bomb-damaged shell of the old Queen's Theatre, and then the company decamped for Brighton and the opening. There had been much speculation, at this stage quite unfounded, as to how a tyro like Christopher had landed such a plum job, and at the costume parade, when he strode to the centre of the stage wearing his Canadian Airforce Uniform he was greeted by Frith saying, 'Oh dear! He looks short in the leg. Terry, you were in the airforce, is there anything we can do to make him look better?' Rattigan, standing in the Dress Circle replied languidly, 'Yes, put him in a battle-blouse. He's got a good bottom.' At which there were explosions of delight from the wings.

Worse though was to befall Maureen Delany. As Madge she had to lean through a ground floor window, stage-left to castigate those on stage for their decadence. Frith standing on the same side of the auditorium asked her to lean in further. 'I can't, I can't,' she shouted back. 'Me private parts is hanging on a nail!'

The notice in *The Sussex Daily News* was the first rumble of the storm that was to erupt later in London. 'Mr Ackland,' wrote Derek Granger (later the well-known television and film producer), 'has chosen a slice of the shabbier life, so fundamentally inartistic in conception, so careless in form that no drama or conflict ever begins to shape itself from the ruins.' Thus entirely negating the play's two greatest strengths. He found himself 'very nearly moved' by Hermione Baddeley, however, but it was 'the pathos, as it were, of utter unattractiveness'.

At Brighton Rodney engaged in some frantic re-writing. Christopher found him 'sweet and intense' as always, but Sam became a smaller part, and rehearsing the new script by day and playing the old one at night, was a routine to which he was unaccustomed.

The audience at the First Night at Hammersmith on June 18, was not overly appreciative. After the close, Rodney disconsolate, passed the gallery entrance from which were emerging two very obvious queens:

'*Well!*' said the one to his friend, 'all I can say is *Poor Totie!*'

The next day's notices were appalling, and although W. A. Darlington in *The Daily Telegraph* was the only one honest enough to admit it, the subject matter was what the critics found distasteful. The characters naked in their fears, desperate in their escapism, made the reviewers uncomfortable. They make extraordinary reading – for not since the first English Ibsen productions sixty years earlier had a bunch of critics been so collectively *angry* rather than just dismissive; and anger only happens when a raw nerve is struck or when expectations are dashed. It was not expected that a dramatist should write such unflattering truths: that an underbelly of society should be so exposed. It was not Binkie Beaumont who felt that an insult to the British people had been committed, but Fleet Street.

Nothing written during that week however, was a preparation for Harold Hobson's notice in *The Sunday Times,* a review which, because it had such an effect on Rodney, needs considering, as does the character of the critic.

Hobson, who had suffered from polio as a child, was disabled. He was also a devout Christian Scientist and was full of wonder at, and gratitude to God's love that he had been given so much in spite of this disability; the penniless boy who had triumphed at Oxford; the ugly young man who had married a sought-after girl; the junior journalist who had succeeded the great James Agate as Theatre Critic of *The Sunday Times.* He was moved to compassion by plays in which there were spontaneous acts of kindness – as a drunken bully had shown kindness only to him at Oxford. He saw the spirit of goodness at work everywhere, and the theatre for Hobson was at its greatest when it was life-enhancing and spiritually uplifting – for that, as he saw it, was the truth.

The Pink Room was about a world he had not experienced, and he did not believe in it. Christian Scientists say that what is bad – like illness – cannot come from God and therefore must be a man-made illusion: a lie. (In later years he refused to believe that Joe Orton's *Diary* with its descriptions of sexual adventures was anything but fantasy.) What he considered evil must be untruthful because his faith taught him only goodness was truth – thus *The Pink Room* was obviously a lie.

'On Wednesday evening,' he wrote, 'the audience at Hammersmith had the impression of being present, if not at the death of a talent, at least of its very serious illness.' He continued, 'One of its scenes – in which an elderly female critic has her wig pulled off must be one of the least creditable to author, players, producer and management in stage memory . . . At the end of an evening of jaw-aching soul-obliterating boredom he appears to have no idea how to finish off a play that a wiser man would never have begun.'

No amount of yawning through boredom makes a jaw ache as much as clenching it in anger. These people did not fit his view of the inherent goodness and nobility of mankind. A bald woman having her dignity destroyed by the forceable removal of her wig was deeply shocking to him. He was affronted. Did he guess that this bald woman was meant to be Agate? The removal of the wig a metaphor for meretriciousness exposed?

Rodney, over-sensitive to criticism and on the look out for slights at the best of times, was shattered. Hobson, who was to follow this blow with a *coup de grâce* five years later became, for him, an object of obsessive resentment, one which started to block his creativity. His self-confidence was so greatly damaged that it never really recovered.

After this review, there was no chance of a run, and plans to publish the play were shelved, but the cast seemed to keep their spirits up. Christopher Taylor found Totie 'A kind good-natured soul. A very extraordinary person who was able to be that effortlessly on stage.' He also found that she could be difficult to act with, 'Because she was so in control that she could play variations that could throw the inexperienced. She could be very naughty.' As in the love scene between Sam and Liz, where Totie would stand in the wings delaying her entrance so they had to adlib and push the temperature of the scene higher than it should go, before she consented to enter. So when the notice of closure had gone up, Christopher and Heather Stannard decided to punish her.

There is a moment when Christine asks the horror-struck Liz to show her the photographs of the death camp she is holding. She then gazes silently at them for a moment before saying, 'I'll fetch you a large scotch, darling!' Before one performance, Christopher drew stick-figures of couples fornicating on the prop-photographs hoping to 'corpse' Totie, naturally showing them to Heather first. But, on stage, Totie looked at them, gave a loud moan of salacious delight, sat down, and still looking, rocked herself and continued moaning – and it was Christopher and Heather who corpsed uncontrollably.

The Pink Room was the only really great modern play that Frith ever directed. It closed after four weeks. Totie, naturally, best summed up the experience: 'When you get a lovely play, with a lovely cast, it's always a flop. But you've only got to do a show with Gingold . . .'

When *The Pink Room* was re-written as *Absolute Hell*, for performance at the Orange Tree Theatre, Richmond in 1988, obviously Rodney was able to introduce certain aspects which, had they appeared thirty-six years earlier, would have fallen foul of the Lord Chamberlain: Hugh was now in a homosexual relationship, failing because of his accidie and his drinking, rather than married to a nagging wife objecting to his hours spent in the club; the unappealing Maurice Hussey and his camp little secretary, Cyril are made more obvious, and, throughout, language is stronger and situations, formerly implied, are now clear and frank. But, without doubt, the major development is the swelling into monstrous proportions of the lesbian critic now called R.B. Monody. No longer is she just a gay joke about Agate but something far more savage: Harold Hobson with a sex change, the wig now a metaphor for Hobson's walking sticks. And portraying the pious and morally innocent Hobson as a grotesque lesbian with a bogus intellect, whose baldness is revealed before her public and humiliating death is sheer wish-fulfilment. Hugh's speech to her is greatly expanded and is now the play's big set-piece. In it all Rodney's hurt, lucidity, pride, intelligence and childishness are blazingly revealed:

Do you mind if I ask you a question Miss Monody? It's something I've wondered about for some time – for several years now – it's something I'd be very interested to know – you've probably no idea who I am, in any case my name means nothing and less than nothing to you – but do tell me Miss Monody when you're writing a really appalling notice condemning and belittling someone's work, do you get some kind of kick, some kind of malicious pleasure – a big belly-laugh, I suppose you get, do you? – out of imagining the writer's face when he reads it? – or do you just dash the notice off and the thought just never enters your mind that it's a fellow human-being – and even perhaps, some kind of creative artist – who's to be publicly humiliated by you the following Sunday? Do you never *consider* or *mind* in any way what you do to people? Do you never stop and ask yourself what *right* you have to risk extinguishing the – maybe small, and maybe not so very steady – flame of some aspiring writer's talent with an utterly destructive, not to say vindictive notice dismissing him as of no account – when in actual fact you're completely unacquainted with his work which you've scarcely even troubled to glance at – let alone tried to perceive, or to search for 'significant values', or to decipher its symbolism or analyse its method or listen for its undertones, or penetrate its over-riding theme, etcet'ra etcet'ra, and all the rest of it – as you would have done in the ordinary course of civilised criticism and common courtesy if you'd thought there was any intellectual snob-value attached to the author's name.

Two years later, after the disappointing reception of John Whiting's *Marching Song,* the Acklands asked Frith and Christopher Taylor to dinner at their flat on Putney Hill. Also present was Moura Budberg, who Christopher considered 'an arselicker' (Frith, more delicately, observing that 'she was inclined to say what one wanted to hear').

Rodney and Mabbie had recently bought a pretty Victorian doll, and as they had so few possessions, it was treasured. This doll lived on the mantelpiece.

Frith started to talk about John Whiting and what bad luck he had suffered in his life and with his plays. Rodney, who greatly resented anybody's luck being worse than his own, suddenly exploded; '*He's* had bad luck, what about *me?*' and launched into a tirade of bad luck competition with Whiting. Every time he said how disgracefully he had been treated by the world, Moura Budberg sympathetically agreed, 'and by Harold Hobson in *particular*'. So Rodney became quite hysterical. Eventually Mabbie rose from the table, picked up the doll and threatened to smash it, unless he stopped – which he did. But it had been a terrible manifestation of the anger and self-pity which were to cause him so much distress from then on.

Shortly after this incident, there was a series on television called *Famous Trials,* and, for one episode, Rodney wrote a dramatisation of the Seddon case of 1912, *A Dead Secret.*

Frederick Seddon, a forty-year-old insurance agent had been accused of swindling his squalid and unappetising old lodger, Eliza Barrow, out of her savings, and then murdering her by the administration of arsenic. The trial had been notorious because, after the judge had put on the black cap for the death sentence, Seddon had made a Masonic sign, (the sign of the Widow's Son), and had sworn his innocence by 'The Great Architect of the Universe'. At which, Mr Justice Bucknill had burst into tears and admitted: 'From what you have said, you and I know we both belong to one Brotherhood, but our Brotherhood does not encourage crimes,' and had sentenced him to be hanged.

Rodney had written the television script so that it could easily be converted into a stage play – and that was what was originally delivered to Frith: an adapted screenplay, divided into Three Acts, the last being a big courtroom scene, which was considered unsatisfactory and uneconomical. Instead, the content of this Act was transferred to a long duologue between Frederick Dyson (the Seddon figure), (Paul Scofield), and the powerful barrister Sir Arthur Lovecraft (Laidman Browne), who comes to interview him at home before deciding whether or not to accept the brief. Unfortunately, the scene between Dyson and Lovecraft never quite takes wing, and its twists and turns are not gripping enough. It fails to be the theatrical climax to which the play seems to be leading, and the Masonic Sign of Distress and the reaction it causes is far weaker when made only to a potential barrister in private, than to a judge in open court after a verdict of guilty.

The plot of the play is in fact not paramount. Any crime-buff in the audience will know the result before the action even starts, but it is the theme that is all important and that theme makes it, in some ways, the most interesting of all Ackland's plays, for into it went his Buddhist faith, and his deepest beliefs: that all evil stems from the spiritual sickness of self-imprisonment, of people unable to extend imaginative sympathy to those close to them by locking themselves up in their own egos, by being emotionally unapproachable.

Ackland's intention is not to tell us the story of a murder. The play, therefore, is not a thriller – and Rodney was annoyed when, on John Perry's instructions, it was billed as such at the Liverpool Opening. We have little sympathy for the victim, the repulsive Miss Lummus (Madge Brindley), who dies, or is killed in the interval between the First and Second Acts. It is not even certain to the audience who it is that has killed her, so Ackland's intention is clearly not to examine a probable miscarriage of justice. Only in his Preface and for the sake of the actors, does Ackland make the position clear: that Dyson is guilty in intention only – his objective pre-empted by the mad maid and self-styled 'nurse' Henrietta Spicer (Jane Henderson). They both suffer from the same spiritual sickness of self-imprisonment but, in her case it has toppled over the edge into complete schizophrenia, which, it is suggested, will be the end result for all those whose sense of separateness makes then concentrate on the Self alone – and Dyson himself is well on the way to this dementia.

How exclusion of others' feelings can sicken the mind into thinking that other people are just images to be played about with is examined all through the play. Mrs Dyson (Megs Jenkins), a kind-hearted woman who has become unfocused and frightened by being excluded from her husband's thoughts and feelings replies to his statement that 'no one can know what it feels like to be someone else' with: 'I don't see why not, Fred. I mean religion and that, we're not supposed to be shut away inside ourselves like, but sort of "part of one another", and I mean if only we *could* feel like that.' (Act I)

By her sympathy, Mrs Dyson has opened herself up to the spiritual influences which lead to a revelation in the witness-box at the inquest.

'In a way,' she says, 'I was outside myself and there was this person called Margaret Dyson being cross-examined there; but I couldn't feel it was me . . . I've always felt frightened of everything . . . but standing there in that police court today with heaven knows what hanging over us, I felt *safe* . . . just in this moment when I sort of stopped being myself, I suddenly got the idea – well, like as if I *knew* – that whatever happens, even dying, there's nothing to be frightened about at all.' (Act III)

For all her simplicity, Margaret Dyson has come close to discovering the dead secret – the secret of human personality: our only hope of salvation is understanding that we are all part of one another and of all creation. It is back to Tagore's 'more and more union with the All'. Secretiveness and concentration on the Self alone will lead to the death of all our finer feelings and, finally, to cruelty and evil. We can only overcome cruelty and evil by discovering that this very sense of separateness, which is fostered and encouraged by people like Spicer and Dyson, is an illusion.

Dyson may not be the murderer but his obsession with Self makes him a guilty man all the same. It is his tragedy that when he finally frees himself from his self-inflicted prison and tenderly embraces his wife, it is only to be put into a man-made one, to await hanging. Yet he has given Margaret the physical contact she has yearned for. She confides to Dyson's embarrassing, shabby father (Harold Scott):

> He was such a funny fellow, you know Pa – he never let you really see what he thought about anything. *(She raises her head and, her cheeks still wet, gives her nervous flickering smile.)* One thing, though, he showed he loved me, didn't he – he did show he loved me in the end. (Act III)

Nor are the other characters entirely free from the same guilt, if to a lesser degree. The Dysons' teenage daughter Peggy has the self-centredness of the adolescent; Miss Lummus's cousin Vokes and his wife (Arthur Lowe and Gretchen Franklin), are pitifully concerned with 'keeping respectable'; and Sir Arthur Lovecraft, because Dyson is repugnant to him as a person, shuts his mind and will not try to identify with the man he has been asked to defend. Had he kept his mind open he would have seen that Dyson was most probably innocent. And the lordly arrogance with which he treats a man who is a social inferior in his own house, makes it clear he is not the gentleman that he is considered to be. The jury too that condemn Dyson, are only revenging themselves on him because he has outraged their sense of decency by taking a commission on the victim's funeral arrangements.

Ackland's ability to penetrate psychological oddity is intriguing, and his sense of place so sure and atmospheric that the temperature of the stuffy lower-middle-class household during the action's long, hot summer can almost be felt. (A large part of the run was during a heatwave.) Not only the topical references but the speech patterns, vocabulary and rhythms of Willesden Park of 1911 are minutely and truthfully observed and must come from memories of the servants' talk of his early childhood and to the world his family found themselves part of only a little later. As always with Ackland the intertwining of plot and theme is of an extreme intricacy and one is in dumb admiration at the complexity of his structure, and the ingenuity of his devices: a black play showing a sinister side of human nature as well as its potential for goodness. Outstanding in the way it is crafted, and vivid in its depiction of that particular class. Every character has their own voice and individuality, from the cheeky clerk, Gooch (Dinsdale Landen), to the pompous and vulnerable little lodger, Bert Vokes, whom Dyson throws onto the street to facilitate his designs on Miss Lummus – and who is denied the five pound loan for which he appeals to Dyson as a fellow Mason.

Paul Scofield, then thirty-five, was approached to play the middle-aged miser Dyson. He came round to St James's Terrace for a discussion, and he and Frith sat on the balcony in the sun.

'Well, Paul,' began Frith cheerfully, 'I think I know you pretty well by now and –'

'No you don't,' said that most private of great actors.

In spite of this unpromising start, Scofield accepted and – Frith's solecism forgotten – remembers the rehearsals as 'Always good-humoured and enjoyable. As an actor himself [he] was full of interest in the contribution that can be made by the actor.'

He thought the play 'very powerful and atmospheric and full of psychological insights into criminality and its essential pettiness and short-sightedness', and gave what Frith and others consider to be one of the most remarkable performances of his career. He played the part of the hard-headed businessman with hardly any make-up – just a waxed moustache and slicked down hair, and the inner transformation was so complete that on the First Night when the leading actor customarily received an entrance round, Scofield unrecognised, went without one.

Frith remembers him giving an absolute character performance rather than playing on his own ambiguous personality as he had done in *A Question of Fact*. He was inhabited by Dyson.

'His imagination was so strong, that he converted the illusion into the reality as you watched it at rehearsal. What seemed *unreal* was when he stopped rehearsing, and what was *real* was when he was acting. It was like a light going on – I've never had this feeling quite with anyone else. When he started to be Mr Dyson a light went on and it went off when he became himself.'

One of Frith's favourite actresses, Megs Jenkins, was cast as Margaret, a choice about which, to begin with, Scofield had his doubts. Frith's letter of explanation is eloquent in her defence: she was an actress of such truth who obtained her effects so economically. Also, it might be added, one of openness, and warmth without sentimentality. Whether the leading man changed his mind or not is unknown, but her performance was certainly highly thought of by the critics.

For the rest, as Frith observes, 'Nowadays only in T.V. and films could you get these small characters played with such verisimilitude and importance by such good people.' Arthur Lowe and Gretchen Franklin were the Vokeses; Harold Scott (of The Cave of Harmony and *Waters of the Moon*), Pa Dyson; Laidman Browne, Lovecraft; the young Dinsdale Landen, Archie Gooch; Maureen Delany (who helped Rodney re-write the role from Cockney to Irish) Mrs Culff, the cleaning woman; and, as the mad Henrietta Spicer, Jane Henderson who Frith thought gave 'a marvellous performance. She was unpredictable and erratic but had a strange quality – the best Mrs Solness I've seen – an emotional lady who eventually killed herself – there were always husband dramas.' Reece Pemberton's two-level set (Miss Lummus's room visible Upright) was heavy, circumstantial and detailed – atmospherically exact in its stuffiness.

Hugh Beaumont, astutely predicting a moderate commercial success, presented the play by Tennent Productions, so its profits could be redeployed, and put it into the fairly large Piccadilly Theatre, where, opening on 30 May 1957, it ran for 193 performances – just over five months.

The notices were universally favourable, although all the critics missed the theme of the play – which as it is stated over and over again says little for their listening – and concentrated on the plot, the atmosphere, and above all on Scofield's performance which drew the very highest praise, as, indeed did Frith's production, *The Times* stating boldly, 'The author is not only very lucky in his producer – for Mr Banbury has a genuine flair for the creation of period atmosphere – he is also lucky in his company and especially lucky in Mr Paul Scofield.' It was poor Rodney whose press went by the board. He had been obsessed with his hatred of Harold Hobson, who had by now in his mind become a demon from hell, bent on destroying Ackland, so when he opened *The Sunday Times* on 2 June he must have been looking out for the worst – and, by his lights, he found it:

The review was headed 'Master of Repose' and it must be one of the longest Hobson ever wrote. Its first two sentences give the context:

'Of English actors under 40, Paul Scofield is the most outstanding. But is he a great actor or only a very good one?' He then discusses this for *nine* very lengthy paragraphs (coming to the curious conclusion that he is not great because, 'a quality of voice he at present has not got'), and only in the tenth does he reach Rodney, and then only to say, 'The development of Seddon's character is slow, and there is an impossible Dickensian servant; but otherwise Mr Ackland has dramatised the story – and it is a highly interesting story – well.'

That was all; and Rodney's rage at, and paranoia about the critic of *The Sunday Times* was now complete. Effectively, he allowed it to take him over and finish him as a creative writer.

He was only to write one other original play, and that never had a professional production, but nine years later his Hobsonphobia was still as active – and as obsessive – as ever, so Frith decided to tackle the problem at source, and, in November 1966 he invited the critic to lunch. He wisely decided to concentrate only on *The Pink Room* review:

'Do you remember a play at Hammersmith in 1952 called *The Pink Room?'* he began. Hobson looked vague,

'Was that the one set in a club?'

'Yes. Do you remember what you said about it?'

He did not, so Frith reminded him.

'Goodness! Did I say that? That's a bit strong, isn't it?' and he munched away contentedly.

'Well, the author was so shattered by your judgement that he hasn't been able to work since.'

Hobson stopped eating, 'Oh, dear! That will never do. We must get him writing again, mustn't we?'

So, in his column the following Sunday, he decided to sign off, quite incongruously with a 'Playwrights which we are so lucky to have' list: 'Pinter, Ackland, Osborne, Wesker, and Fry.' Frith wrote to thank him, saying that Rodney's inclusion had been 'restitution. I know it meant a lot to him.' But, if it did, the respite from his resentment was fairly temporary.

Soon after *The Pink Room* in 1952, Rodney was engaged to write a film-script in Egypt for the director Gregory Ratov. The film, which was never completed, concerned the downfall of King Farouk who, for the film's purposes, had been re-christened Abdullah. Ratov was also playing the title role. Rodney took Mabbie with him, and there they had the most bizarre and amazing Acklandish adventures, most amusingly recounted in his cinematic memoirs, *The Celluloid Mistress* (1954).

In the early sixties Frith persuaded Rodney to transmute some of these experiences into a comedy, and obtained backing from America for him to write it. Rodney and Mabbie took the money and rented a villa at Sanary near Toulon, where he buckled down to his task.

Rodney did not find the process of writing easy, and always had difficulty meeting deadlines, so Frith was pleasantly surprised when, quite soon, he received a message asking him to come and stay, as the play was finished.

When he arrived, it was quite obvious it was not – there was no last act – so Frith, his patience finally run out, exploded and accused Rodney of bringing him to France under false pretences – at which there were floods of tears and, from the next room into which he had run, terrible sobs which continued for some time.

The next morning Rodney was gated, and shut in his study to scribble while Frith and Mabbie went to the port of Sanary for a walk.

There an incident took place which so sums up the spirit of Rodney Ackland's plays, that it should be told in Frith's own words.

COMIC AND TRAGIC IN LIFE STORY

There was a street, on one side stalls of food and trinkets, on the other side, the sea. In the distance, there was a disturbance. A car was careering along the road, but half on the pavement so that these stalls were being mowed down. Screams and shouts from the French, you can imagine . . .

Then we saw that a very fat lady was sitting on the bonnet with her legs out – clinging to the bonnet. A complete Jacques Tati film. It was so funny we could hardly believe it – yet terrifying. It passed us; the woman fell off the bonnet; and the car went right over her – all four wheels – and this body spun round and round after the car. By that time she was dead. Eventually the car came to rest because it ran into the War Memorial when it got to the square. Along came a gendarme, and the next thing we saw was that this gendarme had a tiny, tiny, little old lady in his arms. She had been the passenger. She must have been ninety if she was a day – and she'd fainted, of course. And it turned out that the man at the wheel had had a heart-attack, and the car had lost control. The little old lady was powerless to do anything. In the middle of this ghastly tragedy, the gendarme with this tiny little old lady. *It was the Tragic and Comic so completely intermingled so that you remembered it as neither one nor the other.* Of course, if you had known the poor lady who had been run over, the comic aspect wouldn't have prevailed, I suppose.

The Other Palace, as it was finally called, is a very funny play indeed, with a freakish but recognisably true gallery of various nationalities. Frith felt it required an international cast – a Kay Kendall, Peter Ustinov, Leontovich cast – not just to do the play justice, but to do it at all. He was never able to find one, so the play remains unperformed professionally. It was eventually put on by amateurs at the Questors Theatre, Ealing in 1965 – a sad fate which made Rodney very disillusioned. He re-wrote three of his old plays *(The Pink Room* into *Absolute Hell: Birthday* into *Smithereens;* and a second version of *After October)* but, never again produced any original work.

His childlike irresponsibility over money continued. Frith remembers an evening when he summoned and paid for a mini-cab – to go down the road to the local tobacconist to fetch a packet of cigarettes. He was also generous to a foolish degree and most of any renumeration that came his way was spent on others. Just before Christmas one year, when bankrupt, he arrived by taxi at St James's Terrace to give Marjorie Sisley an expensive present; kept the taxi waiting, and, when he found out that she was just off to the country, took her to the station in it.

Then, in 1968, it looked as if his fortunes might change. That January, out of friendship, the chief critic of *The Stage*, R.B. (Ray) Marriott, wrote an appreciation – and a very good one too: 'The truth is Rodney Ackland broke down barriers and conventions, and was the first English dramatist to pave the way that led to the new dramatists of the last ten years; that his light comic touch is an integral part of his expression. It is interwoven with a profundity of feeling. It requires the impetus of people going through spiritual turmoil as well as worldly mishaps and hazards, for it to convey the basic intention of the plays.' But, unfortunately, *The Stage* has only a limited professional readership.

The year before, Hilary Spurling, reading without any pleasure, some plays of the twenties and thirties, started on one of Rodney's. She became hooked; and 'tracked down a further handful of his plays, which gave me a second shock as powerful as the first.' Reviewing Frith's production of Dodie Smith's *Dear Octopus* that December, she asked why time was being wasted on such a sentimental exercise, when Ackland remained unperformed. Frith contacted her and told her of his feelings and his involvement. Spurling then wrote the major article which appeared in *The Spectator* on 22 November, 1968.

Rodney was naturally touched and, for the first time in a long while, excited about the future. Hilary Spurling became a close and supportive friend, and she and Frith were now the team who sought professional recognition and financial assistance for Rodney. In this, they were aided by the agent Robin Dalton and Rodney's agent, Eric Glass. Later, under Hilary's aegis, Rodney started to receive a small pension from the Royal Literary Fund; an institution to which he would appeal, sometimes successfully, for settlement of bills. (One quarterly telephone bill came to over £600 – and this was in the seventies!)

The articles however, seemed to lead to no resurgence of interest in his plays, and Frith felt that what he really needed was an expression of confidence in his work, and therefore commissioned at different, times, two further plays. But Rodney only provided one promising synopsis, unable to come up with the finished articles.

Then in 1972 Mabbie contracted a cancer of the throat which was to prove fatal. Rodney wrote Frith a piteous cry for help from the shabby bedsit in Cathcart Road where they were both laid up – Rodney with shingles and Mabbie, bald, immobile and dying. Although, even these circumstances provide a great shaft of humour. After describing the scene as 'a Dostoevskian picture' he continues, 'although unlike the Marmeladoff's we've no Sonia to hawk her ass on our behalf'. Crime and Punishment – he often said he felt like Kafka's Joseph K., being tried for a crime he had not committed.

At her death, Rodney's devastation was absolute. His misery manifested itself in acute writers' block, and he spent a short time having treatment in Bethlem Hospital in Kent, where his spirits proved not entirely repressed. Frith asked Marjorie Sisley, who by then lived nearby, to visit him. She took him out for the day with strict instructions to deliver him back at evening curfew. First of all he spent all the money he had buying her chocolates, and, at the end of their day, refused to return as he was enjoying himself too much. When Marjorie eventually delivered him back it was so late at night that he had to climb through the dormitory window.

Meanwhile, in London, Frith was trying to promote Rodney's interests with the new *régime* at The National Theatre. Peter Hall initially showed an enthusiasm, which he swiftly lost. Frith also wrote to Mabbie's brother-in-law in the House of Lords, explaining just how much he was shelling out for Rodney, and implying he would welcome some assistance. He received rather an abrupt brush off. Lord Donaldson had already taken some trouble to find out about Rodney's financial situation by contacting his solicitors. They had replied that Rodney seemed incapable of opening any letter with 'Inland Revenue' stamped on it, and therefore Lord Donaldson considered him to be a lost cause.

In 1980, *Before the Party,* his adaptation of a Somerset Maugham short story came to the West End from the Oxford Playhouse. To mark this a journalist went to interview him, and found a man who was not in a benign mood:

'The theatre is my life and I've been excluded from it, through no fault of my own, for years.' When the interviewer suggested he might find posthumous fame, he replied, 'Screw posterity. I want it now when I am still alive.'

One evening, a more than unusually disconsolate Rodney went for a long walk from his new council flat in Richmond and ended up in a pub at Turnham Green. There he fell into conversation with a strange young man called Terry Todd. Terry's mother had recently died, and Rodney had lost Mabbie, so they talked about coping with grief. The bond of sympathy and understanding between them was obviously immediate and strong. They walked some of the way home together and Rodney asked Terry to visit him the following morning. When he did, Terry found the flat, near the top of a high rise block, to be a tip. Rodney offered him a weekly salary to be his cleaner. Terry pointed out that, as Rodney obviously had no money, that might be difficult, but, although broke himself, he would be happy to clean for free.

Terry was an Acklandish character if ever there was one. Rodney's friends frequently complained about him, but from the first moment of meeting until the day he died Rodney was Terry's entire life, and he saw no reason why he should not be everyone else's entire life too. There was clearly an element of two unfortunates finding solace in, and receiving strength from, each other. But Rodney gave Terry a purpose in life, and Terry gave Rodney reasons to stay alive. One reason was that Terry wanted Rodney to have the acclaim he realised he so desperately wanted before he died, and he coped with this in two ways: by pestering people on Rodney's behalf until they were distracted, and (although this, I think, was unconscious) keeping Rodney's anger on the boil by always holding out the possibility of hope just around the corner. Later, when he married, Terry's wife, Debbie, had to take on Rodney as well. Although he referred to him as his 'father', and Debbie's children called him 'granddad', Terry really adopted the parental role of looking after and organising him. During the long final illness both the Todds were selfless – and Rodney was very lucky in them.

Terry was never backward in coming forward. Out of the blue he presented himself at the Orange Tree Theatre in Richmond and asked to see the Governor. 'Have you ever heard of . . . ? (and he reeled off a complete list of Ackland plays). The artistic director, Sam Walters, let him continue:

'Have you ever heard of Rodney Ackland? He lives here. He's your local author.'

The result of the meeting was a revival of *The Dark River;* staged in the round, in a room above the pub. It received much critical praise and was the start of a mild renaissance. For the last week of the run, Noel Howlett, who played Mr Veness, the old man in the wheelchair, was ill, and Rodney took over the part himself.

The following year, Frith directed *Smithereens,* (a second version of the 1934 *Birthday)* at the Theatre Royal, Windsor, with a cast that included Phyllis Calvert, Andrew Cruickshank, Lucy Fleming, and Gregory Floy.

Lee Menzies co-presented, and there were real hopes of a West End transfer – many not travelling to Windsor because they expected to see it in London – but no theatre was immediately available, and nothing further happened.

Then, in 1988, *Absolute Hell,* the new version of *The Pink Room,* was given a superb production by Sam Walters at the Orange Tree, where the standard of ensemble playing and individual characterisation was of the very highest: David Rintoul especially impressive as Hugh Marriner. One young director said after a performance, 'No wonder it was unsuccessful in its day – he writes with far too much edge.'

Some critics, as they had with *The Dark River,* wondered why on earth the major companies were neglecting Ackland, and the play finally found a publisher: Oberon Books. This had an excellent introduction by Nicholas Dromgoole, and Frith was, rightfully, the dedicatee; the citation reading, 'With gratitude for his unflagging championship of my plays throughout four decades and three lives.' The three lives being Arthur Boys, Mabbie and Terry.

Absolute Hell was also given a major B.B.C. production, directed by Anthony Page with Dame Judi Dench as Christine Foskett, Bill Nighy as Hugh Marriner, and Betty Marsden, the original Treacle Queen, now playing R.B. Monody. At the preview, already very feeble, Rodney sat in his wheelchair in the middle of an aisle, and was quietly overjoyed.

He was, by now, very ill with leukaemia, and before the transmission, was interviewed in bed wearing his favourite lemon coloured pyjamas, and these were what Terry dressed him in when he died on 6 December 1991.

At the funeral, Frith, Hilary and Joss Ackland spoke and read from his works. The perfectly ordinary group of actors, writers and friends who were gathered looked to one observer like a bunch of freaks. Ordinary people frequently took on that guise when around Rodney.

Terry used to say, 'He's like Tchaikovsky – like Tchaikovsky. He'll only be remembered when he's gone.' *The Times,* and *The Telegraph* gave lengthy obituaries complete with a photograph, and Sam Walters wrote a personal memoir in *The Independent.* Hilary Spurling's tribute in *The Daily Telegraph* was, perhaps, the best:

Ackland was Chekhovian in the sense that, virtually alone among the playwrights of his generation, he saw no reason why contemporary intellectual, political, social and sexual undercurrents should not be dealt with on the stage as freely as by any of the other arts. In the context of the well-made West End play between the wars, this was a revolutionary proposition. When the theatre set itself to hold a glamorous and reassuring mirror up to nature, Ackland produced a bright, clear, unflattering glass in which audiences saw their world reflected too clearly for comfort . . . But Ackland remains the only serious playwright whose work will bear comparison, in point of imaginative strength and emotional delicacy, with the novelists and poets – Powell, Waugh, Greene, Spender, Auden – this country produced between the wars.

Christopher Taylor's verbal summing up of his plays too, is accurately succinct: 'Rodney Ackland sees the world as only Rodney Ackland sees it. A unique world, and it's a world we recognise while being surprised; and that, to me, is the essence of all good art: Recognition and Surprise.'

With the arrival of the Royal Court writers, Ackland was undoubtedly left' on the other side of the fence – but only just. Had his major work been written just after, rather than before Britain's confidence in its omnipotence was so damaged by Suez, it might have been different. These writers and their followers tarred him with the same brush as Terence Rattigan and Emlyn Williams, who both so openly admired him – both thought him the best living playwright. Had they openly disliked him, would the English Stage Company have looked on him as a precursor and as an example? I wonder. A lot of people seem to stay blind. In 1993 the Royal National Theatre was still able to turn down *The Dark River* as being 'too slight'. Whatever criticisms can be levelled at that play, slightness is surely not one of them.

Ackland took up a great deal of Frith Banbury's time over the years, but it was time most willingly spent: 'I shall always account it a privilege to have known and been associated with Rodney Ackland, for all the irritations and frustrations that it entailed. Now that he is dead, there remain those marvellous plays, and the memory of the excitement of helping to bring some of them to life.'

Part Five

1954

John Whiting: an Enigma with
the Possibility of a Solution

Towards the end of 1953, Beaumont put into production a play of risky commercial prospects, the rights of which he had held for two years, called *Marching Song*, the fourth play by a former actor, John Whiting. This had been made possible because of the recent success of two of Tennent Productions' offerings: *A Question of Fact*, and, in particular, *A Day By The Sea*.

Whiting was a writer who had stirred considerable interest within the theatre but had not, as yet, found his audience. He was, as Peggy Ramsay (who did not represent him) wrote to Frith, 'an interesting enigma, not without a possibility of a solution'. But, thirty years later, it is one that has never quite been solved.

Whiting's first performed play, *A Penny For a Song*, a fantastic comedy set in Dorset during the Napoleonic Wars, had been a failure at the Theatre Royal, Haymarket in 1951; and the same year his second play, *Saint's Day* (the winner of the Art's Council's Festival of Britain play competition) had been presented at the Arts Theatre. *Saint's Day* was a very intense and unforgettably evocative symbolic drama, which caused, in the writer's word, 'a hullabaloo'. Harold Hobson called him 'a lunatic', which was strange given Hobson's love of French Theatre; for Whiting the serious dramatist was resolutely un-English. At this time, when young intellectuals were looking enviously across the Channel to the post-war expressionist drama of France, or the Marxist plays of an East Germany struggling out of defeat and ruin, Whiting began to represent the exact opposite of the English Safety encapsulated by an N.C. Hunter, or a Wynyard Browne. His influences were Sartre, Camus – Cocteau even.

From the start, theatre people responded. At the Arts, *Saint's Day* kicked some in the stomach with its originality, while others were just bemused and uncomprehending. A year later, an undergraduate called Peter Hall directed it at Cambridge and, as Whiting remembered, 'Out of the University began to come the first comprehensible criticism.' Whiting struck a chord with the intelligent young – those who had been children in the war, and many of that generation were to champion him for a long time.

The idea for *Marching Song* had come from Whiting's experiences in mainland Europe immediately after the war. He was fascinated by the war criminals at Nuremberg, and he knew a professional soldier in the German army, who became the starting-out point for Rupert Forster, just as his conversations with many young Germans who had not fought but had to face the consequences of defeat, created Dido Morgen, General Forster's lifeline to the future.

He had planned the play as far back as 1948 and written it early in 1951. That June, when he was playing small parts in the Shakespeare Memorial Theatre's productions of *The Winter's Tale* and *Much Ado About Nothing* at the Phoenix, he showed it to the leading man, John Gielgud. Gielgud was very impressed and intimated to Binkie Beaumont and John Perry that if they took out an option, he might consider playing Rupert Forster. After a year's dithering he decided against the idea, but by now Beaumont felt enthused by the play and took out a second option, offering the script to Michael Redgrave. (Laurence Olivier, the obvious choice, was never approached as Beaumont needed him and Vivien Leigh for Terence Rattigan's *The Sleeping Prince*.) After a year, Redgrave too cried off and Tennents decided to renew the option for a further six months, at the end of which, if no progress had been made, they intended to drop it.

John Perry was put in charge of the final thrust and he first showed the play to Diana Wynyard, who was astute enough to recognise at once in Catherine de Troyes, the part of a lifetime. Then, with considerable imagination he approached Robert Flemyng.

Following his return from a glorious war, Flemyng had established himself as a West End leading man. On the face of it, an unlikely war hero, with great charm of manner and modesty of nature, he had nevertheless fitted into the army and emerged with honours. After the fall of Monte Cassino, he had been on a nightmare drive to Naples, sharing the back of a transport vehicle with a wounded and dying little boy – an experience on which he would draw for Rupert Forster. His sense of responsibility to his fellows had been as much service to his regiment as it was later to Equity, and his gallantry had been as conspicuous as a soldier, as it was to be when, as an old man, he was forced to overcome pain and lameness. Perry thought quite correctly, that Bobby knew what it was like to fight a battle, and understood what made the military mind function. His reaction to being offered *Marching Song* and his account of the production can be read in Appendix III.

Perry then showed the play to Frith, who was familiar with and a great admirer of Whiting's earlier work. He immediately sensed an important new play, and longed to direct it. Perry, having offered Flemyng the part, then expressed doubts. But Frith insisted: 'If Bobby's the best we can get, we must do it, it's a wonderful play.'

Frith and Whiting then set to work on a revised version of the script, helped by the fact that they obviously liked each other very much. 'A gentle man, beautiful to look at, a darling', is how Frith describes him:

'Nice wife, four children, and a succession of girlfriends. He had met his wife, Jackie, at York Rep. She never spoke. Every two years he kept her quiet by making her pregnant. He was quiet and dry and fascinating to talk to.' Through Frith, Whiting met Wynyard Browne, and the two playwrights, who to the likes of Tynan and Hall must have represented the opposing poles of British Theatre, became the greatest of friends, Wynyard arranging for Whiting to sit on some committees with which he was involved.

Although the theme had been suggested by the fate of war criminals, and the emergence of European states faced with the difficulties of democracy after the victorious occupying forces had withdrawn, Whiting strove, by his choice of names, to give *Marching Song* a pan-European feel, 'avoiding names like Von Runstedt, Von Manstein and so on'. His characters are called Forster, Cadmus, Morgen, de Troyes, Sangosse and Anselm, names which could be 'found in Germany, applicable in France, and found in England, and the same thing with the Christian names which are interchangeable in most European countries'.

The country has been defeated. Before withdrawing, the occupying forces have insisted that the old Chancellor, Cadmus (Ernest Thesiger) institute full democracy complete with an opposition party. This party demands a scapegoat for the country's humiliation who by his trial and death will expiate their guilt.

Seven years before, General Rupert Forster (Robert Flemyng) has paused fatally, during a failed attack on a town on the Eastern Front, and has since been in prison for cowardice. During this imprisonment his hope has been kept alive by the singing of a goatherd, whose song, in *patois,* he takes to be a prayer. He is brought back home to the house of his ex-mistress Catherine de Troyes (Diana Wynyard), where Cadmus gives him the means to escape trial by committing suicide. At the house, Harry Lancaster (Hartley Power), a drunken American film director, has picked up a young prostitute, Dido (Penelope Munday), and in her Forster sees the possibility of future hope. He connects this sense of hope with the song in the mountains and decides to face his trial and whatever that may bring. Only when Captain Hurst (Michael David), the young commander of the escort which is to accompany Forster to the town, tells him that the goatsong is one of obscenity and bestiality does he begin to see that both Dido and the future are tainted. He chooses to kill himself.

The play is largely a portrait of Forster, and its tension derives from us discovering what made him delay in that attack. Why, at the supreme moment of his ambition, did he discover his humanity and the worthlessness of all values – like pride and honour – that he had once held dear? The published text of the play has as its epigraph two quotations from Shakespeare: Cassius's 'Well, honour is the subject of my story,' and then Falstaff's de-bunking 'What is honour? A word. What is that word, honour? Air. A trim reckoning! Who hath it? He that died o' Wednesday.'

All people – even armies – have lines of communication which must be kept open to provide the motivating force for life. For most this is a backward looking line of love to people, places or ideas; but for a soldier the line must look forward, 'to the other side of the hill'. Therefore Forster has to keep himself free of attachment to another person. If he loved Catherine it might cloud his vision. He quotes the Duke of Wellington, 'All the business of war, and indeed all the business of life, is to endeavour to find out what you don't know by what you do.' The soldier is thus de-personalised: cut off from common humanity. Forster considers this forward-flung self-sufficiency offers a greater, more exalted, humanity – that is, until the incident on the Eastern Front.

Forster had intended to occupy the evacuated town at his leisure before crossing the river to engage the enemy army. He was about to give the order for advance, when a church door opened and a little boy stepped out and blew a whistle. At that signal hundreds of children appeared, as if from nowhere, and set about Forster's troops throwing themselves against the sides of their tanks. At this the soldiers laughed but were immobilised. The first boy climbed onto Forster's tank and spat at him, 'I stretched out and drew his head to my shoulder like a lover and shot him in the mouth. I took him by the hair of his shattered head and held him up for my men to see. They understood. The shooting began.' (Act II) It was a children's colony which had been abandoned. Four hundred were killed in the resulting massacre.

The speech which describes this terrible story is the centre-piece of the play, and it is magnificent – but sentimental, because it asks the audience to react merely to its shock effect, and begs their emotional engagement without really earning it. Christopher Taylor thought that Whiting must have begun with that speech and written everything else around it. He may well be right.

The moment he shoots the boy, Forster's values are shattered. The shock of killing the child somehow restores his humanity. Trapped by the event, he is paralysed by inactivity, and the resulting twelve-hour delay in crossing the river means that the battle is lost. Forster is cashiered and imprisoned, *not* for the slaughter of the children, but for cowardice. As a soldier, he is dead.

In prison Forster rigorously and consciously excludes everything from the past. His line of communication is the present, linked to a single, irresistible human voice singing what he takes to be a song of faith. On release this line shifts effortlessly to Dido. (It cannot shift to Catherine as she is the past which he has foresworn.) Had Dido not been at the house he could readily have acceded to Cadmus's request for his death. He does accede finally, because the disclosure that the goatsongs are obscene reveals that even the new life which began for him in the camp in the mountains is fed by a lie, and he therefore feels that his relationship with Dido may be as false as the art of war, or the supposed spirituality of the goatsongs. There is nothing for him but to die.

The play ends with a lengthy scene of frankly unbearable sentimentality as Catherine (who, in an act of great generosity has persuaded Dido to stay on at the house because she has been the one hope of keeping Forster alive) is comforted by the girl and given a reason to continue living.

The play has a number of flaws, the chief being that of construction. Forster tells Dido the story of the Battle of the Children at the half-way point of the Second Act, but does not complete his account – the explanation for his delay – until the scene with Bruno Hurst towards the beginning of the Third. The reason for this is sound enough: Forster has obviously not worked it out in his mind until Hurst asks, as he has previously only dwelt on the moment he shot the boy and the spiritual revelation which that brought him. But it means, as Robert Flemyng points out, that the second half of Act II is one long anticlimax. It could undoubtedly be trimmed more than it was in the first production, but the scene with Cadmus which makes up the bulk of this half-act is essential if we are to make sense of Forster's character at all – for in it he talks about the lines of communication, and describes the song of the goatherd, which Cadmus connects to his feelings for Dido. Yet the audience became – and would still become – restless and bored.

Other facets of Forster do not quite add up. We are told twenty years ago he was a young soldier organising the military for a film directed by Harry Lancaster, in 'my comic opera days'; nine years ago there was a war, and two years later he was imprisoned for cowardice. At the start of the play, he is upstairs having sex with Catherine, and nothing he does or says from his entrance onwards suggests the commander of authority and extreme discipline described by Cadmus, or the flawed hero of Hurst's soldier games.

There are other vagaries, for instance the campaign is not very well thought out. What are the infantry doing on the flanks? And why does their commanding officer not carry out his original order to cross the river that night? And what on earth is the poison that Cadmus gives Forster? He says mysteriously, 'The substance within, I'm told, is also used for extracting gold from its ore,' and later, when Forster has taken it, 'He'd only to break the glass before his face. He knew well enough.' (Act III)

In hindsight, Whiting felt that although *Marching Song's* arguments were absolutely valid, and that it was watertight on the level of human behaviour, it was ultimately unsuccessful as a play because it was too enclosed, too much of a conversation piece, too shut in. He felt it needed to be opened out. 'And, of course, it is glacial on a human level. The sex business with Forster coming back to Catherine and the girl. It doesn't work because they are frozen to death before they can develop. And I could never do anything with it. The whole thing is weighted so heavily – on one side. There is Forster the soldier, and Cadmus the Chancellor who don't exist below the eyes, they are simply all head. On the other side the only person who is more than that, who comes towards any reasonable sort of humanity, is a fool like Lancaster, the film director. The girl is terribly cold. She, too, reasons – picks it up like an infectious disease.'

He is perhaps rather hard on his work. *Marching Song* still has the power to fascinate and sometimes grip with its theatricality. It is a serious play about a moral dilemma and completely un-bogus in its account of man's moral position and human responsibility. But it is emotionally cold, and when Whiting wants sympathy for his characters he becomes sentimental (unlike Browne or Ackland). It is truly European in feel and, because of this un-Englishness and Whiting's intellectual stature, it is easy to see why the younger generation of the day were so attracted to its difference from the rest of contemporary drama, and so impressed by its argument and language.

As Catherine, Diana Wynyard was able to capitalise both on her aptitude for what Tynan would call 'hostess acting' (for the role requires the
charismatic stylishness of a West End Leading Lady) and on her ability
to give a characterisation substance and depth. Catherine's self-centred
superficiality turns into unselfish generosity when she asks Dido to stay
('She was fighting like hell at that moment,' says Dido), and after Forster's
suicide she suffers from terrible despair. After Diana's early death, Frith
wrote a perceptive obituary for *The Times,* which produced a letter from
her old school-friend Peggy Ashcroft, thanking him for his kindness,
('you're a true friend') and telling him that she knew that working on
Marching Song had been one of the most important events of Diana's
life. Frith – and Christopher Taylor – thought her wonderful in the part,
as they also did Ernest Thesiger, a natural for Cadmus, and Penelope
Munday, the young actress who played Dido, 'a star if ever there was
one'. She had played in *The Lady's Not For Burning* on Broadway, and
along with Whiting had been in the Stratford Company at the Phoenix.
All who worked with her considered she had a very special talent and
predicted a remarkable future, but after *Marching Song,* she married and
left the profession.

It was *Marching Song,* too, that brought Christopher Taylor into the
centre of Frith's private and professional life. Frith had sent him the play,
thinking he might be suitable for Bruno Hurst, the young Captain in
the last act. Christopher thought the play flawed, and when they met for
lunch at the Lyons Corner House, he told him so. It was at this meeting
that Frith realised the full quality of Christopher's fine analytical mind:
the scientist's training with the artist's temperament. Christopher pointed
out the incongruities that he felt made Forster an incomplete characterisation, and drew attention to the play's sentimentality. Frith asked him
to write these criticisms down, and pretending that they came from him,
presented them to Whiting with suggested changes, most of which were
not accepted. I think Christopher must have stressed the importance of
Forster's 'lines of communication' dialogue with Cadmus in the second
half of the Second Act, and because of that, Frith was loath to make any
cuts there. It is indeed a problem. This discussion and the information
about the goatherd is necessary at this point, but, after the great speech it
is not the right moment for the audience to receive it, because the act has
lost its focus and therefore its energy. They disagreed about the character
of Hurst, which Christopher never played. Frith – and Bobby Flemyng
– wanted Forster to meet a copy of himself twenty years earlier, but

Christopher rightly thought Hurst far more complex than that: his reaction to the fallen hero is a mixture of hero-worship, curiosity, contempt, and finally cold fury at Forster's betrayal of military ethics.

The lunch followed what for Christopher had been 'a rough summer: selling my clothes to buy cigarettes; of having to walk from Sloane Court West to the Corner House for my one meal of the day, for that's where you could eat as much salad and rollmops as you wanted for 3s 6d.' But he was still being wooed by a large Canadian company who were offering him a salary of $20,000 a year to buy chemicals in Montreal. Frith tried to dissuade him from returning to Canada, and suggested that he become one of the Tennent Contract Players. At this, Christopher just laughed, for any young actor would have given his eye-teeth for that chance. Frith said, 'I'd put you under contract if I had a company like that,' to which Christopher replied, 'Why don't you then?', at which Frith looked taken aback, 'Well, maybe I could, I'll have to talk to my partner Jimmy Wax.' For the present Christopher waited.

Rehearsals started in January and the play opened in Cardiff three weeks later, Frith's salary the usual £200 plus 1.5%, (rising to 2% after the recoup) of the Box-Office Gross. The notices during the six week tour were mixed and the houses poor. At Glasgow, Frith claims the company morale was so low that he had to travel up to bolster it – a claim denied by Flemyng who remembers the company as happy and optimistic throughout.

Frith thought Flemyng had the right idea of the part, but lacked the vocal resources for the long speech, and the stature necessary for a man, who the other characters say has an authority which is never shown in the text: an A.D.C. rather than a General. Bobby, in his turn, felt that Frith had not blocked the play particularly well, and he disliked Reece Pemberton's set which he found too heavy and circumstantial – both surprising criticisms as, from the prompt copy, the movement seems up to Frith's usual high standard and, from photographs, the set fulfils all Whiting's requirements of 'a shell caught within a web of glass and steel,' and looks stunning. He repeatedly begged Frith to cut the second half of the Second Act (he was correct there) which was refused, so he finally said that he would approach Whiting over the director's head, which quite rightly, the director forbade. The disagreements, happily, were purely professional; their close friendship survived the production undented.

Frith says, 'I directed the play as Whiting wanted,' and the author was pleased with both production and the leading man's performance:

'Many people thought the original production lacked warmth, but that was the way I wanted it. The same goes for Robert Flemyng's performance. I admired it very much but it wasn't moving – it wasn't supposed to be.'

On the London opening at the St Martin's on 8 April 1954, Flemyng remembers receiving bad notices. His memory is false: Derek Granger in the *Financial Times* found his performance 'full of integrity and fine moments', while Hobson in *The Sunday Times* thought he told the story of the massacre of the children in the sunlight 'with a fine, cold, self-accusing and controlled fury'. The critics' opinion of the play was respectful, *The Times* saying that the author could 'scarcely be said to court popularity, but it deserves an attentive hearing. It is refreshingly sincere, it deals with a contemporary dilemma intelligently and interestingly, and though it swerves in the end to an otiose sentimentalism it creates for the greater part of the evening a genuine tension. If this tension is more intellectual than dramatic that is because Mr Whiting appears more interested in ideas than people.'

Some complained that it was all too portentous, but Hobson, at last, had tuned in to Whiting's wavelength: 'He has a troubled and uneasy poetry whose shadowy tides never wash against the shores of our own land of cricket bats and football pools, of bells in the old school chapel, and the Welfare State. This perhaps is only another way of saying that the play extends the boundaries of English drama.'

The production was generally lauded – John Whiting, Binkie Beaumont and Frith obviously had a *succès d'estime* rather than a commercial hit on their hands – and the run was only for six weeks. Loudest in their praise were theatre people, and Whiting's stock within the profession – already high – was even further enhanced. To one matinee came Sir Laurence Olivier and Vivien Leigh, and they showed extreme enthusiasm. Afterwards, Sir Laurence seemed displeased, 'Why wasn't I sent this play?' The answer was that Binkie Beaumont thought his talent more profitably utilised playing a Carpathian Grand Duke in a light comedy by Terence Rattigan. Vivien Leigh could well have played Catherine. Had the Oliviers appeared in *Marching Song,* maybe Whiting's future fortunes would have been different.

There were some who thought the killing of four hundred children too far-fetched, but Bobby Flemyng says that if this was so at the time, it was prophetic as similar incidents were shortly to be recorded, one in the Hungarian Revolution, and another during the Suez conflict.

Frith tried unsuccessfully to interest Stewart Granger and Jean Simmons (who were then married) in a New York production, but in Germany the great actor Gustaf Gründgens played Forster. Frith and Whiting travelled to Düsseldorf where they thought the production bad, but Gründgens very good: the all-important centre that perhaps the superior London production had lacked.

It looked as if the public would fail to respond fully to anything Whiting wrote. His dark comedy *The Gates of Summer* closed on tour in 1956. Then, in 1961, The Royal Shakespeare Company – at their new London home, the Aldwych Theatre – put on *The Devils,* a psychological drama about supposed demonic possession taken from Aldous Huxley's *The Devils of Loudon.* It was the one success of his lifetime. The following year, the R.S.C. revived *A Penny for a Song* in a disappointing production which had a disappointing reception. Also, in the sixties it became the subject for an opera by Richard Rodney Bennett.

He remained suspicious of the Royal Court writers with whom he did not identify. When asked in an interview how he hoped to achieve his ambition of writing a masterpiece he answered, 'By not going to the Royal Court Theatre', and said that he felt Arnold Wesker thought he had no political convictions. 'The last time I talked to him [he] obviously thought I was nothing at all, that I had achieved a marvellous situation of being quite non-partisan except for occasional snarls, and that I didn't exist with either foot on the ground.' He said he refused to use political or religious philosophies as arguments. When Christopher Taylor said that he felt Osborne and Wesker had their hearts in the right place, he replied, 'It's not their hearts, but their tiny little heads I'm worried about.'

In 1963, he gave Frith the news that he had undergone an operation for cancer and had been given a 50/50 chance of survival. His wife Jackie, and girlfriend, the actress Susan Maryott, nursed him together at his house in Duddleswell. Three months later he died at the age of forty-five.

A month after his death, Susan Maryott dined alone with Frith and they spent the evening talking about John. She seemed to Frith to be beginning to accept his death, but two days later she killed herself.

Some of the generation that had championed and been influenced by Whiting in their extreme youth were now running theatres themselves and able to mount his plays. There was a general feeling that these had only failed first time around because of insufficient presentation, and there were some revivals both in London and the regions. But either they were done badly second time around as well, or it was not the acting and productions that had originally been at fault. *Saint's Day*, at Stratford East in 1965 drew enough interest for transfer to St Martin's, but the public stayed away. After a revival of *Marching Song* at Greenwich, Harold Hobson, who had become such an adherent of Whiting, wrote a derogatory review which was dismissive of the play, and Bobby Flemyng wrote to him in remonstration. But Hobson's reply was blunt and final: 'No, we were wrong about John Whiting.'

In 1992, at the Theatr Clwyd, Mold, the director Toby Robertson, following what he claimed was Whiting's original intention, produced *Marching Song* with Dido being given a sex-change and becoming a rent-boy called Aeneas. Before he died, Whiting had apparently expressed a wish to re-write the play with this substantial adjustment. My first reaction was that the idea was preposterous (Whiting had certainly not shared it with Frith) – but my second was that it might make all the difference: strengthening Forster's identification of Dido / Aeneas with the goatherd, and giving a real point to the line 'It might have been you,' on his realisation that Dido / Aeneas and the boy he had shot are the same age. Catherine handing over her love of Forster to a boy would then be a greater act of generosity and a genuine struggle, and, by having an affair with someone who could have been the child he had shot, would somehow make Forster feel it was possible to be cleansed of his past crime.

On a personal level, *Marching Song* had brought Christopher Taylor into Frith's employment and daily contact. After talking to Jimmy Wax, Christopher was engaged as Play-reader for Frith Banbury Productions, 'And a lot of plays came in in those days'. A small house in the garden of St James's Terrace was rented to him at £5 a week (which included alterations and refurbishments), which was exactly half his weekly salary. 'Shakespeare at the bottom of the garden', Coral Browne called him. Now Dido Milroy was married he became the greatest professional influence of Frith's life and his greatest friend.

Soon enquiries from students worldwide started to come in, asking questions about Whiting and *Marching Song* – especially from America. No play that Frith has ever directed has aroused so much academic interest – and that continues to this day – students hoping that Banbury will write their theses for them.

There is still a vocal minority, now approaching old age, who claim Whiting is neglected and has never been given theatrical justice. The truth is perhaps that without him new writing would not have gone quite in the way it did. He was a precursor: his workshaped others. He was a considerable influence on major theatrical figures – but not, I think, one himself.

Old Vic Interlude

In 1953, Michael Benthall, whose pictorial and intelligent productions at the Stratford Memorial Theatre had been praised, was appointed Artistic Director of The Old Vic. He announced that the theatre would undertake what he called, The Five Year Plan: all the plays of the First Folio (which constitutes the whole canon excluding *Pericles* and *The Two Noble Kinsmen*) to be given over a period of five years. It was a goal that was reached, although some plays *(Twelfth Night, Macbeth, Richard II* and *Hamlet)* received two productions, and *Titus Andronicus* and *The Comedy of Errors* were presented as a double bill. Benthall hoped that his company of mainly young actors would stay for the duration, but after a very successful first season his four leads: Richard Burton, Claire Bloom, Michael Hordern and Fay Compton had departed for Hollywood or the West End.

Of the six productions in that season, he had directed three himself, given two to George Devine, and one to the dancer, actor and choreographer Robert Helpmann, with whom he then lived. It was his intention to open the second season with his own production of *Macbeth,* (which had already been seen at the Edinburgh Festival on the open stage of the Assembly Hall) at the beginning of September, 1954; run it for a month and a half, giving the company time to adapt to a proscenium arch and become used to each other, and then open the second play, *Love's Labour's Lost,* which he planned to direct himself, in mid-October.

In the absence of Horden, Bloom and Burton, he engaged Paul Rogers, a principal actor of Hugh Hunt's previous Old Vic *régime,* and the film-star Ann Todd, who had no experience of classical acting, to play the Macbeths; and for the younger leading roles Virginia McKenna, and a young man who had played supporting parts during the first season, John Neville.

Macbeth took a while to settle into the smaller confines at the Waterloo Road, but once adjusted, was considered a fine production with Rogers giving one of his most acclaimed performances, and Ann Todd – thrown in at the deep-end – giving a more accomplished Lady Macbeth than anybody had dared expect.

At some stage (Frith cannot recall exactly when) Benthall, because he was to direct *A Midsummer Night's Dream* in New York, decided to relinquish *Love's Labour's Lost*. The risk he had taken with Ann Todd was so far justified; he was already considering Cecil Beaton as a possible designer for the second play; and with his gaze obviously towards the commercial theatre, he asked Frith, now the most successful 'commercial' director, to take his place.

As it was Frith's first and only professional Shakespearean production, and the only time he worked for one of the subsidised National Companies it deserves to be considered.

Love's Labour's Lost had only come into its own recently. This 'delightful ostentation, or show, or pageant, or antic, or firework' has been taken to the hearts of audiences in the second half of the twentieth century after three-hundred-and-fifty years of comparative neglect. The complex wordplay, ornate courtliness, and satire on euphuism needs more attentive listening than audiences of the 18th and 19th centuries were prepared to give it. Furthermore, from the viewpoint of 1954, the last three productions of what was still a connoisseur's piece had been uncontested triumphs: Guthrie's of 1936 (Ernest Milton as Armado); the young Peter Brook's at Stratford in 1946 with designs inspired by Watteau, all silvery poetic distances, and Scofield's Armado looking like Don Quixote; and, just five years before in 1949, Hugh Hunt's at the Old Vic with a beautiful summer lakeside setting, and Redgrave's Berowne stepping straight out of a miniature by Hilliard or Isaac Oliver. (The play actually should take place in September, the deer-hunting season.)

Hard acts to follow, and maybe Benthall was glad not to have to try. Perhaps he thought that two untried Shakespeareans – Frith and Beaton (now confirmed as designer) would approach the piece with fresh eyes, and bring to it what the commercial theatre at its best could deliver: namely style, taste and elegance.

In many ways it should have come off. Frith loved the play and clearly understood it. Its educated humour and (until the final pages) its optimism is much like his own. It requires great subtlety of acting and he was a director famous for bringing out subtlety in actors. The stylishness which Granville Barker rightly sees as an essential of the play's presentation is one that his imagination easily encompasses; even the maddening pedantry of Holofernes and Sir Nathaniel is not a million miles from one aspect of his own nature, and, from the prompt copy, his blocking is elegant and exactly right psychologically. Some of the groupings must have looked quite beautiful, especially after Mercade's entrance when the company groups, re-groups into a lovers' pattern, and forms again into the contrasting courts of Navarre and France with the commoners separate and excluded.

Cecil Beaton, too, should have been a good, if bold, choice. He was never a great set designer – unable to draw groundplans and not adept at communicating his ideas to those in the workshop – but his costumes, if sometimes over-extravagant, always had flair and beauty. He understood social history; knew the microcosmic life of great houses, indeed conjured up an atmosphere of Arcadian hedonism in his own country houses – so what went wrong?

The first mistake seems to have been Frith's. At his opening talk, he said how much he looked forward to rehearsals 'as he had never directed Shakespeare before'. A reasonable enough pleasantry one would have thought, but one which seems to have lost him the confidence of the cast. Then Beaton told them that the predominant colour would be green, an idea that presumably came from Moth's observation that green is the colour of lovers and wit. The young company of serious Shakespeareans decided not to like this precious double-act from the West End, and, at the first run-through all turned up dressed in green from head to foot, while Michael Benthall sat in the back row of the stalls handkerchief stuffed in mouth, enjoying himself hugely – behaviour which must have seriously undermined Frith's authority, and given the cast the licence they were seeking to gang up on the director.

On paper, this cast looks splendid: Eric Porter and John Neville as the King and Berowne; Ann Todd and Virginia McKenna as the Princess and Rosaline; Paul Rogers as Armado; and, in the smaller roles; Rachel Roberts as Jaquenetta, Robert Hardy as Longavill, and Charles Gray as Mercade. But most of them seemed to feel they had little to learn from Frith, and, apart from Paul Rogers who had played his part before for Hugh Hunt, the acting was not much praised.

Green is not perhaps a very suitable colour for the set of a Shakespeare comedy. Stage green never looks like the natural colour of grass or foliage, and is apt to look artificial and tawdry. The style Beaton aimed for was what he described as 'impressionist realistic' i.e. impressionistic sets with realistic or rather naturalistic, costumes. From the black and white photographs the sets look hideous. Cardboard cut-out topiary with everything looking as if made of cheap materials, set off by a badly painted and wrinkled backcloth; the whole ensemble aesthetically most unpleasing. The majority of the critics found the same: 'Cecil Beaton's set seemed to me to be a disaster,' said *The Times,* 'glum topiary and those cloth bowers of viridian cotton which are trundled about in ice-shows,' while *The Spectator* called the set 'exceedingly unfortunate . . . like an enlarged nursery farm, full of tufts of green wool that stand for hedges'. Only Derek Granger in *The Financial Times* saw what Beaton was aiming at, 'by imagining what Braque or Bérard might have done given a similar commission in Paris'.

The costumes were another matter: quite splendid but, to my eye ludicrously extravagant. What fashion plates from an Elizabethan *Vogue* might have looked like, not what anybody would have actually *worn* in the country – yet Beaton said he was aiming for 'realism'. He might have found his terms of reference in the miniatures of the day rather than the great formal portraits and discovered that women wore 'nightgowns' as they were called in the country, not cumbersome far-thingales, and men flat shoes or soft boots, open-necked hero's shirts, and casual doublets. In the sixteenth century as in the present, the upper class had easy country clothes to contrast with formal court or London dress. Here Armando is dressed in a plumed bowler and a padded hose; the farthingaled women are straight from Zuccaro, and Mercade's ornate purple magnificence, was thought by Frith to be one of the most superb costumes ever seen on a stage. The comics were dressed as conventional Shakespeare comics.

Such visual style in Shakespeare, to us, looks very dated. Soon the fashion was to move away from the striving after pictorial effect with the cunning use of cheap materials to a greater simplicity and the use of natural fabrics. Wood, leather, beaten metal, and John Bury were not far off; paint, canvas, and gold-painted lavatory chains around velveteen jerkins had had their day. This was not Cecil Beaton's fault, nor Frith's. It is a cause for tangential reflection that the expressionistic designs of a Bérard, that must have seemed so modern after the war with their rela-tionship to abstract painting, were not to be the theatrical influence that once seemed likely. Simplicity was the order of the day until the arrival of High Tech. – and the painters of the thirties and forties who did leave their mark on stage design forty years later, were to be the surrealists.

Frith felt that with three and a half weeks rehearsal, he had not been given enough time. 'I was used to energies being directed to the matter in hand not diversified into other productions.' These were *Macbeth,* which was playing every night and *The Taming of the Shrew,* which was waiting to start rehearsing as soon as *Love's Labour's Lost* had opened.

The strain was beginning to show on Ann Todd who was playing Lady Macbeth eight times a week, preparing Katharina, and rehearsing the Princess of France. Added to which she had domestic difficulties; 'I need to lie down. I'm playing Lady M. tonight, and my husband's leaving me. I won't be able to go on unless . . . '

It is a pity that Frith directed no further Shakespeare or major play of the 16th, 17th and 18th centuries, for his Classical ethos is so right: 'I ask an audience to make an effort of imagination to go back in time, rather than bring it to an audience'. He is the antithesis of the conceptual director who may greatly illuminate one aspect of a play by concentrating on it exclusively, but will never present the whole of the author's intention. Frith wants to reproduce to a 20th-century audience as far as possible what life was like in those times. Unlike some, however, he has enough self-confidence not to take up an attitude about other directors' methods:

> I don't approve or disapprove. If it comes off it's good enough. But when it's not it's irritating and boring. Like *The Man of Mode* with Alan Howard in a bubble-bath [at the R.S.C.]. I feel I still haven't seen *The Man of Mode*. Directors have to make their mark so they show off, which is fine if intelligent and inventive. Class and education come into it. You presuppose that audiences are not conversant with other manners and mores, so you update the play because they don't have the terms of reference.'

The opening was on 9 October 1954 and most of the critics felt that the set marred what would otherwise have been an enjoyable evening. Only W.A. Darlington in *The Daily Telegraph* was unstinting in his praise, 'I do not remember to have seen a production in which the different elements were better balanced,' but *The Times* and *The Financial Times* were also very complimentary to Frith, if a bit reserved about some of the performances. Cecil knew the sets had failed but could not see why they had gone wrong. Frith felt that with more time they could have been righted – but I doubt it: they were simply too ugly. From New York, where he had departed for his next assignment, Beaton wrote Frith a typical letter: the mixture of warmth and coldness that was his nature. In it he thanked Frith with genuine gratitude for the opportunity given, agonised over letting himself and the director down, and then bitchily rounded on the actors; 'It isn't a good cast, and includes a few howlers and you managed wonders in spite of them'. In his turn Frith loved working with Cecil. He relished his enthusiasm – a compliment Cecil returned – and appreciated his erudition and panache.

Lack of familiarity with the play rather than reaction to the production meant that the stalls were not full during the run – but the cheaper seats upstairs, with the Old Vic regulars, were a different matter. Many liked it very much. Both Alec Guinness and Norman Hunter wrote to Frith full of praise – the former asking him not to be disheartened by any adverse criticism for his 'charming *unaffected* production' – and John Gielgud wrote flatteringly to Cecil. Cecil and Frith remained friends, and Frith stayed in touch with Michael Benthall during his sad, alcoholic decline.

The readers (or critics?) of *Plays and Players,* a magazine for the captive audience, were not so happy however. In an end of year summary for 1954 called 'Credits and Discredits' *(Marching Song* was best play) and under the heading *Please don't do it again,* it said 'Noel Coward adapting someone else's play as a musical; Frith Banbury directing Shakespeare'.

He never did.

Part Six

In the Face of the Royal Court

Reaction Against Aunt Edna

Between them, Terence Rattigan and Binkie Beaumont had invented a matinee lady whose sensitivities needed consideration when a script was being honed and readied for rehearsal; she did not like hearing about sex, and found any aspect of life which was ugly extremely distasteful. They called her Aunt Edna. In the Preface to the second volume of his collected plays in 1953, Rattigan defined her as, 'a nice respectable, middle-class, middle-aged maiden lady, with time on her hands and the money to help her pass it . . . She is, in short, a hopeless lowbrow.' He added that she had lived since the time of Sophocles and 'if the bomb doesn't fall is immortal'. To the younger playwrights, as Rattigan him-self would admit, she was 'the enemy', symbolising everything that was wrong with West End writing: the fact that dramatists had to write down to her level because she was bored by matters of consequence. Although Beaumont's attitude to her was healthily ironic and amused, he took her presence in an audience to be a fact of life, and in discussion with authors and directors invoked 'not suitable for Aunt Edna' often – much to Frith's exasperation, who thought that taking her assumed opinions into account, led often to truth being avoided.

Then, in 1964, eight years after 'Look Back in Anger . . . initiated what has been called the Theatre of Revolt', Rattigan, in a Preface to his third volume of plays, attempted to reassess her. Here Aunt Edna, offended by his earlier reference, takes him to court for libel. But the playwright defends himself eloquently enough. He admits that the theatre of the thirties really lasted until the early fifties because 'the five years of war and the seven years of pov-erty and austerity that followed, provided an atmosphere hardly conducive to a theatre that would force audiences to face uncomfortable facts. It needed increasing affluence and a growing sense of security from war . . . to do that.' He denies that there is such a thing as a highbrow play – highbrow playwrights yes, but 'a highbrow play would appeal only to an audience of highbrows.' All plays have to touch the emotions of their public and that is why Aunt Edna will always be around; 'It's only Aunt Edna's *image* that changes, and

191

changes constantly from generation to generation . . . she herself remains the same, she always has and she always will. *She knows what she likes* and there is nothing she likes better than *a nice change!* She is liking one at the moment, but that doesn't and cannot change *her!*'

In the first half of the 1950s, she was still in her earlier manifestation, and over the years, Frith says he had several arguments with Binkie over her unwillingness to hear a spade called a spade – but as yet, like Gwendolen, Aunt Edna was probably glad to say that she had not seen many spades – and Binkie felt disinclined to show her any. Rattigan was right, she will always exist in different guises, but at this point, young radical writers seemed not to know this fact, and rather than asking her to come along with them, they wanted to banish her altogether.

The Welfare State, introduced by Attlee's post-war Labour Government had produced a young generation of university educated and newly articulate working-class people who were now, in the mid-1950s, old enough and secure enough in their values to have their voices heard. Mandatory grants for further education at the universities meant that far more from poor families were being exposed to literature and philosophy, and were then becoming both practitioners in and audiences for the theatre. Discretionary Local Authority Grants for drama schools provided a means of entry into the theatre, too, for a new working-class actor who had little wish to learn to speak with Received Pronunciation nor to pour out drinks on stage like Rex Harrison.

Frith thought a change was due: 'Osborne and Co. were right to rebel. The pendulum was bound to swing as years before it has swung in favour of Ibsen and Shaw instead of Henry Arthur Jones and Pinero. It was just unfortunate that I was left on one side of it.' Could he have found himself on the other? 'I think class came into it a good deal.'

Class did indeed come into it a good deal. To the new wave (a press-term from the French 'Nouvelle Vague') whatever may have come after cocktails and laughter rather paled against bravery and gaiety in the face of genuine deprivation. Hester Collyer in *The Deep Blue Sea* at least had choices: pain, anger, and defensive humour stemming from poverty, exist because there are no choices at all.

There was a genuine effort to return the theatre to what was considered to be its working-class roots. The theatre's roots are not, of course, working-class but religious, cutting across all classes. But it was true that since the demise of melodrama, eighty years earlier, the theatre had been a predominately middle-class entertainment.

At the Theatre Royal Stratford East, Frith's R.A.D.A. contemporary Joan Littlewood, was running the Theatre Workshop, and her intention was to make her theatre the heart and focus of a poor working-class community. The house-style was Brechtian with a dash of Music Hall. Elsewhere the philosophy of Antonin Artaud abounded: shock the audience out of their complacency by any means: absurdity, cruelty – which was a long way removed from the gentlemanly rebellion of Frith's generation: the genteel anarchy involved in annoying the Admiral.

Working-class plays in the twentieth century were not, of course, exactly new. There had been the Manchester School which had produced two classics: *Hindle Wakes* by Stanley Houghton in 1912, and *Hobson's Choice* by Harold Brighouse in 1915; and, in Ireland, after all, the Abbey Theatre had presented the plays of Synge and O'Casey. While in England plays like *Love on the Dole* by Ronald Gow and Walter Greenwood, had been commercial successes as well as social commentaries on poverty. But these plays had been exceptions. The Abbey Theatre's visits had created a stir because what they offered was so unlike anything else then found in London.

Like all ideologues the new wave went too far: by rightly condemning what was wrong with the British Theatre, they refused to acknowledge what was good. Reticence over sex and the fact that plays nearly always dealt with a specific social order gave the West End many problems of which the worst were superficiality and cosiness, but the literary standard could be high, and the quality of acting was sometimes very distinguished indeed.

If many people active in the theatre of the time were scarcely aware that a revolution was taking place at all, historians like crystallising into a moment, of finding a symbol, an event that pushed the British Theatre forward – and they find one, of course, in John Osborne's *Look Back in Anger* in 1956.

The English Stage Company was, in fact, a theatrical management set up with George Devine as Artistic Director, in association with the poet Ronald Duncan as Literary Advisor, its aim being primarily to persuade poets and novelists to try their hand at playwriting; to give interesting foreign plays London productions, and to encourage new writing. In 1956 it leased the Royal Court Theatre and planned a season of plays in repertoire, which as Hugh Beaumont quite correctly pointed out, would be financially impracticable.

Two plays by established novelists came first: Angus Wilson's *The Mulberry Bush,* (which had already been seen at the Bristol Old Vic) and Nigel

Dennis's adaptation of his own novel *Cards of Identity*. Only then was a new play risked.

Nancy Seabrooke, Frith's friend and stage-manager, met Devine's mistress the designer Jocelyn Herbert at the Arts Club one day, and asked her what the Royal Court was putting on next. 'A marvellous play by someone in the company called John Osborne. It's called *Look Back in Anger*. It's a really good play.' This really good play received the attention which led to its pre-eminence among avant-garde work by some strokes of fate.

A few weeks into the season, George Devine asked Kitty Black, who was then Angus Wilson's agent, to come to his office at the Court. He admitted Binkie had been right; the repertoire system was a mistake and the financial consequences of the policy looked like being disastrous. Regretfully both *The Mulberry Bush* and *Cards of Identity* would therefore be dropped. He could only run one play, which would have to be *Look Back,* because it had just one set and five characters. He proposed to keep the production going by sending it out on tour while the other plays finished their runs in London. Then it would be brought back to the Court for a further run. It was on return that it made its impact. Excerpts were shown on television, and it was this more than Tynan's celebrated review 'I doubt I could love anybody who did not wish to see *Look Back in Anger,'* that changed its fortunes. Jimmy Porter and his blazing iconoclasm had arrived and the theatre had its first rhetorical playwright since Shaw.

Frith and Osborne had not met, yet they had an associate in common in Jimmy Wax, who now had three jobs: as a partner in Frith Banbury Productions, as a practising solicitor and as a playwright's agent. In this latter capacity he represented Christopher Fry and Denis Cannan, and was soon to add Harold Pinter to his list of clients. Osborne found Wax 'as morose as the playwrights he discouraged . . . his office was directly opposite Frith Banbury's who seemed to be his only theatrical contact. When I gave him both *Epitaph for George Dillon* and *Look Back in Anger* he said despairingly, "Well I gave it to Frith and he didn't like it".'

'It' suggests that he only gave one of the plays to Frith. Which one was it? Did Frith really turn down *Look Back in Anger?* Frith states categorically that he was shown neither. But would it really reflect badly on him if he had not considered *Look Back* commercially viable in 1955? 'Yes. I would have considered myself worthy of great reproach if I had read it and displayed no interest in it.' Then did Jimmy Wax lie to Osborne? He may have wanted to rid himself of the young writer, but he was strictly honest and as straight as a die. Perhaps Osborne's memory is faulty? Frith was certainly not Wax's 'only theatrical contact'. Through Christopher Fry alone he must have had dealings with Alec Clunes at the Arts Theatre, Binkie Beaumont, John Gielgud, Laurence Olivier, Edith Evans and Richard Burton to name only a selection. Osborne's picture of the gloomy agent receiving his opinions from the West End director and manager is quite funny. But Frith, in his time has turned down plays that have found success elsewhere, and is quite ready to admit it.

Ironically, the finances of the English Stage Company's first season were saved by a revival of Wycherley's *The Country Wife* with Joan Plowright and Laurence Harvey, but in Kenneth Tynan their new writers had found their champion and with the Royal Court, Tynan had found his cause. What is astonishing is that his assessment of the West End theatre of the mid-1950s 'a ruthless three-power coalition consisting of drawing-room comedy and its two junior henchmen, murder melodrama and barrack-room farce', was until recently widely held to be the correct one. Now Ackland and Rattigan are far enough away to be 'period', while many of the Royal Court writers seem just dated.

In 1956, the first year of the Royal Court, Frith directed two new productions which hardly fall into any of Tynan's three categories. The first, at the Lyric Hammersmith in April, was an adaptation by Louis O. Coxe and Robert Chapman of Herman Melville's *Billy Budd* called *The Good Sailor*. 'Twenty-four men, twenty-two of them heterosexual!' said Marjorie Sisley, who thought the production's virility and energy made it Frith's best, a view shared by others. Philip Bond was Billy, André Morell Captain Vere and Leo McKern superb as the villain Claggart. In supporting roles Christopher Taylor played Gardiner, and a young Sean Connery, O'Daniel. Then, in November, a fully commercial (H.M. Tennent Ltd) production at the Phoenix of a play which had already won a Pulitzer prize in America: Frances Goodrich and Albert Hackett's dramatisation of *The Diary of Anne Frank*. The adaptors wanted a carbon copy of Garson Kanin's New York production. The set (by Boris Aronson) – the room behind the warehouse door in Amsterdam – was basically and necessarily the same, but although Frith was made to acknowledge Kanin's original production (which he admired) in the programme, much of the staging and all the directing of the play's inner life was his own.

Frith had many conversations and a correspondence with Otto Frank, Anne's father and the family's only survivor, and no play he ever directed produced such a volume of letters. Some from Jewish people who had survived the Holocaust, others from ordinary theatregoers surprised that they found the whole terrible story inspiring; the thirteen-year-old girl's youthful wonder and adolescent candour, an affirmation that simple humanity can stay bright in conditions of horror. Perlita Neilson played Anne with George Voskovec as Otto Frank, and Max Bacon (formerly the drummer of Ambrose's band) and Miriam Karlin as the tiresome van Daams. The adaptation does not perhaps quite capture the eloquence of Anne in the original diaries, but only Noel Coward, famously, stayed quite unmoved, loudly saying when the Gestapo were heard breaking into the warehouse below, 'She's up in the attic!'

In 1956 at the Phoenix Theatre, people were having their spirits uplifted and their perceptions altered just as much as they were being mentally and emotionally stimulated in Sloane Square. Both *The Diary of Anne Frank* and *Look Back in Anger* fulfilled the same purpose. The purpose of theatre at its best: to alter people's lives a little by enlarging their understanding.

Frith, the avid theatregoer, went to the Royal Court often and 'rather enjoyed it for what it was'. He thought the standard fluctuated: some plays much better than others. Binkie, once he realised that what George Devine was up to in Chelsea was going to be fashionable, tried, not entirely successfully, to get on the bandwagon. But most of the new plays left him cold. He thought Arnold Wesker's *Roots* in 1960 was like a bad stage version of *The Archers*.

From the vantage point of being a successful and sought-after actor, Paul Scofield perhaps saw what was going on with the greatest clarity. He thought that the work of the English Stage Company during the fifties and sixties was of the greatest importance but that it never really tipped the balance of public favour against the West End. But because the work of H.M. Tennent and other West End Managements had reached such a peak, there was bound to be a trough. As for the critics who praised the Royal Court at the expense of the West End, Scofield says, 'That is a matter of selling papers and of being conspicuously controversial. Most actors I knew were happy to work in the West End just as they were happy to work at the Old Vic or the Royal Court or at Stratford.'

So perhaps the strict division of West End / Royal Court was fair nonsense after all. There was, for instance, one new play-wright of considerable talent who had all his plays presented by H.M. Tennent – by choice – because he felt that their standards were higher than the pioneering managements as well as there being more money in the West End for the writer. He was lower middle class, Grammar school educated and a former card-carrying member of the Communist Party. His credentials as a new playwright of the 1950s were thus faultless, and his first two West End plays were directed by Frith Banbury.

Robert Bolt:
If You Want a Non-Naturalistic
Production, Write a
Non-Naturalistic Play

'About the brightest playwrights' agent that there's ever been I should think' listened to a play on the radio – one of twelve written over six years by an Exeter schoolmaster called Robert Bolt, and she immediately took him on as a client. Bolt, at this stage thought the theatre 'just flighty and also impossibly glamorous and bohemian' and 'had seen no more than half a dozen stage plays in his life'. So when he wrote his first, he decided to use Somerset Maugham's *The Circle* as his model, analysing its structure and even following the same lengths for each act. Surprising because *The Critic and the Heart*, which the agent placed for production at the Oxford Playhouse in April 1957, bears no resemblance to Maugham's work at all either in substance or in style, but is the work of a writer of individual voice who has an obvious gift for creating tension in dramatic confrontation, and who can instinctively interest an audience in his characters and their situations.

His second play, *Flowering Cherry*, was sent to Frith who read it over a weekend, and passed it on to Christopher Taylor, who after reading a few pages turned to Marjorie Sisley and said, 'Peggy Ramsay's on to something here.' Frith decided to take an option and present the play himself. He thought it 'rather raw, but my instinct was that it didn't want too much fiddling and faddling with'.

Everything seemed to fall into place quickly and smoothly. Ralph Richardson and Celia Johnson he thought obvious choices for Jim and Isobel Cherry. Celia Johnson's acceptance was conditional on Richardson's, and Richardson – in New York playing General St. Pé in Anouilh's *The Waltz of the Toreadors* – accepted at once. His only stipulation was: 'I think we should do it with Beaumont' (He always gave the name a French pronunciation). Armed with this package of play and two stars, Frith was easily able to set up a co production with the profit-making arm of H.M. Tennent, the first time he had been connected with it. Richardson may have had another reason besides feeling safe with the management's production machine for this request: he was to receive 5% of all profits. The production was lavishly capitalised at £4,000.

There was talk then and later of the play's similarity to Arthur Miller's *Death of a Salesman* written six years earlier. But Bolt did not read Miller's play until after the comparisons were drawn. Indeed he knew next to nothing about other playwrights or the world of theatre. At thirty-two, he had never heard of either Hugh Beaumont or Frith Banbury. He came to London to talk to them – the meeting was at St James's Terrace – 'I knocked on the door. I had never seen anything like it, you know. I went to the bathroom and saw a bidet – never seen one before – so I peed in it.'

Marjorie Sisley, who met him that day thought him, 'bucolic, rather like a farmer, and highly strung. He was very overawed to start with. Binkie was amused at the shy little person at the beginning and how he changed!'

Robert Bolt had been born in 1924 in Manchester, where his father kept a small furniture shop. After an unremarkable time at Manchester Grammar School, he worked for a year as a junior clerk in an insurance office. It was a year that he loathed with passion: the routine of uninspired office life, the small-mindedness of the agents unstimulated by any of the finer things of life, and most of all, his own inadequacy at a job for which he felt he was too good. It was this experience which was to form the basis of *Flowering Cherry*.

After a year, he met by chance one of his brother's old teachers, who remarked that this hatred for his job was the first positive reaction he remembered him having towards anything, and he wondered if Robert would be interested in a place at Manchester University if one could be wangled for him. At university, Bolt joined the Communist Party and remained a member for five years, including the three that he spent in the airforce and army. Communism was against regulations, but, surprisingly, 'there was always a Party cell in every camp.' Here also he met public-school boys for the first time and, against his better judgement, was charmed by their way of life and good manners. It was the first of his conflicts: riches and privilege both repelled and seduced him. Intellectually he was a Marxist, emotionally a hedonist. This basic conflict would expand: when on demobilisation he left the Party, interest in mysticism began to take the place of communism and when, in turn, success brought access to pleasure, it was greatly enjoyed but undermined by his own puritanical disapproval. So too as a writer: intellectually he wanted to be an expressionist, but his gift was for naturalism.

Richardson returned from America in June, and because Celia Johnson could not begin work until after her children's summer holidays were over, rehearsals were postponed until September (to Binkie's disapproval) which left Sir Ralph with rather too long to kick his heels and reflect, unhelpfully, on the play. Because of this delay and because the author lived in Somerset, nearly all the pre-production discussions were by letter. Bolt wrote endlessly, both excited and worried, to Frith, Peggy Ramsay, and Binkie. Peggy Ramsay's letters, mainly to Bolt (with covering notes on copies sent to the others), were astute, caring and idiosyncratic; Binkie's, blue-typed on very thin blue paper, were reassuring and succinct; and, at the centre, Frith was the go-between and referee.

Jim Cherry (Ralph Richardson), has worked for twenty years in an insurance office which has been made bearable by his dream of owning an orchard in his native Somerset; a dream which gives him the excuse to escape from reality and evade responsibility. His wife Isobel (Celia Johnson), has to hold the home together, dealing with the great child who is her husband and seeing his bad traits emerge in their son (Andrew Ray) and daughter (Dudy Nimmo). When Jim loses his job, he conceals it from her for some weeks by lies, but she finds out and makes one last effort to help her husband. She tries to sell their London house so he might buy his dream orchard. But he is unable to turn his dream into a reality. When she finally finds the courage to leave him, he tries to bend a poker – symbol of his country-bred strength – and dies of a stroke, still dreaming of Somerset.

Cherry has never even taken his wife and children for a holiday in Somerset because any contact would make reality of a necessary fantasy, yet Bolt insists he is a Hero, 'a dreamer in the face of the terrible nine-to-five of his job – all the time he harked back to his childhood, which was all nonsense.'

Bolt's hatred for the whole ethos of office life is encapsulated in his description of Gilbert Grass (Frederick Piper), who replaces Cherry after he is sacked:

He is an undersized, bespectacled man with a face boldly designed to express fear, but wearing the covert confidence of those not hampered by self-respect. Either he was formed by Nature for office life or office life has formed his nature; either way he is a condemnation of it. (Act I)

Boasting to Grass that he has had a row with the boss rather than the other way round, that it is he who has given in his notice, Cherry says: 'But I can't, I can't give myself to a job like that. Those green lampshades every morning and that blasted rubber carpet! D'you know what it makes me think of?

> GRASS *(ready to take the joke)*. No?
> CHERRY. It's like walking on corpses. (Act I)

His hatred of office life drives Cherry into fantasy and his fantasies include scenarios where he tells Burridge, his boss, where he can put the job for daring to criticise his inefficiency. But, until towards the end of the play, he is incapable of using violent words to achieve ends. Then, when Grass returns to offer Cherry an inferior agency and, embarrassed at seeing Isobel about to walk out, he slinks off, Cherry rounds on him:

> (He *turns suddenly on* GRASS) Little rat!
> (GRASS *exits exactly like one.*) (Act II)

In Hampstead, Sir Ralph ruminated long and hard on the text at this point and telephoned Frith,

'I say old fellow, about "Little rat!" I can't say that. This man wouldn't say that.'

'Well, I'm speaking to the author tonight – I'm ringing him in Somerset, and I'll tell him and we'd better go from there.'

'Well, I know I can't say it, old cock.'

Bolt was aghast at this announcement; 'The most important line in the play!' (it is certainly the most important *moment* in the play for finally Cherry is truly heroic).

'I've got to get the design in by Monday,' Frith continued. 'Write a letter to Ralph with a copy to me explaining why you think "Little rat!" is so important.'

Bolt did – he wrote pages, ending 'But if after this, with due consideration, you feel on your conscience as an actor you can't bring yourself to say it, I will bow to the inevitable.'

At the first read-through, Celia Johnson waited for the line before saying 'I'm going, Jim.' No cue came.

'Aren't you going to say that?' she asked, sounding rather like the Queen.

'Why? Do you think it's good?' queried Sir Ralph.

'Yes I do rather – don't you? – Oh well, it doesn't really matter.'

By the third rehearsal Sir Ralph was saying it. Frith said to Bolt,

'Now don't say, "Oh you decided to say it after all," in case he changes his mind.'

Some critics felt that Richardson had too large a personality for such a little man. But Cherry's dreams are grandiose; like most dreamers he is a poet, and Sir Ralph, in Frith's exact description, was 'the poetic extension of the ordinary chap'. But Frith did not find him an easy man. 'He was a cussed old thing, but so first-rate. Bolt said, "You go up to an attic, put a towel around your head, juggle with a phrase until it's right. Along comes Ralph and chops it up and puts the end of one sentence into the next one. It's driving me mad!" and I said, "Yes, but he brings something of his own which, in some ways may be as good as you have written – or better. And you have to face the fact that if you've got a Ralph Richardson that is how it's going to be." Afterwards we all agreed he brought so much to the play particularly when he was on form. He was like Sybil Thorndike – allowed an audience to control him sometimes, and very often would pull a face – "oh they're very nice tonight, I'll give them something extra to bite on!"'

Richardson was at his best at an evening performance following a matinee: after the top had been taken off his energy. On the first night at the Haymarket, after a four week pre-London tour, Binkie, as always devious, persuaded Celia Johnson to ask for a run-through that afternoon at three-thirty. It fell to Frith to break the news to Sir Ralph,

'I wonder why the old girl wants it?' He was puzzled. 'Oh well if she wants it I think we should do it.'

Binkie's astuteness paid off, for that night he was magnificent.

To begin with, Richardson thought Cherry lacked charm and humour, and Bolt says that he provided the part with the charm it lacked – although on the page Cherry is as endearing as most childlike dreamers. What he must have provided was stature: a sense that in other circumstances Cherry could have realised his vision. Like Celia Johnson he acted instinctively, but unlike her he did not much like being directed.

For Frith, Celia Johnson was at the very top of the first division. 'She was incapable of telling a lie on stage. It all seemed to be so effortless with her.'

At the start of the pre-London tour in Liverpool, Frith went to her dressing room: 'It's such a relief to do something one knows one can do,' she told him. He asked her what she meant.

'I'm so bad at being a wife and mother.'

'In that case, we've all got the wrong end of the stick,' he said.

'All the cast,' recalled Bolt, 'were so nice to me.'

How had he liked his first London play being given such preferential treatment?

'*What?* I was over the moon. I remember I walked down the Haymarket and I thought "What?" and I walked back and it said: 'NEXT. FLOWERING CHERRY. BY ROBERT BOLT WITH RALPH RICHARDSON AND CELIA JOHNSON. I could not believe it!'

Bolt himself later criticised *Flowering Cherry* for being an awkward mixture of naturalism and non-naturalism. He spoke of 'The dreadful struggle to get over into non-naturalism . . . I tried it by dumping here and there a big poetic speech and extra-natural effects of music and vision. The result was a kind of uneasy wobble, which presented the actors and director with hellish problems.' In fact, he overstates the case: the only really non-natural effect is the vision of the orchard which appears illuminated at the start of the play and again at the end when Cherry dies. This effect was achieved by having the rear wall painted on to a gauze, which, when the lights came up behind it; revealed the orchard: two short moments when the audiences's minds are expanded and lifted out of the naturalistic kitchen. There is also a superb speech in which Cherry describes how Jesse Bishop – his ideal specimen of country manhood – becomes Lord of the Harvest. This is written in heightened language and it gives Cherry a controlled poetic imagination and ordered use of phraseology unlikely to be heard in any ordinary man.

That's right. He was the Lord of the Harvest, as they used to call him in those days. Oh, harvest time was something glorious then, the horses and the men. They used to bring up huge parcels of bread from the farm, a perfect mountain of bread, and real Cheddar cheese, and cold boiled bacon under the hedge on a tablecloth; the dogs used to sit round in a circle with their tongues hanging out, the dogs the men brought, terriers and collies, they came from miles for the rats, the hares and rabbits in the corn. The dogs my father had were beautiful. From our big field you looked right over the Plain of Somerset; nothing but pasture and orchards, it's too wet for crops, it's not much above sea level; green and blue as far as you could see. The men were a rough lot and I wasn't much better than the men, but the place was something all right . . . The way those old-time squires planted trees – there was an avenue of elm trees two miles long that didn't go anywhere; it's still there I'll bet; ecclesiastical property, they won't have cut it down. That's another thing we could see up there, the old cathedral. They used to set their watches by the bells and my father said, 'Allow nine seconds for the distance.' It's a noble pile, that building, a gem of architecture; yes, many's the time you could bend down and look between your legs – (He *does it.*) with the sweat running into your eyes – (He *rises.*) and see this thing the Normans built crumbling away like something soft in the sunshine we had then . . . We were as brown as – pieces of furniture!

A big set speech and also a tremendously vivid way of conveying a soaring poetic temperament suddenly released from repression – surely no one could doubt that here was an astonishing writer. The 'hellish problems' Bolt gave his director came from his own frustration. He desperately wished he had written an expressionist play when all the evidence on the page said he had written a fundamentally naturalistic one. Frith felt duty bound to listen to his author's wishes although he told him repeatedly – then and later; 'If you want a non-naturalistic production, write a non-naturalistic play.' But he did try to make concessions towards non-naturalism and was criticised for so doing. It was not until *A Man for All Seasons,* when he adopted a Brechtian-epic structure that Bolt was able to free himself from the form in which he worked best: the well-made play. In *Flowering Cherry,* Bolt writes quite cerebrally until the characters reach crisis point and then suddenly involves strong emotions. Basically it is a play of family tensions, and the relationships between sad almost downtrodden mother, lying husband and father, potentially dishonest but bright son, and daughter who has taken her emotional allegiance elsewhere are well drawn – all the more so because, although these conflicts have often been shown on stage before, they seem new. And as Bolt points out the play's title is a pun – the flowering cherry is a suburban tree that puts out clouds of pink blossom but nothing happens. No fruit.

It is difficult to imagine anyone other than Sir Ralph Richardson as Jim Cherry – surely the main reason for the play's lack of major revival. Bolt thought that 'What he came up with was lovely. When the play opened at the Haymarket on 21 November 1957, Kenneth Tynan in *The Observer* found him 'interesting without respite' and implied that his personality was too large for the role. But it was an isolated criticism. Derek Granger in *The Financial Times* noted that 'Few players could be better suited to enact the death of the heart than Sir Ralph Richardson and Miss Celia Johnson. Sir Ralph is a player of greatness . . . He is seldom better than as here, assuming the bemused suet-faced identity of the common man suddenly suffused with secret longings. Miss Johnson's doggedly patient wife reminds us how much we miss in this splendid actress's long absences. There is none to touch her for achieving such moving effects with such spareness of method.' He thought 'Mr Frith Banbury has produced this close little study in kitchen despair with all the delicacy it needs and, except for a shade too much mood music and clever lighting, all is fine.'

Tynan assessed the play with great perspicacity, noting the not very remarkable similarities it has with *Death of a Salesman* . . . 'But beyond that the analogy will not hold. Mr Miller the sociologist attributes Willy Loman's downfall to social forces outside himself: Mr Bolt, the psychologist, looks inside Jim Cherry for the seeds of his failure. It is the play's major weakness that he never finds them . . . The play moves from alpha minus to beta plus. All the same, in a desert of gammas it is a considerable oasis,' and Derek Granger thought that 'This fine sad play was the best thing from an English playwright since *Look Back in Anger.*'

How did the Royal Court writers react to this great new talent happily ensconced in the opposition camp of the West End?

'Friendly, but not too friendly,' says Robert Bolt.

What about the West End – Royal Court divide?

'Balls!'

Was it because of him that it was balls?

'Yes!' – a lengthy pause, then 'The standard of production was better at H.M.Tennent' – then a triumphant grin. 'And more money!'

He finally appreciated Frith's production too: 'He had absolutely the right idea for *Cherry.* He nudged and orchestrated it.'

Three months after the opening Sir Ralph started to overplay and Frith wrote to him:

> I beg you to remember that you have an outsize personality and that, therefore, you need to do half as much as an ordinary actor. The devastating effect that such overplaying has on an audience is to stop them identifying themselves with Cherry, since he seems to come from some strange, remote world with which they can have nothing to do. Yours was such a wonderful performance on the first night. It is my feeling that you are always at your best when you are under the impression that you are doing less than you should!

It was when Wendy Hiller replaced Celia Johnson that Sir Ralph's behaviour left a lot to be desired. He had wanted his wife 'Mu' (Meriel Forbes) to take over, and, this denied him, went into a sulk, and made it quite plain that he resented re-rehearsing the play with another leading lady. He wandered through the rehearsals without bothering to remove his hat, scarf or coat, and even the discreet Dame Wendy remembers his attitude as 'regrettable'. Wendy Hiller was one of Frith's best friends, and Frith bluntly told Sir Ralph to behave himself. The troublesome actor-knight said something amusing but most impolite about Miss Hiller. Binkie Beaumont was sent for. He pointed out that if this state of affairs continued Miss Hiller would surely withdraw, he would then take off the play and Sir Ralph would be out of work. That seemed to do the trick and matters improved slightly.

When the London run ended in December 1958, the play went on a fourteen-week tour headed by Sir Ralph but with a new cast – which included his wife as Isobel. At Brighton he started to over-act again:

'It is essential,' wrote Frith again, 'that they [the audience] regard Cherry not as some strange, fascinating being from another world, but a projection of themselves.'

Sir Ralph may not have liked directors much, but he seems to have respected Frith:

'I greatly enjoyed my association with you,' he wrote after the tour, 'and I hope we may renew it.' They never did, although Richardson sometimes sent Frith scripts, and there were plans and proposals which like the flowering cherry did not bear fruit.

At the end of the following year a New York production was set up. Bolt, still hankering after non-naturalism now blamed Reece Pemberton's London set for being stylistically wrong and wanted the production redesigned for New York. Boris Aronson, who had designed *The Diary of Anne Frank*, was engaged. He arrived from America and Frith drove him to South London to have a look at some English suburban houses. Aronson considered the play to be completely naturalistic, and his set was thus far more representational than Pemberton's had been. Also the American management claimed that Arthur Miller's agent objected to the ending because of its similarity to *Death of a Salesman*, and so the orchard vision went, and it became just a well-made play set in a box-set kitchen.

Wendy Hiller was again to play Isobel with Eric Portman as Cherry. Portman was a fine actor – of the very first rank in Frith's opinion – rated below Olivier and Gielgud only because he had played few of the classics. What no one associated with the enterprise then realised was that he had become an alcoholic. 'He could not,' says Dame Wendy tactfully, 'walk and talk at the same time'. When Bolt was asked what Portman's performance had been like, he replied; 'Drunk!'

At an early rehearsal, much the worse for wear, Portman engaged Frith in forty-five minutes of drunken discussion. Wendy Hiller, exasperated, left the rehearsal, telephoned the management and said: 'It's a very long way for me to come just to act with an alcoholic.' Once she rang Bolt at two o'clock in the morning in despair, 'I can't bear it,' 'Well, what do I do about it?' he asked, reasonably but unhelpfully.

Portman played the day-time dress-rehearsal sober but was paralytic by the time of a press-conference two hours later – thus insulting both the American theatre and the American press. And the next morning Frith found himself apologising on behalf of the entire British people.

After the opening night Robert Bolt, wisely if pusillanimously, left New York by boat, before the reviews came out, which was just as well as they were truly terrible. The play ran for four performances.

'It is sad about Eric,' wrote Binkie Beaumont to Frith, 'but we have learned our lesson.' While Bolt, perhaps feeling guilty for running away, says now with generosity, that the failure was 'entirely the play's fault'.

*

Bolt had told Frith before the post-London tour of *Flowering Cherry* that he was writing a play for Michael Redgrave, an actor whose combination of scholar and man of action he greatly admired. Early in February 1959, the completed script was posted to St James's Terrace.

'My dear Bob,' wrote Frith after reading the play once, 'This is just to tell you that I have read *The Tiger and the Horse* and am fascinated by it!'

Bolt telephoned at once, amazed.

'Is that all you can say?'

'Yes,' replied Frith 'but I will have a hell of a lot more to say when I have studied it further.'

A week later, and Redgrave had read the play one morning in bed. He wrote to Frith:

'After Act I, I went for more tea and started Act II. I noticed by the end of the act I hadn't drunk my tea. I have been laughing and crying by turns all through the play. I shall read it again many times I hope, but I don't need to read it again to know that (if Mr Bolt will pardon the expression, for it is only meant in affection) it is "my" play for I truly love it.'

Bolt and Frith had suggested his daughter Vanessa for Stella, the younger daughter in the play. He continued: 'Of course you are right about Vanessa. She has the vulnerability and essential youthfulness. Also she has a conscience, like her mother's, the size of Grand Central Station.'

The letters continued. Frith to Redgrave: 'Bolt asks me to tell you how really excited he is by your reaction . . . He always told me before I read the play you were the man for the part and, of course, as soon as I did I saw how right he was.'

Redgrave visited the Bolts (he also had a cottage in the West Country) and the playwright reported to Frith: 'How extraordinary to find a man who can both act and *think*. Jo [Bolt's first wife] fell for him instanter during the first few minutes he spent at the cottage. I also; by contrast I can now gauge the extent of our sufferings at the hands of Rogue Ralphie.'

The project could hardly have begun with better omens.

The title of the play is taken from William Blake's *Proverbs of Hell*: 'The Tigers of wrath are wiser than the Horses of instruction.' It is a play about involvement: how lack of involvement in others can destroy their lives, just as how excessive involvement in the ills of the world can be self-destructive. The trigger for all the action is one that was then close to Robert Bolt's heart: a petition calling for complete nuclear disarmament:

Jack Dean (Michael Redgrave) is the Master of an Oxbridge College. Once a pioneering astronomer, he has now settled for writing routine but respected books on philosophy. He married his wife Gwendoline (Catherine Lacey), late in life. The only way she is able to cope with his physical lack of interest is to believe that, like her father, he has saintly qualities and, more worryingly, to blame herself for all the whole wrongs of the world: if such a good man cannot love her, she must be evil. Their younger daughter, Stella (Vanessa Redgrave), an academically gifted girl with a social conscience, is going out with a left-wing Research Fellow, Louis Flax (Alan Dobie) who is neglecting his thesis because of his involvement in C.N.D. He brings a petition for Jack Dean to sign at an inopportune moment – Dean is just about to be made Vice-Chancellor of the University – so there is no question of his adding his signature. His wife Gwen, who has read a horrifying article on how nuclear tests produce deformed children, is willing to sign until the current Vice-Chancellor (Kynaston Reeves) tells her that her signature might do serious damage to her husband's election prospects.

The College's most precious possession is a Holbein group portrait of the founder and his family. In its present uncleaned state the figures are murky, but Gwen thinks one of the children may be a hunchback. When it is cleaned, a deformed child is clearly visible.

Stella is pregnant by Louis who proposes gracelessly, because he is involved with issues rather than with people, and seeing through him, she refuses. She has found her father's old telescope and is trying to continue his astronomical work. When she tells her father of her pregnancy he can only show cliched concern, and later cries, 'I'm not involved. I'm extremely distressed on your behalf, my dear. But I am not involved.' (Act II) Gwen's behaviour becomes increasingly eccentric and it is plain she is heading for a nervous breakdown. Dean visits Stella and her baby in their shabby flat. The news comes that Gwen has cracked up, removed the Holbein from its frame, taken it outside and slashed it to pieces with a pair of secateurs, with Louis's petition attached. Gwen, the mad tiger, appears and, goes mad before Dean's eyes. He, still the horse, stays uninvolved as revelations pour out: how she knew he found her repellent, and how she looked at him asleep in his separate bedroom: 'He sleeps like an angel. *(Almost shouting through her tears.)* Like a pig!' (Act II)

Only when it is clear that he thinks that she will not be allowed to be with her grandchild unsupervised, does Dean admit it is his fault, and in a magnificent gesture of involvement – but with his wife not with mankind – he signs Louis's petition giving up any chance of academic advancement.

Bolt had remembered the Jewish mystic Martin Buber: love is the only thing that can rescue people from isolation. When deeply involved with another person, you open yourself up, and God slips in.

In the first draft this mad scene was much shorter, and when Peggy Ashcroft was offered the part she turned it down. 'That Peggy Ashcroft must be a very stupid woman,' said Bolt, but he rewrote and expanded the scene, and Frith believes that had she seen the finished result she would have accepted, but Catherine Lacey was universally thought to have been excellent as Gwen, by author and director in particular.

The Tiger and the Horse is a play of far more intricacy and depth than is *Flowering Cherry*. Bernard Levin called it 'a talk-all-nighter', and its issues and characters are indeed almost impossible to forget: it is most memorable.

At the time it was called a play about the bomb, and the petition is a central issue. Bolt was deeply involved in the Aldermaston marches and sit-down-strikes which then accompanied the Ban-the-Bomb campaign, and indeed, the following year was to go to prison, along with Bertrand Russell, for demonstrating. In *The Tiger and the Horse* he does seem to be saying that anyone involved in mankind must be involved in Nuclear Disarmament. Around the company he was voluble in his opinions and one member was much influenced by them. Vanessa Redgrave says in her autobiography, that at twenty-three, it was this play and Bolt's influence that started the concern for social issues that led to her present rigorously held political dedication. Bolt himself shrugs in an amused way at the suggestion: 'It may be true. She was a smashing girl,' and, as for her performance as Stella, 'Lovely she was. Superb!'

The Naturalism/Non-Naturalism battle with Frith continued, except this time, perhaps because of Bolt's increased frustration at being hide-bound by the structure of the well-made play, their discussions had an acrimonious edge which had previously not been present. Frith became the playwright's whipping boy, and he was given a hard time. Bolt now concedes that Frith 'was right really but it is half-way to being a poetic play'. It is that, but it is no way at all towards being an expressionist play. As in *Flowering Cherry* the one great poetic moment is a beautiful speech at the end of the Second Act when Stella, hoping to find some pattern and order in the universe to counter-balance her own disordered life is disabused by her father:

> Oh, yes, the moons go round the planets and the planets go round the sun and the sun goes round the Milky Way, but that doesn't matter because the Milky Way is circling round itself as it goes looping from nowhere to nowhere and in twenty-four billion years the sun will be back where it started. None of it matters since happily it leaves no trace, but if all the galaxies were God's Fingers Dipped in Light d'you know what pattern they would make? Scribble! (He *is breathing hard. On a note of going.*) So if you find them comforting – (He *points rather unsteadily at the telescope.*) now's the time to stop.'

Frith lost the first battle which was over the designer. Bolt insisted on his own choice and the results were a most unhappy mixture of artificial and representational with no homogeneous reality. Tattily painted library backdrop and cut-out topiary for the first two acts, and then a completely circumstantial Third Act.

The play starts with Stella sitting at a desk, wrapping a birthday present for her father. During the run, the playwright had the idea that the moment should be symbolic, and that the curtain should rise on Stella posed in the attitude of Rodin's *The Thinker*. It was tried for one performance. He now laughs about it when reminded, 'Did I really? I don't agree with that. Awful!' Bolt was still ever hopeful he had written another kind of play.

Since Frith had directed Redgrave in *A Touch of the Sun* two years earlier, the actor had been knighted and was now unquestionably one of the leaders of the profession. Both playwright and director think, in retrospect, he could and should have been marvellous as Jack Dean, but there were two major problems: he was drinking too much, which meant that on the nights he had imbibed he became unbearably slow, and, as he became grander, he increasingly disliked playing unsympathetic parts. Early on, at the rehearsals which took place at Her Majesty's, Sir Michael seemed to have the exact measure of the part and drew from himself the supercilious manner the Master of the College displays to cover his real feelings. Frith told Redgrave he was on the right tracks, and from that moment onwards he never played the part correctly again – quite deliberately because he thought if he did the audience would not love him.

Why did the actor feel this need for compromise? Bolt thinks it was because of his sexuality: 'He went off kilter because of the drives in him. His wife . . . how she put up with it I don't know. Did Vanessa know that her father was homosexual, or not? He wanted *everything*, right. *He* wanted rough trade . . . A tortured man.'

More worrying to Frith was Redgrave's slowness over learning lines. At the end of the second week of rehearsals, Frith's mother died. He went down to Midhurst to be with her at her deathbed on Friday night, and the next morning was back at rehearsal. Only the stage-manager knew this. He would not normally have called a rehearsal on the second Saturday morning, but Sir Michael's inability to remember his moves, let alone his lines, meant a special call was given at half past ten so he could familiarise himself with the blocking. The company waited. At ten past eleven the stage-manager appeared with the news that Sir Michael would not be attending that morning as he was suffering from 'nervous strain'.

'Of course I hadn't told the cast I'd been up all night at my mother's deathbed, but I had Alison Colvil as stage-manager, and I shall never forget the look on that redoubtable Scotswoman's face as she told me.' They both suspected that it was a hangover.

Five days before the Brighton opening, Frith went to Binkie Beaumont and told him that the opening night might have to be delayed as the leading man did not know his lines. But of the First Night all Frith can remember is the relief that there was not a catastrophe. Following Brighton, the play went to the Manchester Opera House where, by his own unaided efforts, Redgrave put a quarter of an hour onto the running time of the production, which was quite understandably slated by the local press for being too slow.

Frith called a meeting; 'The trouble with Michael was that he was indubitably the star, but everyone knew that half the notes you gave other people were, in fact, for him. The next night he was sober and the quarter of an hour was taken off. When we walked back to the Midland Hotel I said, "That made such a difference when the production was pulled together." "Yes," Michael said, "it makes such a difference when Catherine plays that scene properly." It was always somebody else's fault, somebody else's responsibility. He found it terribly difficult to come clean about anything really, which is why in his book Fred Sadoff, who was his lover for years, is not mentioned once.'

Robert Bolt kept badgering Frith to make Redgrave play Jack Dean. He also felt that Frith 'was getting up the noses of the cast' by talking too much. There was a row and Beaumont asked a willingly consenting Frith to stay away for ten days when the play moved on to Leeds so that Bolt could try and make Redgrave act the part properly. This was a complete failure – and when Frith came back only one move had been changed. The playwright said to him, 'I can't do anything. Every time I say, "Can we have a session? Can we go for a walk?" it's always "I must lie down", always some excuse.'

When it was announced that *The Tiger and the Horse* was going into the Queen's Theatre where Redgrave had just played *The Aspern Papers,* the Front of House Staff asked for guaranteed taxi money home, as they said any production with Sir Michael Redgrave in it became longer and longer and they missed their last buses and tubes home – and it was given to them.

It opened on 24 August 1960 to ecstatic reviews from every paper except *The Times*. Bernard Levin, then of *The Daily Express,* fell in love with Vanessa Redgrave. ('The first of Vanessa's loonies' as Ian McKellen called him.) Of her 'stunningly perfect performance' he wrote, 'I shall have more to say. And now to talk all night. What a play! What a play!' Five days later he did have more to say about her performance: 'Resounding in depth . . . needs an article to itself . . .'

Frith was standing at the back of the dress circle during one of the first matinees, when he became aware of mutterings coming from behind him, 'Get on with it! For Christ's sake get *on* with it!' Turning around he saw the Commissionaire. 'I quite agree with you,' he whispered to him, 'but not so loud!'

Then he visited Robert Bolt at home and noticed a lot of unopened box-office returns on the mantelpiece.

'What are those doing?' he asked.

'I can't bear what's going on at the Queen's,' Bolt answered, 'so I don't open the returns.' It was a kind of protest.

Three months into the run Frith wrote to Redgrave: ' . . . If Dean is such an old duck as we saw on Thursday afternoon we do not understand Stella's attitude to him in Act I ("I can't bear it when you talk like this") or why Mrs Dean is going off her head.'

'There is one other thing that has crept in which I thought to be a definite mistake – that is the kiss you now give Gwen before she goes into the bedroom in Act III. Somehow one feels that this fastidious man – even at that moment – would never make such a gesture before a roomful of people. It seemed to cut across the scene at that moment.'

Then he wrote to Jerome Chodorov, the American playwright and investor in this production:

I am afraid that business has dropped considerably in recent weeks, and I rather doubt that the play will have an enormously long life [it ran for seven months]. Michael Redgrave is now playing the part in exactly the opposite way from that which the author intended, and we none of us seem to be able to get him to do anything different, although I am going to make a great effort next week to do this. The result is that the play's largely incomprehensible to audiences since it seems to be about a very old duck of a man whose wife, for some unexplained reason goes mad, and this is just too unfortunate for him! I could not believe that a leading actor and an artist of what I thought was Michael's character could so twist a part round in order to get what he erroneously believes is the sympathy of the audience. It is a great disappointment to me I must say.

Frith's 'great effort' the next week was to call a rehearsal which Sir Michael declined to attend, probably because he knew what Frith was likely to say. He then retaliated by calling a rehearsal of his own. Kynaston Reeves, the actor playing the old Vice-Chancellor asked whether the director was going to be there, and, on being told he was not, refused to go. So the rehearsal never took place.

Because Redgrave was already committed to play 'H.J.' in his adaptation of Henry James's *The Aspern Papers* which he presented with his lover Fred Sadoff, at the Queen's in August 1959, the start of rehearsals for *The Tiger and the Horse* were held over for seventeen months. During this time, Frith directed Wynyard Browne's *The Ring of Truth* in July, and Frith and Bolt had their disagreeable American experience in the autumn. Meanwhile Bolt had written another play: *A Man for All Seasons.*

Frith rightly claims that, unless production of this had been postponed as well, he would not have been available to direct it – but others have told me that he was desperate to take it on. When Binkie Beaumont compared the play to *Richard of Bordeaux,* Frith told him such a comparison was nonsense; it was the best historical play since Shaw's *Saint Joan.* Bolt, however, still finding fault with what he believed to be Frith's over-naturalistic mind, told him he was seeking a director elsewhere. Bolt remembers; 'He took it like a gentleman. He was not the right director for *A Man for All Seasons* because he was too naturalistic. But his reaction was lovely, superb.' Frith invested in the production, directed by Noel Willman and a triumph for Paul Scofield, and its success must have somewhat softened his disappointment.

After *Flowering Cherry* Frith, who had wanted to put Bolt on contract as he had Wynyard Browne (an idea firmly scuppered by Peggy Ramsay) tried without success to interest Dame Edith Evans in *The Critic and the Heart.* But Dame Edith thought Winifred far too near the knuckle; 'I don't want to live eight times a week with this poor little person. It would colour my *whole day!'* Then their professional paths separated. Bolt returned to the theatre in 1963 with a studiously non-naturalistic play *Gentle Jack,* a mish-mash of whimsy and folk-cults influenced by J.M. Barrie which failed, in spite of the intriguing combination of Edith Evans and Kenneth Williams. Then, with *Vivat Vivat Regina!* in 1970 he wrote another successful historical play – this time about Mary Queen of Scots and Elizabeth I – using almost the same format as *A Man for All Seasons.* Then the cinema claimed him. His hedonism was aroused by Sam Spiegel and his yacht and he became most successful in that most naturalistic of all the performing arts. His screenplays for David Lean: *Lawrence of Arabia, Doctor Zhivago, Ryan's Daughter,* must be among the best and most literate in all film. None of which can have come as a surprise to Frith.

Robert Bolt died on 20 February 1995. In 1978, he had been incapacitated following a serious stroke. Although he found speech and movement difficult, he had a life-force which blazed: an enormous personality with a formidable intellect and almost elaborate good manners. His opinion of Frith surely made amends for any rough times past: 'A lovely man. I think more and more what a gentleman he was. He was more of a gentleman than any other person I have ever met.'

Coda

In 1966, Toby Rowland asked Frith to direct Edward Albee's *A Delicate Balance* with Redgrave as Tobias – but after the experience of *The Tiger and the Horse,* Frith was not interested. 'It's sad to talk of Redgrave in this way,' Frith reflects. 'He was a leader of the British Theatre. Shortly afterwards, Parkinson's Disease showed itself and it then became very difficult for him to do anything. By the time he was in *Close of Play* by Simon Gray at the National where he only had one line at the end, it was very sad: this big star actor sitting on stage just looking. When he went to South Africa touring his one man show, he just gave up. He couldn't remember. It was too painful for everybody. But – I have to say this – it was brought about by his own self-indulgence.'

Directing at the Royal Court:
Moon on a Rainbow Shawl

In 1957, Kenneth Tynan, champion of Royal Court New Writing and drama critic of *The Observer,* persuaded his Editor, David Astor, to set up a play competition. The brief given to the undiscovered authors was that 'the action of all the plays submitted must take place in the period since the last war.' The first three prizes were to be of £500, £200 and £100, and the winning entries were to be staged at the Arts Theatre Club, although this last idea seems to have been abandoned along the way: all the plays being put onto the open market. Five hundred plays were expected, nearly two thousand were received. The judges were Peter Hall (then of the Arts Theatre), Michael Barry, head of B.B.C. Television Drama, Peter Ustinov, Alec Guinness and Tynan himself. The third prize was shared between three plays: Richard Benyon's *The Shifting Heart,* N.F. Simpson's *A Resounding Tinkle,* and Ann Jellicoe's *The Sport of My Mad Mother,* the second went to Gurney Campbell and Daphne Athas's *Sit on the Earth;* and the first was awarded to *Moon on a Rainbow Shawl* by a thirty-three-year-old West Indian actor, Errol John.

It was said by some, uncharitably, that Tynan, keen to be politically correct, steered the jury away from the better works of Ann Jellicoe and N.F. Simpson, so that he and the *Observer* could be seen to champion a play with Black and mixed-race characters set in Trinidad. Yet John's play, about backyard life in Port-of-Spain with its dreams, aspirations and disasters has a haunting poetic timelessness and a homogeneity which made its placing well-deserved.

The story is told through the lives of two contrasting couples: Ephraim (Epf), the young trolley-bus driver eager to escape the tenement for the golden pavements of Liverpool and Rosa his pregnant wife, whom he foolishly leaves behind; and Sophia whom Tynan described as 'a sort of Negro Anna Magnani' and Charlie, her pathetic husband who could have been an international cricketer if he had learnt to keep his mouth shut over racial discrimination. Fearful that his daughter, Esther, will look poor in front of the other pupils at the smart school to which she has won a scholarship, Charlie robs a cafe to buy her a bicycle.

It is a slice-of-life play laced with poetry. Such works are usually strong on atmosphere and rather weak on theatricality, and *Moon on a Rainbow Shawl* is no exception. Trinidadians have made the English language their own as much as have the Irish, and to a middle-class English public, then not so used to West Indian accent and dialect, such speech must have seemed strange and exotic. The appeal of the characters is their buoyancy and courage in the face of deprivation and adversity, and the amalgam of noises (steel-bands, squalling babies, fish vendors) invokes a complete environment most strikingly: a tragi-comedy by a sub-Chekhov of the tropics.

When the winner was announced in the summer of 1957, Binkie Beaumont optioned the play at once, read it and had not the slightest idea what to do with it next. He had rashly promised a West End Production but now clearly thought the piece to be hopelessly uncommercial. The other prize-winners were seeing their plays performed, but *Moon on a Rainbow Shawl* had, to begin with, only a radio production. Beaumont passed it on to John Perry at Tennent Productions (the non profit-making arm), and gave the script to Frith, who thought it showed great promise but needed much further work, an opinion which was confirmed by a public-reading at the Criterion Theatre.

Frith wrote eight pages of closely typed suggestions to Errol John in which the hand of Christopher Taylor is very evident. They objected to the absence of plot, which seems rather literal-minded, as in plays of poetic realism the plot is just used as a pretext to look at the lives of a group; neither was the 'synthetic and fancy' title admired. Where the criticisms were right were over the excess of 'Fine Writing of an amorphos kind, perfectly harmless in itself, but lacking sharpness and bite', and the lack of dramatic development in both Ephraim's character and situation. He was seen packing at the beginning of the First Act, and was seen going at the end of the last. Two radical suggestions were therefore proposed: that the two scenes of the First Act should be played as one, which was an improvement, and that Ephraim should not definitely decide to leave until he has seen Charlie taken off by the police at the end of the Second Act. Errol John accepted all the suggestions bar the change of title, and started re-writing, giving definition to his atmospheric poetry.

Frith, armed with an unaccustomed camera, then travelled to Port-of-Spain to take photographs for the designer, Loudon

Sainthill. Trinidad was not then much on the tourist map and he stayed in an old Colonial hotel which served Brown Windsor Soup and Roast Lamb in the blazing heat. He was assisted by a lady called Electra, who ran the radio station and who gave him introductions to Trinidadian worthies. The physical beauty of the people with their extraordinary variety of racial mixes (Spanish, Portuguese, English, Chinese, Assyrian, Jewish, East Indian, African) and the courtesy and charm with which he was met everywhere made it the most enjoyable of working holidays.

Back in London, he auditioned seemingly every professional actor from a racial minority. The supporting roles were soon filled and some talent was let through, 'Unbelievably I turned down Cleo Laine for Rosa'. At the end he decided that as there were, in those days, no ethnic actors of sufficient experience and stature for Ephraim, Sophia and Charlie, he would import them from America. Black English actors were not pleased and complained to Equity, who now looked at the enterprise without quite their former enthusiasm.

Earle Hyman, whose work Frith knew and admired was engaged for Ephraim, and, at his suggestion, Vinnette Carroll was taken, sight-un-seen, for Sophie – which was a lucky risk for she was excellent – and John Bouie was cast as Charlie.

When these actors arrived in the autumn of 1958, John Perry, who was meant to meet them at the airport, did not do so. Neither did he appear at the small party of welcome which Frith gave at his house. At the first rehearsal at the Apollo Theatre, Earle Hyman asked, reasonably enough, when they were going to meet the management. A few days later, Equity, not overly well-disposed to these visiting Americans, asked Vinnette Carroll to pay up and join. She considered this was the responsibility of the management, and when a message came from upstairs that she should pay the fee herself, she refused, and gave a one-woman sit-down-strike in the middle of the stage. Frith fetched John Perry, who therefore met the leading lady for the first time as she sat, in a foul mood, refusing to work until Tennent Productions coughed up for her Equity subscription.

Rehearsals seemed to continue eventfully. One day Frith, wanting to rush from stalls to dress circle, flung open a door at the back of the auditorium and knocked flying a cleaning-lady who then sued him for assault. She was sent twenty pounds and a note of apology.

Neither at the Manchester Opera House, where it opened, nor at Brighton and Leeds where it then toured, did the management either appear or show any other sign of interest. Frith thought this attitude disgraceful and made even more so (this was 1958) because the actors were black. He felt far more trouble might have been taken.

Binkie, not thinking the play suitable West End fodder, suggested to George Devine that it should go to the Royal Court, an idea which he seems to have shared with no one else. The Americans still thought that they were bound for the West End. To Manchester, Devine dispatched Anthony Page, then one of his assistant directors, to report back. He approved and told the surprised and displeased Earle Hyman it was going to the Court. The company became very unhappy and eventually, at Leeds, Frith telephoned Binkie, and, during the conversation, burst into tears with shame at the way the cast were being treated. John Perry thought it all very funny. Around this time, Robert Flemyng dined at Lord North Street, where he was told by Perry that Frith had become quite impossible: demanding that the play come to the West End because he had fallen in love with Earle Hyman, and being thwarted, hysterically assaulting a cleaning-woman. At the other end of the table Binkie had sat silent, inscrutable – but amused.

The Royal Court opening was on 5 December 1958, and notices were guarded: Harold Hobson in *The Sunday Times* thought the play 'belonged to the romantic past. It is built on that old *Three Sisters* delusion that the place you are is awful, and paradise exists somewhere else.' While, for *The Times*, 'The author's compassion rings true as his attempted lyricism rings false'. But the critic was full of praise for the actors; 'Mr Earle Hyman brings out the wholeness of the man as the author represents him, and makes it easy for us to accept both the devotion and the bitter contempt that the betrayed girl feels for him. Miss Vinnette Carroll could hardly be bettered as the wife who has had the strength to endure conditions which have ruined her man.' And for Doris Lessing, reviewing instead of Tynan in the *Observer:* 'The actors have a quality lacking in most British acting: a warm and tender sensuality which gives the production a deep delicacy of emotion.' Tynan himself was privately furious that Frith had forced Errol John to rewrite.

For six weeks it ran at the Royal Court to poor business; neither white nor black people showing great interest. Frith enjoyed working with the company and thought Loudon Sainthill's set with special front curtain for the Royal Court, first-rate. But after this experience, although they stayed on adequate personal terms, he refused to work with John Perry again. Any sourness there, must have been balanced by the friendships which came out of *Moon on a Rainbow Shawl*. Earle Hyman became and remained a close friend and, judging by her adoring letters, Vinnette Carroll's opinion of Frith was nothing short of hero-worship.

*

That Frith directed at the Royal Court at all (albeit in association with Tennent Productions) is little known. That he did so in a contemporary ethnic play is both surprising and needs to be noted.

Part Seven

*Watershed, Doldrums
and Renaissance*

Watershed

Soon after I began researching this book, Frith, whose attitude to the project had, up until then, been non-committal: 'Well, I won't stop you,' suddenly became far too over-excited. I was bombarded with suggestions: who to see; what to focus on, even what opinions to hold: 'I don't think you should be too dismissive about *Love's Labour's Lost.*' Unexpectedly I felt most insecure and could not bring myself to tell him that although everything I was being given was helpful, I was not yet ready to receive it. Such a weak admission would surely, I thought, be seen as feeble and unprofessional. I took to switching on my answer machine to monitor all calls. Then after one Banbury message – the longest I have ever received from anyone – I disconnected the telephone. Then the letters began: each one opened with dread and later used with gratitude. The most immediately interesting was called 'Watershed':

Late in 1964, after I had had production after production on the trot for 15 years or so, I decided that the time had come to take a sabbatical. So I left Jimmy Wax to look after Frith Banbury Ltd, and, having stopped off in New York and set up a production with Barr-Wilder-Albee at the Cherry Lane Theatre of Charles Nolte's *Do Not Pass Go* for the following spring with Alan Schneider as director, I set off for the Pacific – Tahiti, Bora-Bora, Fiji, New Zealand, Australia – then on to Japan. From there I was about to return home by way of New York for the off-Broadway premiere, when I was offered the direction of the Broadway production of *The Right Honourable Gentleman.* (This had been done in London by Glen Byam Shaw.) So I came home for only a fortnight before returning to the U.S. for five months.

The West End was without a production or projected production of mine for about a year and a half, which it hadn't been, I suppose, for about fifteen years, until I did *Howard's End* at the Albery in 1967. (I did do *Do Not Pass Go*, by Charles Nolte at Hampstead, but that very American piece was a complete flop in this country; it was inadequately performed and did not connect with audiences.) How fortuitous it was, then, that after the flop of *Howard's End,* I met Peter Bridge, one afternoon as I was picking up my car at the garage at the top of St Martin's Lane and he was about to pick up his. 'I say, what are you doing at the moment?' 'Nothing.' 'What about doing *Dear Octopus* with the Hulberts? Patrick Cargill has just told me he won't be free to direct it!' 'Well, why not?' 'Good. Can you come along to the office now?' 'Why not?' Thus I was put in the way of a big success.

So . . . wouldn't it be a good idea for the main body of the book to carry through until the end of 1964 – after *The Wings of the Dove* and *I Love You, Mrs Patterson?* In my mind that interval is certainly a watershed.

John Gale had sent Frith an adaptation of Henry James's *The Wings of the Dove* by P.G. Wodehouse's collaborator Guy Bolton, which was considered possibly producible if improvements were made: the American characters sounding English. Christopher Taylor, given this task, went back to the novel, and letting Frith believe he was working on the Bolton script, wrote in six weeks his own completely different version. Novels are difficult to dramatise for an evening's entertainment because they are too long, and therefore too much has to go – short stories are a better length – but by not starting his play until Milly Theale has already taken the palazzo in Venice, and by incorporating previous material when the other characters visit her, Christopher produced what must be one of the most satisfying – and certainly one of the most literate – stage versions of a novel ever made. Following James closely, his stage directions are extraordinary detailed, giving the actors virtually every thought and mood change, which must have been a great assistance but also imposed certain restrictions on their imagination. Seldom can a writer have wished to exercise such control over the final performances.

Christopher, whose original and autobiographical play *The Velvet Shotgun* had been produced and directed by Frith in 1958, was still living in the garden house at St James's Terrace both as Frith Banbury Productions' play reader and Frith's closest professional and personal influence.

The Wings of the Dove opened at the Lyric Theatre in December 1963 with Susannah York as Milly, James Donald as Merton Denver (Densher in the novel), Wendy Hiller as Susan Shepherd and Elspeth March as Maud Lowder. In April 1964 it transferred to the Haymarket and the following month Jennifer Hilary, Alan Howard, Viola Keats and Nan Munro replaced the original cast. In spite of the praise this civilised and literate project received, the production lost its entire investment – Christopher foregoing author's royalties for the latter part of the run – a case of everybody except the backers feeling rewarded to some degree.

I Love You Mrs Patterson was the first play of a television producer and novelist, John Bowen. Again the literary quality is high – much finer than most other plays of the early sixties. Some critics judged it by its surface level: that of a State school *Young Woodley,* but there is more to it than that. The play concerns emotional responsibility, who can or cannot take it on and why. Hal (Jeremy Bullock), a schoolboy in love with his teacher's wife Brenda (Wendy Craig), believes, 'People don't change. If I could take emotional responsibility, I wouldn't have been running away from it all my life.' Eventually he is forced to take it on because she asks him for help. Bernard Levin, by now of *The Daily Mail,* found it 'a remarkably fine and enthralling play, flawed at times (though never fatally) civilised, literate, and skilful'. Another *succès d'estime,* as again the investment was lost during its short run at the St Martin's Theatre in 1964.

Frith is right to be proud of *Dear Octopus* (1967). It was the first production of his that I saw and it seemed to be everything the West End should and could do: star performances (acting with individual personality yet truth of character, for those who still dislike that word); supporting players of great distinction; subtlety of orchestration yet attack of delivery; an excellent set; period clothes which looked smart and were worn correctly and effortlessly; essential charm, and the whole *ensemble* fitting together as an impressive whole. Dodie Smith's 1930s comedy of a large family coming together to celebrate the golden-wedding of its patriarch and matriarch is a bit cosy but one with which it is pleasantly easy to identify. One remembers Cicely Courtneidge as Dora Randolph imbuing her brood with a new sense of purpose, and Richard Todd as her son Nicholas giving the famous toast: 'Here's to the family, that dear octopus from whose tentacles we are never quite able to escape, nor in our inmost hearts do we wish to do so.'

There was no question that younger critics, playgoers and members of the profession were impressed by the production of *Dear Octopus.* By the late sixties Frith's stock was still high – but only as the director of a certain kind of play: naturalistic and well-made. Superior to most other middle-aged directors in the established commercial theatre but still, to the young, belonging to an older, less challenging tradition. Unfortunately his next assignment, which might have altered some of these perceptions, failed to do so.

After the success of *Rosencrantz and Guildenstern Are Dead* at the Edinburgh Festival and its subsequent production by the National Theatre, Tom Stoppard was a young playwright from whom a great deal was expected. Doris Cole Abrahams, the American producer resident in London, discovered that in 1963 aged twenty-five, Stoppard had written a television play, *A Walk on the Water*, which had later been adapted for stage performance, and performed in Germany without much success. It is really a one-act play distended into two, and this elongation results in thinness. Its importance in the Stoppard cannon is that it served as an exercise for the more mature *Jumpers* (1972). Certainly George Riley in *Enter a Free Man* (as *A Walk on the Water* came to be called) has much in common with George of the latter play – and the same actor, Michael Hordern, played the 'George' of all three versions: on television *(A Walk on the Water)*, in the West End *(Enter a Free Man)*, and at the National Theatre, *(Jumpers)*.

But is also clearly a 'prentice effort of a writer of immense possible promise, who might develop or who might just have a gift for verbal dexterity and quibbles. Some of his puns are, at this stage, fairly laboured. And, as the critics knew from *Rosencrantz and Guildenstern Are Dead*, that he *had* already developed, it is surprising they were so dismissive of this earlier work. 'An idea on a revue sketch level', said Eric Shorter in *The Daily Telegraph;* while Peter Lewis in *The Daily Mail*, noting that it had been written in Stoppard's early years and for television, thought 'he would have been advised to leave it there in the junior league.' Perhaps their expectations were inflated, *Enter a Free Man* is heartwarming – its message: Everybody Fails but Life Still Goes On – and there is one excellently fashioned scene of family breakdown between George, his wife, and daughter, where Stoppard writes with such compassion and truth that the play becomes very moving.

Five years later and now on to great things, Stoppard had lost interest in this early work and it was difficult for Frith to make him concentrate his mind on any revision. Also, because his first marriage was breaking up, he had difficulties at home. Frith and Michael Hordern were not the right actor and director for each other and *Enter a Free Man* did not succeed; Frith's most positive memory of the experience being Megs Jenkins's delightful portrayal of George's wife, Persephone.

But it was sad that Frith, whose past reputation had been founded on directing new work, and whose main pleasure was working with a playwright on a new script, was never again to be associated with a fashionable and successful young writer.

Doldrums

1968 was the most significant year in post-war theatre: the Lord Chamberlain's power of censorship was finally abolished. But this important event had little bearing on the work Frith was doing in that, and many subsequent years. After *Enter a Free Man* he was invited abroad: to Tel Aviv for Peter Nichols's A *Day in the Death of Joe Egg*, which was a happy experience; and to Paris for Robin Maugham's *The Servant (Le Valet)*, which was not.

The following year there was another glossy, all-star revival (ten names above the title) presented by Peter Bridge: Bernard Shaw's *On the Rocks*, which played the Dublin Festival, toured extensively, but, in spite of the cast, the sumptuous Cabinet-room set by Reece Pemberton, and an encomiastic review by Frank Marcus in *The Sunday Telegraph*, came no nearer to London than Wimbledon. In 1970 Frith presented (losing every penny) Christopher Taylor's adaptation of Theo Lang's book about Edward VII's mistress, Lady Warwick, *My Darling Daisy*. In spite of its tourist-entrapping theme of the British Royal Family being blackmailed, neither Christopher nor Coral Browne managed to convey the strange dichotomy of Daisy Warwick as socialite and socialist, and the play folded after two weeks. There was a Tennents revival of Rattigan's *The Winslow Boy* with Laurence Naismith excellent as Arthur Winslow, and Kenneth More miscast but having a brave stab at Sir Robert Morton. After the first night, Rattigan wrote to Frith telling him that this was the best production of *any* of his plays, and he wished Frith had directed *all* of them – but then Rattigan was a great flatterer. In 1971 came Bernard Shaw's *Captain Brassbound's Conversion*, another Tennents revival, this time mounted as a wildly unsuitable vehicle for the film-star, Ingrid Bergman.

We need to pause briefly at *Captain Brassbound* because Kenneth Williams, who played Drinkwater in that production, both in his autobiography *Just Williams*, and later in his published diaries, was rather rude about Frith. No ruder than he was about any other director who had the temerity to give him direction (Guy Verney, Douglas Seale, Cecil King, Peter Glenville, Peter Wood and Eric Thompson) but quite unpleasant all the same.

As so often in these instances, it all seems to have started well. Williams came to see Frith for a discussion and found Frith 'kindness itself'. For the next three hours Williams poured his heart out about his neuroses, anxieties, and sex-life or lack of it. Frith, 'kindness itself', was obviously a sympathetic ear and afterwards, he received a most admiring and grateful letter. (Not, anyway, that Frith was unaware of these troubles, because some years earlier, a friend of his had made a pass at Williams who had reacted like a Victorian maiden in danger of suffering the Fate Worse Than Death.)

Then there was a meeting at Binkie Beaumont's house between Frith, Kenneth Williams, Joss Ackland (who was to play Brassbound) and Miss Bergman. They all seem to have loved each other, and the enterprise was toasted with champagne. Frith, Joss Ackland, already a friend, and Ingrid Bergman who remained a friend of Frith's until her death, continued to love each other – and Miss Bergman and Joss Ackland continued to love Kenneth Williams, as he did them. It was just with Frith that Kenneth Williams fell out.

To begin with (quite uniquely in view of what everyone else who has worked with Frith says) Williams found the rehearsals boring. He claimed that Ingrid Bergman had said to him privately, 'I thought Binkie would get a young and imaginative director so that the play would have the sort of re-interpretation which Zeffirelli gave to *Romeo and Juliet.*' If she indeed equated directing *Captain Brassbound's Conversion* with directing *Romeo and Juliet,* she must have been a complete idiot; but Frith thinks the veracity of the anecdote highly dubious, while Joss Ackland dismisses it out-of-hand: 'I was fond of him but I didn't take anything he said very seriously.'

Williams had two professional flaws: one was that he took even the mildest instruction, for instance, 'move up to the window', as a personal insult; the other that, unlike the rest of the cast, he was so self-centred that he completely failed to see the difficulties placed on Frith by Ingrid Bergman's inability either to learn her lines, or to speak them with any degree of sense. Williams criticised her for 'not grasping a scene once', and Frith for not telling her how to do so – but how can a director start directing the performance of a major star who is still desperately insecure with an unfamiliar language? During rehearsals Frith had written a note to Binkie Beaumont, bluntly asking him whether he wanted a production of Shaw's *Captain Brassbound's Conversion* or a show-case for Ingrid Bergman. 'A vehicle for Ingrid Bergman', had come the reply.

One day, Williams threw a temperament ('It's a dreadful production anyway') walked out of rehearsal, and was found by Frith who had followed him, clinging to a radiator by the stage-door sobbing, 'You're always picking on me.' Frith put an arm around his shoulder and suggested they have a cup of coffee together. He also, according to Williams, said that in future he would give him his notes in private. This kind and sensible offer was recorded in the diary as, 'of course he's mad', which was rather rich coming from Williams. He also records Frith ending every sentence with 'don't you see' – a verbal idiosyncrasy unnoticed by anyone else in either Frith's working or private life.

Ingrid Bergman finally found confidence with her lines during a word-run not attended by Frith. At this run, the cast started to move about as well. Once she realised that she had mastered the text at last, she was able to pull in the focus of the scene towards herself, and take the stage with authority. Absence of a director on such occasions is often a good idea. The actors suddenly have the freedom to experiment and thus make the final breakthrough. Perhaps Frith knew exactly what he was doing by not being there. It might have occurred to Kenneth Williams that here was an experienced director who directed with subtlety – not one who just gave the 'peripheral instruction' with which the comedian taunted Frith in print.

During the dress-rehearsal at the Cambridge Theatre, Williams had another bout of hysteria; this time not aimed at the director. After he had ranted and screamed for a while, Ingrid Bergman appeared in curlers with an old scarf around her head. 'Oh Kenny,' she cajoled, 'do stop this silly-nonsense-talk.'

It seems rather unfair on Frith that so much of Williams's silly-non-sense-talk found its way into his best-selling autobiography.

With his seeming inability to bear a grudge, Frith remembers Williams for being outstandingly and inspiringly funny at the first night party he gave for the cast at St James's Terrace. His improvised comic turns both in public and in private were pyrotechnical *tours de force,* but ones which could slip over the edge into mania. Perhaps he would have been happier at rehearsals had he admitted how rusty and insecure he felt. He had not been in a play for six years, and was never to do one again. His influence on twentieth-century British Classical acting though was considerable: Maggie Smith, Robert Stephens and Derek Jacobi being all so greatly indebted to his voice and style.

Joss Ackland and James Gibson gave the best performances in *Captain Brassbound*. Ingrid Bergman was very charming and watchable, but was hardly the Lady Cicely Waynflete that Shaw had in mind.

Most plays which are given revivals are of some merit. It was not that Frith was working on poor material, but that his productions were seen as catering for an older type of West End audience. If the removal of the Lord Chamberlain's powers made it now possible for almost complete freedom of expression in new work in the West End, Frith was increasingly being distanced from the contemporary. It seemed as if his role in the theatre was now to be that of the man brought in for revivals, adaptation of famous novels, and as a guest-director abroad: joining the breed of distinguished old has-beens, in other words. Perhaps too that after *My Darling Daisy* and *Captain Brassbound* his confidence, for a brief time, was not as unassailable as it had been once. His work sometimes lacked theatrical *frisson* and even had lapses of taste, while his casting, formerly so exact, was now sometimes questionable: not only because the right leading actors were unavailable, but in the supporting, particularly the younger, roles.

In 1982 he was seventy. Moyra Fraser and her husband Roger Lubbock gave a drinks party for his birthday in their Hampstead garden. For the first time in nearly forty years he was out of work in England; and it seemed as if his career here had effectively ended.

He had sold his much-loved house, 4 St James's Terrace, to a property developer. Christopher Taylor, in charge of negotiations, cleverly obtained the exact amount above the original offer that Frith had lost on *My Darling Daisy*. Symbolically, as if relinquishing his base was an omen, the house itself began to crumble – quite literally: lumps of plaster and masonry fell, and damp swamped the basement. The Italian couple who had looked after him moved on and he was left for the first time, servantless. At the end of the year he departed for Florida and a subsequent long stay in America. Jose Ferrer, then running the Coconut Grove Playhouse in Palm Beach, had invited him to direct Noel Coward's *Fallen Angels*.

Renaissance

During the 1980s, a more right-wing political climate and an emphasis on expensive living led to a nostalgia for the opulence of the past. Television productions such as *Brideshead Revisited* and *The Jewel in the Crown* both promoted and followed this trend. Duncan Weldon of Triumph Apollo was able to put on all-star revivals at the Haymarket and the Duke of York's. *The School for Scandal* in 1982 appealed so strongly to the spirit of the Sloane Ranger and the new upwardly mobile that it became the most sought-after ticket in London.

On his return from America, Frith moved into a temporary flat in the street behind his old house, and in 1984 Weldon invited him to direct Michael Redgrave's adaptation of Henry James's novella, *The Aspern Papers*, with Vanessa Redgrave, Wendy Hiller and Christopher Reeve – who had just made his name as Superman – in Redgrave's old part of Henry Jarvis. A link was provided not only with Henry James, whose *The Wings of the Dove* had been one of Frith's most noteworthy productions of the early sixties; but with Wendy Hiller (now a Dame) who had been in that production; and with Vanessa Redgrave, whose first West End appearance in *A Touch of the Sun* had been under Frith's direction. *The Aspern Papers* at the Haymarket, was West End Theatre at its best: magnificently designed and lit, and acted with authority and individuality by the whole company. The next year, again for Weldon, he directed *The Corn is Green* with Deborah Kerr as Miss Moffat. If she and Frith had hoped that this would be a repeat of their successful partnership a decade earlier, when Frank Harvey's version of Thomas Hardy's *The Day After the Fair* had played to packed houses in London, Canada and Australia, they were to be disappointed. Miss Kerr was most unhappy in a part which proved to be outside her range. The author, Emlyn Williams, had wanted to play this character, based on his own inspirational schoolmistress Miss Cooke, himself – even going to the lengths of having photographs taken of himself wearing a grey wig and an old dress, in the hope that Frith might agree to the scheme. Maybe the evening would have been more entertaining if he had. The choreography of the production: the bustle of the makeshift classroom in the Welsh front-room was faultless, and so were some of the supporting performances but, with the pace being continually slowed down by a leading lady unfamiliar with the words, the overall result lacked shape. Three years later, there was another Triumph Apollo offering at the Haymarket: J.M. Barrie's *The Admirable Crichton* with Rex Harrison as Lord Loam – but the situation here was difficult: Harrison was nearly blind, and Frith had been called in at the last moment to salvage the work of another director.

Frith took his leave as a manager (although not as a director) in 1989 with a new play *Screamers* at the Arts Theatre Club. This play had a homosexual theme, doubtless one of the reasons he had been drawn to it. (He had openly 'come out' in an interview with Sheridan Morley in *The Times* in 1985.) The demands the play made called for all Frith's best qualities: his skill at working with a writer (Antony Davison) on a new script; at giving a truthful and unflamboyant production; and at drawing a superlative performance out of his leading actor, William Osborne. And it was with this play, and the rest of his work during the 1980s, that Frith achieved recognition from a new generation of actors anxious to learn from the high standards of one of the last and most gifted representatives of his era.

Young actors working for Frith found that, far from being outmoded, his methods were revelatory. Used to university educated directors, strong on concept but of little use in giving help with the actual process of acting, they discovered, many for the first time, a director who could assist them in realising technically the content of a scene. William Osborne, whose sensitive and delicate performance as Rodney in *Screamers* was astonishingly impressive, is perhaps the last of the actors, Evans, Ashcroft and Scofield, for whom Frith felt a loving and fascinated admiration. In his turn, Osborne was, at first, predictably struck by Frith's energy and, in maturity, spareness with words. When asked to play the part by 'a very eccentric voice' on the telephone, he had never heard of Frith; and was then quite surprised, once he discovered how long Frith had been a manager, that the organisational side of the production had not been better planned. But in spite of this:

'His remarks are always so sharp and acute. He doesn't tell anecdotes well, but always gets to the balls of them. I like his lack of pretention – he got on with it: sometimes the cast wanted to work improvisationally but Frith said, "Come on, let's get on with it!" But that's good if you work instinctively as I do. I've worked with X [a very fashionable director] who is marvellous at concepts, but the guts of a scene are often to be found at the point where a scene changes. X was of no help there, Frith was. He can tap a word on the head which reveals a whole speech or scene. He's great at defining things, at helping you in your choices. Sometimes as an actor you need to put a bit of moisture in, in order to take it out later. Frith understood that. He cut the play very well: all corny sentiment was OUT. The production was very good on the text.' Had Frith contributed to his performance? 'Oh yes!' Why? 'Because he hit the nail on the head; I could have been lost.' I asked where he thought Frith's dislike of sentimentality might have come from.

'He's not sentimental about himself. People who are financially secure feel guilty about being sentimental. They're not up against the wall. Sentimentality keeps people going in hard times. He's chin-up because of his father who sounds aggressive and brutal.' He also liked the director's 'formal' way of working, i.e. blocking first. 'We worked in shorthand, going straight to the point. I hate a director saying about a speech, "I would like that laced with a little more regret." Osborne found himself "fascinated" by the old director 'because of the different class backgrounds, but he transcends that. I always feel I'm with someone young.'

He is perspicacious too about Frith's endless theatrical curiosity: 'He is frustrated at not quite grasping what is going on now. He sussed what was going on under the conventions of the day, so when the kitchen-sink stuff came along it wasn't really a shock to him, but he couldn't *own* that it was a different class and life-style. His way of being anarchic was more genteel and civilised.'

What are Frith Banbury's great virtues as a director? and why – apart from stamina and longevity – has his reputation surpassed and outlasted such contemporaries from the same theatrical stable as Peter Ashmore, Peter Glenville, and Murray Macdonald? Among his papers there is an undated cutting, an article from *Plays and Players,* presumably from the late fifties:

'It is difficult to say why Banbury's Productions have impressed so strongly for he has no gimmicks or idiosyncrasies of style that stamp his productions with something of his own personality. He is, in fact, so sensitive to the intentions of the authors whose plays he chooses that nothing seems to intrude between playwright and audience. He is an excellent "actors" producer too, directing his players with the utmost patience and drawing them out to give of their best.'

Frith's closest theatrical colleague, for the last forty years, Christopher Taylor says this:

His great strength is his total devotion to the work – to the text – not using it to show off. It's the old dictum of Stanislavsky: Frith is somebody in the theatre who really loves the art in himself; the art he can bring to something, rather than himself in art. He exemplifies that. This certainly carries through in his work with actors where he is infinitely tactful and very imaginative – like a wonderful squash professional I used to play with, who never got impatient, or showed he was tired with you however inadequate you were. If one way of persuading you to do a stroke didn't work, you could see his mind ticking over, and by the time you had your next lesson with him, he would have thought of a different imaginative approach, a different image to present you with to try to persuade you to get your swing the right way. Frith's like that with actors.

Paul Scofield, too, stresses this identification with the actor:

He was easy to work with, and as an actor himself was full of interest in the contribution that can be made by the actor. As I remember, and, as I write this I remember, that one of his favourite comments was 'How interesting' with the emphasis very much on the first syllable. It was not necessarily a favourable comment! Frith I think is a good and wise man, a good friend. I recall not always being in agreement with him and if, as can happen, I ever ignored him or went against his directorial wishes – he never harboured any rancour or any (perfectly justifiable) complaint.

Certainly he has integrity, that accolade given to too many who do not deserve it. Lies on stage deeply offend him. To Noel Coward's dismay he turned down *Waiting in the Wings,* a play about old actresses in a retirement home, because he thought it did not tell the truth about old age.

Frith has fulfilled nearly all his ambitions. One of his only regrets is not having directed *John Gabriel Borkman,* the last act of which, I think he considers one of the great cosmic experiences of world drama.

As a director, whose career spans the greater part of the twentieth century, Frith might conceivably be criticised for missing out on an entire theatrical movement: the kitchen-sink – but it is more constructive to confine criticism to work he has done. What were his weaknesses?

Like many Jewish people, he finds it difficult to take 'yes' for an answer: there always *must* be something else to discover in a text: another angle, a greater depth. In so exploring he can lose sight of the whole. Christopher Taylor explains:

> The big weakness with Frith – partly because he identifies so strongly with actors giving them confidence, and finding so much in a scene, exploring it in such depth, and discovering so many unexpected facets – is that in their excitement, and in their probing, they can lose sight of the whole. They can't see the wood for the trees. I've sat there thinking, 'How can they reconcile what they're doing now with what they're going to be facing two scenes on, which is going to give the lie to all this?' – but Frith usually gets wrenched back at the next run-through.

It is true that sometimes, in conversation with Frith, the twigs of the branches of the trees are being so minutely examined that one wonders whether he remembers that there is a wood there at all. William Osborne considered that in *Screamers,* by ensuring the maximum detail and veracity of content, his production thereby lost out on style. Yet he certainly can be a stylish director: knowing the correct form for a particular play. In *The Wings of the Dove,* no white was seen in any of the costumes, stage decorations or props (even the writing paper was coloured) until the dying Milly Theale's entrance in a white dress in the last act. This effect must have enhanced the 'moment' without the audience being quite conscious as to why. Yet, paradoxically, that brings up my second criticism: that in his studious avoidance of cliché in acting and direction, his productions can miss obvious theatricality. There are sometimes too few 'moments': points where all stage action and emotion are suddenly crystallised. But his theatrical instincts are marvellous, and deficiencies in style or theatricality never take place in his work when he allows himself time to stand back and away from his burrowings for detail and truth.

In a recent radio interview he said something that was, for me, deeply revealing: 'Truth is relative; one man's truth is another man's lie'. He is like Bacon's 'jesting Pilate' I thought. For some of us truth is *not* relative – truth is truth and universally recognisable because it *is* truth. A moral absolute. Who is right? I have learnt never to dismiss a maxim of Frith's simply because it jars at the time. Flexibility of mind, and the humility to revise former profoundly held beliefs, are two of Frith's great personal virtues. The closed mind is the start of cerebral atrophy. In his eighties, it is not only Frith's long-term memory which is excellent (usual in an old man) but his short-term memory is prodigious as well – and that is because his mind has always been kept open.

It is an indelible truth that the greatest influence of his life, and the person to whom he owes his successful career is his father, the Admiral – but that is not a truth Frith welcomes.

His rebellion against his father made him embrace the theatre; his contempt for his father's values made him into an artist; by turning the Admiral into a joke-figure he became a mimic and a raconteur. But also his wish for his father's approval gave him the drive to make a success of his life and career – subconscious perhaps – but a determination to prove the Admiral's supposed opinion of him wrong. Admiral Banbury died in 1951, during the run of *Waters of the Moon,* so he just lived long enough to see his son become an unquestioned success.

The greatest gift that his father gave him was the one of naval discipline – by which Frith has always lived his life. It has been this discipline which has meant that having independent means, usually such a hindrance for a creative artist, has for him not been so. Financial security has only been the underpinning for emotional security. It is that discipline which has given him his staying power. It is why Frith has had twenty working years more than most of his contemporaries. It is the discipline which has kept him free from self-indulgence: one has only to contrast his old age with Binkie Beaumont's decline and death at sixty-four.

The truth is that Frith has done the Admiral proud.

Coda

In his seventies, Frith learnt to cook and fend for himself for the first time, with an admirable alacrity. His move to his new flat, in a smart apartment block exactly on the site of his old house, coincided, almost exactly, with the Michaelmas Summer of his career. A gleaming new phoenix arising from elegant old ashes; the apartment, on first sight, is straight from *Dynasty.* Frith's modern artistic tastes are a matter of surprise to some people. They expect quite a different kind of flat: one full of antique furniture and personal mementos. But Frith does not look back in that way. Always interested in what is around the *next* corner, his furniture is strikingly modern (the dining-room table and chairs might have been designed by Gordon Craig for the Banquet Scene in *Macbeth).* Through Christopher Taylor's influence, he has been a careful collector of modern art and an early buyer of David Hockney's works – in the days when such paintings could be acquired for a few hundred pounds.

These tastes also embrace music. The grand piano is his most valued possession and much of his solitude is spent playing it. There is little of the nineteenth-century romantic about Frith – and here he is unlike most of his generation who, because of parental influence, have a fundamentally romantic appreciation of art. Both by temperament and taste Frith is different: Handel and Debussy are favoured composers – one eighteenth century; the other, at least in spirit, twentieth. Mahler is a villain: sentimental and overblown, the overall sweep of whose music quite fails to carry Frith away. Romantic opera, too, is not really appreciated; and that must be the main reason why such a musically gifted theatre director has done no work to speak of on the lyric stage.

He continues, too, his assiduous theatre going. No one I know visits the theatre as often, to both the mainstream and the fringe. And his enthusiasms for, and perceptions about the latest actor or writer, are seldom conventional and always stimulating.

Christopher Taylor now lives in the apartment opposite, and their relationship seems to be one where the complexities, amazing to outsiders, are necessary for both parties. Without question he was the love of Frith's life, but this passion was not reciprocated. A fact that Frith seems to have accepted without rancour.

It is impertinent – and impossible – for an outsider to analyse the relationship between two people; but to outsiders, it seems that Christopher is understandably irritated when it is assumed that he and Frith are a 'couple'; while Frith worries about Christopher's supposed misanthropy and love of solitude. But equally obvious are the bonds between them which look strong enough to withstand friction. Although Frith likes to cast himself as the stable one during the *froideurs,* he is quite capable of needling people into childish behaviour so he can be seen in a calm and mature light. Frith can be alternately wonderful and infuriating, and never more infuriating than when he turns situations to his own advantage.

Professionally I think Frith's behaviour has nearly always been above reproach, and Christopher is right to cite him as the paradigm of Stanislavsky's exhortation for artistic ethics in the theatre.

Two tributes from those I have spoken to remain with me: as she walked me to her front door, Dame Wendy Hiller's, 'Frith was at the very centre of what is best in commercial theatre – as a man, actor, director and manager;' and Robert Bolt's: 'He was more of a gentleman than any other person I have met.'

Appendix I

Frith Banbury's Career from Who's Who in the Theatre?

BANBURY, Frith, actor, director and manager; b. Plymouth, Devon, 4 May, 1912; s. of Rear-Admiral Frederick Arthur Frith Banbury, R.N., and his wife Winifred (Fink); e. Stowe School and Hertford College, Oxford; studied for the stage at the Royal Academy of Dramatic Art; made his first appearance on the stage at the Shaftesbury Theatre, 15 June, 1933, walking-on in 'If I Were You'; after touring, Jan., 1934, in 'Richard of Bordeaux', appeared at the Shaftesbury, May, 1934, as Barry Green in 'The Dark Tower'; at the New, Nov., 1934, played the Courier in 'Hamlet'; appeared at the Ambassadors', Mar., 1935 in 'Monsieur Moi'; Arts, June, 1935, in 'Love of Women'; Duke of York's, Oct., 1935 in 'The Hangman', and at the Little, Dec., 1935, played the Unicorn in 'Alice Through the Looking Glass'; appeared at the Perranporth Summer Theatre, 1936-8; at the Gate Theatre, Sept., 1936, played Eustace in 'Oscar Wilde'; Victoria Palace, Dec., 1936, Gerald Perkins in 'Adventure'; Arts, Feb., 1937, Michael in 'First Night'; next appeared at the Players' Theatre, Jan., 1938, in 'Ridgeway's Late Joys'; Vaudeville, Oct., 1938, Peter Thropp in 'Goodness, How Sad!'; Chanticleer, Nov., 1939, in 'Let's Face It'; Apollo, Jan., 1940, Quetch in 'Follow My Leader'; Comedy, Apr., 1940, appeared in *revue* for the first time in 'New Faces'; at Stratford-upon-Avon, Oct., 1940, played Algernon in 'The Importance of Being Earnest' and Horace Bream in 'Sweet Lavender'; 'Q', Jan., 1941, in 'Rise Above It'; Ambassadors', July, 1941, in 'The New Ambassadors' Revue'; St Martin's, Feb., 1942, played Peter Blakiston in 'Jam To-day'; Ambassadors', July, 1942, appeared in 'Light and Shade'; from Jan., 1943, played a season at the Arts Theatre, Cambridge, appearing as Gregers Werle in 'The Wild Duck', Quex in 'The Gay Lord Quex', Muishkin in 'The Idiot', the Actor in 'The Guardsman', Joseph in 'The School for Scandal', Sneer in 'The Critic', Cusins in 'Major Barbara', etc.; Westminster, Sept., 1943, played Astrov in 'Uncle Vanya'; appeared at the Arts Theatre, London, May-July, 1944, as Lord Foppington in 'A Trip to Scarborough' and Cyril Beverley in 'Bird in Hand'; Palace, Dec., 1944, the White Rabbit and

White Knight in 'Alice in Wonderland'; at the Citizens Theatre, Glasgow, Feb., 1945, Hlestakov in 'The Government Inspector'; Piccadilly, June, 1945, the Gestapo Man in 'Jacobowsky and the Colonel'; toured on the Continent, Sept., 1945, as Colbert in 'While the Sun Shines'; Globe, Dec., 1945, took over the same part; Lyric, Hammersmith, Nov., 1946 played Capt. Hawtree in 'Caste', and appeared in this part at the Duke of York's, Jan., 1947; has since directed the following plays: 'Dark Summer', 1947; 'Shooting Star', (co-presented) 1949; 'The Holly and the Ivy', 'Always Afternoon', and 'The Old Ladies', 1950; 'The Silver Box', 'Waters of the Moon', 'All The Year Round', 1951; 'The Deep Blue Sea' (London and Broadway) and 'The Pink Room', 1952; 'A Question of Fact', 1953; 'Marching Song' and 'Love's Labour's Lost' (Old Vic), 1954; 'The Bad Seed', 1955; 'The Good Sailor', and 'The Diary of Anne Frank', 1956; 'A Dead Secret', and 'Flowering Cherry' (co-presented) 1957; 'A Touch of the Sun', 'The Velvet Shotgun' (co-presented) and 'Moon on a Rainbow Shawl', 1958; 'The Ring of Truth', and 'Flowering Cherry' (Broadway), 1959; 'The Tiger and the Horse', 'Mister Johnson', 1960; 'A Chance in the Daylight', 'Life of the Party' (co-presented) 1960; 'Big Fish, Little Fish', 1962; 'The Unshaven Cheek' (Edinburgh Festival), 'The Wings of the Dove', 1963; 'I Love You, Mrs Patterson' (co-presented), 1964; 'Do Not Pass Go' (co-presented) (New York), 'The Right Honourable Gentleman' (New York), 1965; 'Do Not Pass Go', 1966; 'Howard's End', 'Dear Octopus', 1967; 'Enter a Free Man', 'A Day in the Death of Joe Egg' (Tel Aviv), and 'Le Valet' (Paris), 1968; 'On the Rocks' (Dublin), 1969; 'My Darling Daisy' (co-presented), 'The Winslow Boy', 1970; 'Captain Brassbound's Conversion', 'Reunion in Vienna' (Chichester and London), 1971; 'The Day After the Fair' (co-presented), 1972; 'The Day After the Fair' (co-presented) (America), 'Glasstown' (co-presented), 1973; 'Ardele' (co-presented), 'On Approval' (South Africa), 1975; 'On Approval' (Canada), 1976; 'On Approval' (London), 1977; 'Equus' (Kenya), 'The Aspern Papers' (America), 1978; 'The Day After the Fair' (Australia), 1979; 'Motherdear', 1980; 'Dear Liar' (co-presented), 1982; 'The Aspern Papers', 1984; 'The Corn is Green' (Old Vic), 1985; 'The Admirable Crichton', 1988; 'Screamers' (co-presented), 1989.

Recreation: Piano.

Appendix II

Dido Milroy and Frith Banbury's Mise en Scene for 'Waters of the Moon'

Assuming that we are in 1950, that means John Daly (who is twenty-two) was born in 1928 which means that he was called up for the army in 1946. He could therefore have been invalided out in '47. *But* it is highly unlikely, with his chest, that he would ever have got through the initial medical at the time of his call-up. It would be far more probable if his 'chest' were to have been discovered *at* this same medical, and therefore in 1946. This, however, is up to the author, it is just that it makes a difference of one year in the length of time that Mrs Daly has been running this house as an hotel. For the purposes of the play, obviously the longer the better. In any case the Dalys have *only been here 'since John's chest'* (i.e. since '46 or '47).

*

The late Mr Daly and Mrs Daly lived somewhere else – an altogether more urban district; not London, the Midlands perhaps and nowhere near the West Country – where Mr Daly was in business or maybe he was a solicitor. He wasn't rich or especially successful, but he made enough to give his children a decent education and things were quite comfortable for his wife who had never really thought about money, being quite content with her lot, until a) her husband died and b) John became ill – two events which happened quite close together.

Mrs Daly was slightly her husband's social inferior; he was 'well connected' on his mother's side, well connected enough that is to inherit this rather lovely, late 17th – early 18th-century Palladian gentleman's residence from a spinster aunt who died somewhere around 1930.

There was never any question of the Dalys corning to live in this house which was already quite profitably let (unfurnished) on a long lease to good tenants at the time of the aunt's death. They weren't rich enough, Mr Daly had his job in the Midlands, and anyway all their roots and interests were there. Nor, even had they been able to afford it, was this a part of the country that especially appealed to them and this wasn't their kind of house (certainly not Mrs Daly's; she preferred something modern, labour-saving, more compact and far less pretentious and 'fancy'). *Torbridge Court* was just a windfall, a bit of real estate that represented another couple of hundred or so to add to the Daly's modest annual income. It was jokingly referred to as 'Our Stately Home in Devonshire', but it meant no more to Mrs Daly and the children than 'Our Railway Shares'; what it *might* have meant to Mr Daly is another story.

In 1939-40 the lease expired and the tenants decamped to America. The empty house was immediately requisitioned. In 1944 it was empty again though rather the worse for wear. It was now impossible to let; the demand for big houses had gone. Anyway it needed doing up. Mr Daly endeavoured to sell it but there were no takers. This (distinctly dilapidated) 'historic gem' was still on the agent's books when Mr Daly died in 1945.

In 1946-7 (preferably 6) it was discovered that John was ill and must live in the country. The house was unsold (and therefore a dead loss). Mrs Daly did not have enough money to buy a cottage or a bungalow in some healthy spot (which is what she would have liked) and keep John and herself without either of them working, so she decided to come and live here and try to run it as an hotel. With the proceeds of their existing home, she did the house up as cheaply as she could and bought hotel furniture from sale-rooms (this accounts for the awful cocktail lounge furniture which should war with the beautiful and ornate architectural proportions and ornamentation of the house) and set up here calling it the *Torbridge Court Hotel*. This type of house is usually called 'Something Court' in the West country; the manors are older, mostly Tudor.

Mrs Daly does not like the house: the back premises are dark and inconvenient, the boiler is too small and 'it's not what she's been used to'. She does not see it as beautiful; she simply puts up with it because of John's chest and because it provides a means for eking out a bit of cash, but it's all a carking care.

Evelyn does not like the house, because it is associated with the loss of her fiancé, with John's illness, with taking orders from people she does not like and with drudgery. She also suffers from the back premises and even more from the ornamental niches and italianate embellishments which might have been specially constructed to collect dust.

John loathes the house. To him it spells exile, prison and frustration.

There is no sympathy between the Dalys and the house. They have demeaned it and it has demeaned them.

Humiliation is one of the corner-stones of this play.

The set must *not* be a 'little room' (Mrs Whyte: Act 1 ac.1 p.5) or a 'little sitting-room' (Mrs Daly: Act 1 sc.1 p.10). It should be one of the principal rooms with fine proportions and lovely windows and doors and fireplace and cornice, in fact masses of architectural stimmung. In this lovely framework or background I see typical hotel furniture; club arm-chairs and settees, upholstered en suite in leatherette and railway carriage material, grouped round nasty tables, nasty neutral beige-caca-coloured curtains and a large red turkey carpet, a hotel double-sided desk etc.

*

Here follows a list of the more obvious places in the text for bringing about a cleared definition of the *mise en scene:*

Act 1 sc.1 p.5 MRS WHYTE: ' . . . *cooped up in this little room* . . . '
The room should not be 'little'.

Act 1 sc.1 p.10 MRS DALY:' . . . *This is the little sitting-room* . . .' See above. Here is the first opportunity for a comment on the house from Helen. If Mrs Daly were to say *'This is the lounge'* and Helen, taking in the noble proportions of the room before she notices the ghastly furniture were to reply *'But it's far too nice a room to call a lounge – such an awful word don't you think? And it's got a fire!'* After all Helen doesn't yet know that Mrs Daly is the owner and anyway she always says exactly what comes into her head.

Act 1 sc.1 p.11 MRS DALY: ' . . . *no bed in the single room* . . . ' Better to say 'dressing-room' it sounds more like that sort of house, and anyway there must be more than one single room.

Act 1 sc.1 p.19 HELEN: ' . . . *Can you imagine living here . . . just look at that dreadful thing.'* This passage wants reframing to build up what the house was and what, from its anach-ronistic furniture and other obvious indications it has become. Helen begins here to speculate and Julius can enlighten her quite a bit. He knows the story from his intimacy with Evelyn.

Act 1 sc.2 p.3   Robert and Mrs Whyte scene. The house can be intro-
                 duced here from Mrs Whyte's point of view. Why she
                 came to live here (apart from its being cheap). At least
                 it was a country house; affinity with her own Manor in
                 Wiltshire.

Act 1 sc.2 p.5   HELEN: ' . . . *I'm beginning to like it here* . . . ' Something
                 here about the house and its atmosphere and beauty in
                 spite of what's happened to it. And then straight on about
                 the boiler not being big enough (hot water system con-
                 temporary) and the house not being meant for an hotel.
                 A bit more of the story can slip out here.

Act 1 sc.2 p.8   TONETTA: ' . . . *Hello darling! We've had a ridiculous*
                 time . . . ' Something here about the garden like this:
                 TONETTA: ' . . . *It's lovely out there, all sugary and crisp.*
                 The garden's enchanting with all these grottos and statues
                 and that absurd little ornamental lake. It's just like some-
                 where in Italy with the colours frozen out. We found an old
                 pair of skates in the stable . . . *etc.*'

Act 2 sc.1 p.3   HELEN: ' . . . *Once, of course, it was a private house* . . .'
                 This fact will have been stated much earlier, probably
                 in Act 1 sc.1 p.19, which means that if Julius has said
                 it to Helen, Helen will not now be saying it to Julius.
                 But this is certainly the moment in the play when
                 Helen should enter discussing the house and continue
                 to hold forth about it and sum up the situation. All
                 this passage which includes the Helen – Robert duo-
                 logue (Act 2 sc.1 ps.6-8) lends itself to this. The key to
                 what Helen feels (in her case this is synonymous with
                 what she thinks) about *Torbridge Court* and its inhabit-
                 ants is to be found in her words on p.4 ' . . . *The world*
                 is getting duller and duller . . . ' What has happened
                 to this house is what is happening to the world and
                 vice versa. She draws the parallel. This house ought to
                 belong to people who love it. It was built for that. To
                 be lived in by one family who would appreciate it and
                 cherish it and beautify it. Now it is merely 'somewhere
                 to go' for an ill-assorted collection of people who none
                 of them 'belong' and who wouldn't care less about it.

Mrs Daly to nurse a sick son in and try to squeeze money from.

Evelyn to be a sex-starved drudge in.

John to be ill in.

Mrs Whyte to economise in.

The Colonel and Mrs Ashworth to come to because they've nowhere else to go.

Julius to be a refugee in.

The Lancasters to wait for their car to be hauled out of the ditch in.

The house was *created* for a small unit of people to be happy in.

It is now *used, faute de mieux,* for a larger disunited group of people to be unhappy in . . . Oh dear! *What* a depressing thought! And *How* like the world!

Act 2 sc.1 p.11   The Tonetta-John duologue. Any details in the story of the Dalys and their relations with the house that have still to be told can be introduced quite easily and naturally here. Very little alteration of the existing text would be necessary, just a few insertions and a little building up and the cutting of John's lines on p.13: ' . . . *Every now and then mother tries to sell but the sales always fall through* . . . '.

After which the house ought to be able to look after itself.

Appendix III

Robert Flemyng on 'Marching Song'

M*arching Song* was the third play of John Whiting's to be presented in London, and opened at the St Martin's Theatre in April 1954. His two previous plays were *Penny for a Song* and *Saint's Day,* both produced in London in 1951. Neither of these plays had been a commercial success, but both had aroused much interest, and in the later case controversy, and Mr Whiting's work had gathered a number of admirers in the professional theatre.

Mr Whiting was at one time a professional actor himself, which may well have contributed to his wonderfully pronounced sense of theatre, and he was a member of Sir John Gielgud's company in 1951 during Sir John's production of *The Winter's Tale.* About this time he gave *Marching Song* to Sir John to read. The latter was impressed by the play and caused it to be bought by Tennent Productions Ltd, of which he was a director, and which was at that time a non-profit-making company controlled by the great theatrical firm of H.M. Tennent Ltd.

It is perhaps necessary to explain here that between the end of the war in 1945 and 1958 (when all taxation on theatre seats in Great Britain was abolished) there were a number of these non-profit-making companies, the most important of which was Tennent Productions, in which the capital for such companies was privately subscribed and controlled, but in which taxation was abolished provided also that profits (if any) were ploughed back into further similar productions. Since the abolition of tax on all theatre seats such companies have of course become obsolete.

During the years 1952 and 1953 Tennent Productions retained an option on the play but Sir John, I think it would be fair to say, felt that the play was somewhat too difficult to appeal to a wide audience, and since he had at the time a great popular success with *A Day by the Sea* (N.C. Hunter) he finally decided not to do the play himself.

Towards the end of 1953 I was playing at the Duke of York's Theatre in *The Moon is Blue* when Mr John Perry, one of the directors of H.M.

Tennent Ltd, gave me the play to read. I was immediately and tremendously impressed by it, and experience has led me firmly to believe that one's first impression of a new script, however subject to modifications later, is on the whole the correct one. It seemed to me that the play was enormously exciting theatrically and at the same time immensely stimulating intellectually, not only on the subject of war itself but on love and death and indeed over a wide area of human involvement and responsibility. I accordingly reported to Mr Perry that I found the play of single importance and substance, but I did make two reservations – firstly that I was unsure of its success commercially, and secondly that the part of Forster might well demand Sir John or Sir Laurence if the play was fully to be realised. I could only say that I believed in the play completely, and that I would regard any chance of acting in it as a distinction.

Finally in late 1953 Mr Hugh Beaumont, the Managing Director of H.M. Tennent Ltd, ordered the production of the play and as always he and Mr Perry gave every possible support and encouragement. Miss Diana Wynyard was also much impressed by the play and agreed to play Catherine de Troyes, and Mr Frith Banbury undertook the direction.

The play was cast and went into rehearsal in January 1954 and opened at the Prince of Wales Theatre, Cardiff, on the 8th of February 1954.

Rehearsals proved very exciting, and as with all good plays the more one worked the more one found layer after layer of meaning beneath each speech and each scene.

In addition one became aware of a rhythm and tension in the writing which is always the mark of the born dramatist. Actors recognise this quality at once and respond to it accordingly, but meet it only too seldom. Terence Rattigan has it to a marked degree – *The Browning Version* is a model of dramatic dialogue – sparse, lean, taut and immensely actable. Of course Mr Tennessee Williams has it. It can extend to quite minor plays. Some of the comedies of the late Mr John van Druten appear on reading to be thin and trite, but they are at their best immensely actable, and a competent actor should be able to hold an audience firmly on the edge of laughter and sentiment. Among the new dramatists it is to my mind the quality that so very much distinguishes the work of Mr Harold Pinter.

There were however difficulties. The very definite and somewhat curious rhythm of the dialogue led us into a tendency to sound portentous. I never quite understood why this was, unless it could have been that we found it difficult to resist enjoying the theatrical effect which the writing seemed to be making. This is a trap that is always fatal, and for some reason particularly difficult in this instance to resist.

For example in the first act where the Chancellor, superbly played by the late Ernest Thesiger, confronts Forster and intimates to him that it is essential for him to kill himself, it appeared to us imperative that the scene should not be played for emotional effect. I remain convinced that this approach was correct, and yet it led paradoxically to the impression that the play was cold.

Again in Forster's great speech in Act II it seemed to me essential that the speech should be delivered objectively, almost as if it was an experience that had happened to someone else, despite the fact that it contains a description of the events that led directly to the climax of Forster's life. It is a wonderful speech – indeed on the first night in Cardiff, when I delivered the lines about the shooting of the boy, the audience gave a gasp of horror such as I have seldom heard in a theatre – but in spite of the fact that they were gripped and shocked, they were not moved by Forster's personal predicament. Whether the fault was entirely mine, or whether there was a certain lack of sympathy in the part of an English audience for the type of soldier in Forster's position, I cannot altogether be sure. I think I am right in saying that the play was received with more sympathy in Germany, where not only was Forster played by Gustaf Gründgens, but it might be thought that the audience were more sympathetic to the character, and to say nothing of the fact that German audiences are trained to *listen* far better than English and American audiences.

Incidentally, as Mr Whiting has remarked in the preface to the collected edition of his plays, many people talked a great deal of rubbish about this speech, reading into it all manner of symbolism. In fact he meant it to be taken factually. I always regarded it as such, and attempted to play it accordingly. And indeed two years later at Suez and in Hungary such events were realised in history.

Then again the placing of this speech, coming as it does half way through Act II, posed another problem which I was not able completely to solve. The sequence of events describing the battle is broken at the point where the audience want to know why Forster lost his power of decision and waited before continuing the attack. The resolution of this situation is not disclosed until the scene between Forster and the young Captain Hurst in Act III. This piece of construction is of course entirely legitimate and extremely effective, but after the effect of the big speech I found it difficult to hold the audience through the latter half of the second Act, containing as it does some highly sophisticated argument and thought. It tended to become anti-climatic, and though an anti-climax can be wonderfully effective in the theatre it is generally required that it should be short and sharp. Here, however, the play turns to the central issue of Forster's suicide, and I found the scene between Forster and the Chancellor, where as a result of his meeting with the girl Dido, Forster declares his intention to live and face his trial, extremely difficult. I thought it a wonderful scene, and intellectually and emotionally I understood it completely, but I could not always hold an audience through it. It is somewhat oblique and I felt might have been slightly cut. Banbury however did not agree with me on the question of cutting.

Similarly in Act III after Forster's death, when the play is resolved and the thread of the dilemma snapped, the final curtain comes after a long dying fall. This was certainly fascinating, and as a part of the play's orchestration, I think correct, but, beautifully though the scene was played by Miss Wynyard and Miss Munday (Dido), it did tend, in my view, to be slightly too long. But this may not be so.

The opening at Cardiff was for us a remarkable experience. Naturally the first performance of any new play is always remarkable for actors, anxious after weeks of rehearsal to find out how the play will go and what precisely is effective and what is not. It leads to an entirely new phase in the history of any play, and to more weeks of altering and polishing, and adding and rejecting. Usually, however, one has some definite idea of how a play is likely to be received, and it is often a matter of confirming one's hopes or realising one's fears. Here we literally had no idea what sort of reception we would have. In the event it was more than encouraging. The audience were utterly still and receptive and accorded the play a most warm welcome, and the notices in Cardiff were good.

We continued to tour the English provinces for some eight weeks. As I remember, though, we worked hard at our own performances, not much alteration was made to the play. The receptions and notices varied from town to town, but considering that it might be termed a somewhat difficult play, they were encouraging and business, though far from good, was not disastrous.

The opening in London at the St Martin's Theatre was full of interest and respect but somewhat cool. I think it is true to say that in London critics can sometimes make a play, and quite often kill a play, but I do not think that the effect of their notices is based directly on the actual report made nor the opinions expressed, but far more on the general atmosphere that they emanate. Respectful notices can kill, and bad notices can sometimes do the opposite, or at any rate, can be safely ignored. In this case they were of the former kind, and business was extremely poor. Despite this, Mr Beaumont and Mr Perry kept the play on for six weeks and gave us every chance, but to no avail. Nevertheless the audiences, though small, were often extremely appreciative; many actors were most enthusiastic about the play if not always about the playing and production; some people came two and three times. I think that it may fairly be said that it was something of a *succès d'estime,* and that it finally secured John Whiting's position as one of the leading dramatists of the day, a position he was to consolidate some years later in 1961 when he wrote *The Devils* for the Royal Shakespeare Company.

For my part I was subjected to much criticism, and I think that in feeling I did lack the full authority and ruthlessness that the part demanded and that technically I did not bring enough variety of tone and inflection. I was accused of being cold, and of being on one note. Some of this was deliberate and some of it was not. There were numerous problems which, as an actor, I could not solve – chiefly, I agree, the question of variety. The character of Forster seemed to impose on me a certain feeling of one who was already dead, apart from the briefly glimpsed feeling for life gained through his contact with Dido, and this perhaps made my own performance monotonous and the play cold. Nevertheless, it remains for me a landmark in my own life, and if I have regrets that I did not carry it off better than I did, I have none that I attempted it, apart from the fact that I wish I could have served Mr Whiting more fully.

Robert Flemyng,
Brighton, 1962

Notes

Preface

xv 'deeply interested and earnest young men' . . . Sir Henry Irving, speech in Edinburgh 1881

xv Robert Morley was never directed by F.B., although he was part manager of Wynyard Browne's *The Ring of Truth* in 1959. Their friendship was close but not always serene. Morley said, 'our bone of contention was that we both cast each other in smaller roles than we thought we deserved'.

Introduction

i Deeply Interested and Earnest Young Mm

4 F.B.'s sister Joan (1918 – 1979) later married Peter Cadogan.

5 The contemporary who remembers F.B.'s father is Geoffrey Wright.

6 Mrs Patrick Campbell 1865 – 1940 actress and *monstre sacré* of the English stage. The original Paula in Pinero's *The Second Mrs Tanqueray* and Eliza in *Pygmalion,* which Shaw wrote for her and with whom he was platonically in love.

8 *The Chinese Bungalow,* 1925 by Marion Osmond and James Corbet.

8 *Carnival,* Matheson Lang's adaptation of Compton MacKenzie's novel (1912).

ii Training with Joan Littlewood

11 Some young actors of the 1930s, like Robert Flemyng, had this opinion of Violet Vanbrugh.

11 *A Royal Divorce* 1891, a Romantic Drama by W.G. Willis and C.G. Collingham.

Part One: An Actor in the Thirties

i The Worst Unicorn I Ever Had

17 F.B.'s advice to young actors was told me by his ex-secretary Marjorie Sisley.

17 Frith tried to join the Liverpool Repertory Company in 1934.

17 There were, of course, a few excellent new plays coming from the provinces to London in the 1930s. Walter Greenwood and Ronald Gow's

Love on the Dole from the Birmingham Repertory Theatre introducing Wendy Hiller in 1935 is an obvious example.

18 *Richard of Bordeaux* was Gielgud's first collaboration with the design team of Motley, whose colourful sets and costumes contributed much to the play's success. It also started the Commercial managements' policy towards Gielgud later crystallised by Binkie Beaumont and John Perry as 'Give her a crown, and shove her on'.

22 The People's National Theatre had not yet produced its two great successes which both dated from the following year, 1936. These were *Lady Precious Stream,* H.S. Hsiung's adaptation of a traditional Chinese play, and *Whiteoaks,* Mazo de la Roche's adaptation of her novel about a Canadian family warring over the will of the a hundred-and-two-year-old grandmother, played by Nancy Price. There is a sensitive grandson called Finch (who receives a love letter from another man) and the play is now considered one of the earliest to take a homosexual character seriously. F.B. was shortlisted for this part but lost out to his R.A.D.A. contemporary, Stephen Haggard. He does not remember being particularly struck by the homosexual aspect.

ii *Eagerness and Concentration*

25 Richard Ainley was the son of the great Romantic actor Henry Ainley; Constance Lorne later achieved fame in the Drayton and Hare farces, British Films, and, in real life as Robertson Hare's girl friend. She acted for F.B. in *The Ring of Truth;* Nicholas Phipps was a high comedy actor and author of Revue numbers like *Maud (We're Rotten to the Core),* for Beatrice Lillie. He came to a sad alcoholic end; Pamela Brown, who later acted for F.B. in *A Question of Fact,* was an excellent actress who died too young; Pauline Letts is an excellent actress.

25 'Flat above a boot shop': this was Robert Morley's description of the home in which Peter Bull said they would all be living.

25 Robert Morley's *Responsible Gentleman* written with Sewell Stokes Heinemann 1966, says F.B. began playing small roles at Perranporth.

27 Robert Morley and Norman Marshall worked together again. Morley played the Prince Regent in Norman Ginsbury's *The First Gentleman* which was directed by Marshall. Said Morley: 'Norman Marshall was very shy. One day during rehearsals Sewell (Stokes) found him sitting on one of the staircases at the Savoy (Theatre) of which there are many and said: 'I thought you were directing,' and he said, 'I can't direct Robert in this scene he's so terrible.' I was very fond of Norman who was very sweet'. It seemed to be a habit of Marshall's who some years later left the auditorium when F.B. was rehearsing Adolphus Cussins in the final scene of *Major Barbara,* because he did not think his acting bearable.

29 Peter Brook directed Robert Morley in Nancy Mitford's translation of André Roussin's *The Little Hut,* in 1950.

31 Elsa Lanchester became, of course, Mrs Charles Laughton, and Harold Scott later acted for F.B. in *Waters of the Moon,* and *A Dead Secret.* The Cave of

Harmony was the song-and-supper room in Thackeray's *The Newcomes*.

31 When the Players Theatre moved to Albermarle Street during the war, plays were put on again after the Music Hall.

32 The cast of *Let's Face It*, were Michael Wilding, British film star and second husband of Elizabeth Taylor; Dorothy Hyson, daughter of the musical comedy actress Dorothy Dickson and later wife of Sir Anthony Quayle; Charles Heslop, a very successful and amusing comedian; and Bunty Payne, who married the legendary boxer Kid Berg and afterwards a Jamaican judge.

34 F.B. had taken William Douglas Home for a walk in St James's Park shortly after the outbreak of war. F.B. warned him that once a member of the services he would have to obey orders unconditionally and that his conscience could play no part. It was not advice that he took.

Part Two: A Conchie in the Theatre of the Forties

i Revue and After

40 In *Rise Above It* F.B. sang a 'most unsuitable' romantic number dressed in Regency Buck's clothes with top hat and cane to the very pretty Carole Lynne. In 1983, during the run of *The Aspern Papers*, F.B. took his designer, Carl Toms, for a celebratory dinner at the Mirabelle where also dining were Sir Bernard and Lady Delfont. 'I'll give her a fright,' thought F.B., went up behind her and sang this terrible song. The poor woman 'nearly had a stroke'.

42 'Bezer' was Benedicta (real name Kathleen) de Bezer; jazz pianist, and later religious painter, indeed religious obsessive, who always wore either trousers or a monk's habit. She developed a passion for Antonia White *(Frost in May.)* Susan Chitty, (Antonia White's daughter) says in her edition of her mother's diaries, 'Benedicta now church-crawled with the passion that she had once pub-crawled'.

47 *The Gay Lord Quex* by Max Beerbohm; *The Wild Duck* by Henrik Ibsen; *The Idiot* by Dostoevsky; *The Guardsman* by Ferenc Molnar

47 James Bridie wrote to Flora Robson after her Old Vic Lady Macbeth telling her that when she said:

The raven itself is hoarse,

That croaks the fatal entrance of Duncan Under my battlements.

That he expected her to add that she was about to give it some Soane's Lineament; and called Dame Edith Evans giving one of her greatest performances in his *Daphne Laureola* 'gloriously miscast'.

52 F.B. played Ferdinand Gadd in Pinero's *Trelawney of the Wells* for a short run in May 1952 'to see whether I could still do it'. The production, by Peter Ashmore, received bad notices – Ashmore being accused by W.A. Darlington in *The Telegraph* of not trusting his author, but he thought 'F.B. and others could act the play beautifully if allowed'.

Kenneth Tynan in *The Spectator* said, 'Mr Frith Banbury playing an ambitious tyro, caricatures without affection a part written without nicety,' but then he begins his review: 'Even in the 1890s, when it was written, Shaw found Pinero's peep into the 1860s sentimental and inept, and the subsequent half-century has, I'm afraid, quite staled its small bouquet,' which is inept criticism in itself. But Dorothy Primrose told me, 'Frith and Yvonne Mitchell got it right. It's a difficult scene the Avonia / Ferdy one. They got it just right'.

ii The West End 1940s

56 *The Creaking Chair* originally called *The Man in the Wheelchair* was an adaptation by Roland Pertwee of Mrs Allene Tupper Wilke's novel. In the cast in addition to C. Aubrey Smith and Tallulah Bankhead were Nigel Bruce, Sam Livesey, and Eric Maturin. It opened at the Comedy Theatre on July 22, 1925.

iii Wynyard Browne: Quiet Plays from a Quiet Man

70 Selma Vaz Dias who replaced Joan Miller in *Dark Summer* can be read about in the collected letters of Jean Rhys, whose life she rather took over. F.B. thought her 'rightly cast, but not a very interesting actress'.

71 Basil Thomas killed himself a few years after *Shooting Star* by taking an overdose in a bedroom at the Savage Club.

81 The film of *The Holly and the Ivy* was released in 1952. It was adapted by Anatole de Grunwald, and directed by George More O'Ferrall with music by Malcolm Arnold. Ralph Richardson plays Gregory, with Celia Johnson as Jenny, Margaret Leighton as Margaret, Denholm Elliott as Mick, John Gregson as David, Hugh Williams as Richard, and – the best reason for seeing the film – Margaret Halstan and Maureen Delany repeating their stage performances as the aunts.

Penelope Houston wrote: 'This type of direct translation to the screen, using none of the cinema's resources, can only do harm to the play itself.

The play is heavily cut; too much of the final scene between Margaret and Gregory is lost for there to be a satisfactory resolution, yet the ensemble playing is very good, and if anyone is still misguided enough to think that actors of the early fifties could not play subtext, they should watch when the film is next shown on television at Christmas time.

87 'Paul Scofield remembers *A Question of Fact* . . . ' Scofield to author 8.1.92

94 Charles Marowitz is an American director and writer, who worked in London during the 1960s. He was thought of as the epitome of the innovative and the *avant garde*.

Part Three: A Producer in the Fifties

i The West End 1950s

107 John Deane Potter's article appeared in *The Daily Express* on April 9, 1959; John Osborne's reply on April 16, 1959.

ii N.C. Hunter

125 I made my first professional appearance as an actor in a later N.C. Hunter play, *The Adventures of Tom Random* at the Yvonne Arnaud Theatre, Guildford in 1967. He attended every rehearsal and I remember him as a charming man who was very kind and encouraging to a teenage A.S.M.

iii Terence Rattigan and The Deep Blue Sea

127 Anthony Maurice's real name was Goldschmidt. He was killed in the war.

130 From his performance in *The Deep Blue Sea,* Kenneth More was cast in the film *Genevieve,* about the London to Brighton Vintage Car Race. His successful film career followed.

131 Dame Peggy Ashcroft's husbands were: Rupert Hart Davis, the publisher; Theodore Komisarjevsky, the director; and Jeremy (now Lord) Hutchinson, Q.C.

132 Margaret Sullavan's most noted films were: *The Good Fairy, So Red The Rose* 1935.; *Next Time We Love, The Moon's Our Home,* 1936; *Three Comrades, The Shopworn Angel, The Shining Hour,* 1938; *The Shop Around The Corner, The Mortal Storm,* 1940; *Back Street, So Ends The Night, Appointment For Love,* 1941; *Cry Havoc,* 1943. Her one film since the war had been *No Sad Songs For Me* in 1950. She was at the time of *The Deep Blue Sea* on Broadway, married to the producer Leland Hayward. Her previous husbands had been Henry Fonda and William Wyler. The story of her life is told by her daughter Brooke Hayward in *Haywire.*

Part Four

Rodney Ackland – Either Fog or the King Died

140 'Joe Orton . . . ' quoted in John Lahr's Introduction to *Joe Orton, The Complete Plays,* Methuen, 1976.

140 'The house was sold . . . ' F.B.'s programme note for a German production of *Absolute Hell,* Staats Theater, Stuttgart 1992. Unpublished in English.

140 'Acting, Rodney later claimed . . . ' *The Celluloid Mistress,* Allan Wingate, 1954.

141 'His aim being 'to tell the truth . . . ' Ibid.

141 'Having been brought up . . . .' Banbury, Stuttgart.

141 'They are uncertain of their jobs.' John Gielgud, *Early Stages,* Macmillan, 1939.

142 'The distinctive rhythm of his plays', Ibid

143 'Man's individuality . . .' quoted by Frank Granville-Barker in an article called 'Why Don't They Listen?' *Plays and Players,* September 1957.

147 'silly fool of a woman' author's conversations with F.B.

147 Mary Clare was the original Lady Marryot in Noel Coward's *Cavalcade,* 1931.

148 'Always the play came first,' F.B., Stuttgart.

149 'it is the skill with which these intertwine' Nicholas Dromgoole, Introduction to *Absolute Hell,* Oberon Books 1990.

151 Insomuch as any character in a play is modelled on someone from real life, the following probably gave Rodney Ackland the idea for some of the personages in *The Pink Room | Absolute Hell:*

Christine Foskett: Olwen Vaughan of The French Club.

Julia Shillitoe: Gwladys Evan Morris – Rodney's eccentric actress friend who kept lodgers, and who had first played Vera Lyndon in *Strange Orchestra* (on whom she was based). By 1952 she could not remember lines.

Elizabeth Collier: Mabbie's relation, Dorothy Donaldson-Hudson.

Maurice Hussey: The film producer and director, Brian Desmond Hurst, who at his best (i.e. *Scrooge* with Alistair Sim 1957) showed considerable talent. He was still hanging around Knightsbridge pubs in the 1970s.

Nigel Childs: Arthur Boys.

Lettice Willis: Brenda Dean Paul, socialite and dope fiend.

Ruby Bottomley / R.B. Monody: James Agate / Harold Hobson

152 Donald Crutchley of *The Pink Room* 'A plain soldier. Member of the upper middle-class', became Butch, the American G.I. in *Absolute Hell.*

160 'Scofield . . . remembers the rehearsals . . .' Letter from Scofield to author 8 January 1992.

160 'He thought the play . . .' Ibid

165 'The Theatre is my life . . .' quoted in *The Times,* Obituary 7 December 1991.

167 'Ackland was Chekhovian' Obituary by Hilary Spurling in *The Daily Telegraph* 7 December 1991.

168 ' . . . both thought him the best living playwright,' author's conversations, on separate occasions, with Robert Flemyng, and Allan Davis.

168 'I shall always account it a privilege.' Banbury, Stuttgart.

Part Five: 1954

i John Whiting: An Enigma with the Possibilities of a Solution

171 'an interesting enigma . . . ' Undated letter from Margaret Ramsay to F.B. c. 1954.

171 'out of the University . . . ' Anonymous interview with John Whiting from an unidentified magazine headed *Writer as Gangster*. Newspaper cutting in F.B.'s possession. c. 1962.

173 'If Bobby's the best we can get' author's conversations with F.B.

173 'A gentle man . . . ' Ibid

173 'avoiding names like von Runstedt . . . ' *Writer as Gangster*

176 'Whiting was dissatisfied with *Marching Song'* and following. Ibid

177 'a star if ever there was one' author's conversations with F.B.

178 'a rough summer: selling my clothes' author's conversations with Christopher Taylor.

179 'Many people thought the original production lacked warmth' *Writer as Gangster.*

180 'By not going to the Royal Court Theatre' Ibid.

ii Old Vic Interlude

184 'The only time he worked for one of the subsidised National Companies.' Frith was asked by Sir Laurence Olivier to direct Coral Browne in Shaw's *Mrs Warren's Profession* at the National Theatre in 1970. He was unable to accept as he was contracted to H.M. Tennent to direct a revival of Rattigan's *The Winslow Bay.*

184 'delightful ostentation . . . ' spoken by Don Adriano de Armado, *Love's Labour's* Lost Act V Scene 1.

187 '(Beaton) wrote Frith a typical letter' Cecil Beaton to F.B. 1954, headed '1 Nov. The Ambassador, 341 Park Avenue. New York.'

188 N.C. Hunter's letter to F.B. 1954, undated.

188 Sir Alec Guinness's letter to F.B. 24 Oct. 1954

Part Six: In the Face of the Royal Court

i Reaction Against Aunt Edna

191 'a nice respectable middle-class, middle-aged maiden lady . . . ' *The Collected Plays of Terence Rattigan,* Volume Two, Hamish Hamilton, 1953.

191 *'Look Back in Anger* . . . initiated what has been called the Theatre of Revolt' *et seq. The Collected Plays of Terence Rattigan,* Volume Three, Hamish Hamilton, 1964.

194 'as morose as the playwrights he discouraged . . . ' John Osborne *A Better Class of Person* Faber and Faber 1981

196 'like a bad stage version of *The Archers'.* Author's conversation with Robert Flemyng.

196 'Paul Scofield perhaps saw what was going on . . . ' Scofield to author 8.1.92.

ii Robert Bolt

199 'Bolt . . . thought the theatre "just flighty" . . . ' quoted in interview with Ronald Hayman in *Robert Bolt*, Heinemann Educational Books, 1969.

199 *'The Circle* as his model' Ibid.

200 'I knocked on the door' Bolt in conversation with author 9.4.92.

200 'There was always a Party cell in every camp.' Hayman.

201 'a dreamer in the face of the terrible nine to five of his job' Bolt to author.

204 'The dreadful struggle to get over into non-naturalism'. *Encore* interview with the Editors March – April 1961.

204 Frith was criticised for using too much music and clever lighting by Derek Granger in his review of *Flowering Cherry. The Financial Times,*
22.11.57.

206 'I beg you to remember that you have an outsize personality . . . ' F.B. to Sir Ralph Richardson, 4.2.58.

207 'It is essential', wrote Frith – to him again. F.B. to Sir Ralph Richardson, 29.12.58.

207 'I greatly enjoyed my association with you.' Sir Ralph Richardson to F.B., 3.4.59.

208 'It was sad about Eric' Hugh Beaumont to F.B., 5.11.59.

208 'I have read *The Tiger and the Horse'* F.B. to Robert Bolt, 13.2.59.

208 Sir Michael Redgrave's letter to Robert Bolt with a copy to F.B. is undated but is from the last ten days of February 1959.

209 'Bolt asks me to tell you' F.B. to Sir Michael Redgrave, 27.2.59.

209 'How extraordinary to find a man' Robert Bolt to F.B., 2.3.59.

210 'Bernard Levin called it a "talk-all-nighter"', Levin, *Daily Express,* 25.8.60.

213 'Miss Vanessa Redgrave whose stunningly perfect performance . . . ' Ibid.

213 'resounding in depth', Levin, *Daily Express,* 30.8.60.

214 'If Dean is such an old duck . . . ' F.B. to Sir Michael Redgrave, 6.12.60.

214 'I am afraid that business has dropped' F.B. to Jerome Chodorov, 2.12.60.

215 'I don't want to live eight times a week . . . ' Dame Edith Evans to F.B., undated.

iii Moon on a Rainbow Shawl

217 'The action of all the plays submitted . . . ' *The Observer Plays*, with a Preface by Kenneth Tynan. Faber and Faber, 1958.

217 'a sort of Negro Anna Magnani' Ibid.

Part Seven: Watershed, Doldrums, and Renaissance

229 *Just Williams, an autobiography.* Kenneth Williams, J.M. Dent 1985.

236 'It's the old dictum of Stanislavsky . . . ' In *Building a Character,* Stanislavsky says, 'That is why in our world of theatre we must learn to hold ourselves in check . . . follow the principle: love art in yourself, and not yourself in art'.

236 'He was easy to work with' Paul Scofield, letter to author 8.1.92.

237 'In a recent radio interview . . . ' F.B. interview with Martin Jenkins, Radio 4, 6.6.93.

239 ' . . . why such a musically gifted theatre director has done no work to speak of on the lyric stage'.

Frith was engaged to produce Donizetti's *Lucrezia Borgia* for the Wexford Festival Opera in 1968. Although the production went out under his name, disagreements with the management over the non-availability of singers caused him to depart before the dress-rehearsal.

Select Bibliography

Books

Joss Ackland *I Must Be In There Somewhere* Hodder & Stoughton 1989

Rodney Ackland and Elspeth Grant *The Celluloid Mistress* Allan Wingate 1954

Michael Baker *The Rise of the Victorian Actor* Croom Helm 1978

Jean Batters *Edith Evans, A Personal Memoir* Hart-Davis MacGibbon 1977

Michael Billington *Peggy Ashcroft* John Murray 1988

Kitty Black *Upper Circle* Methuen 1984

Denys Blakelock *Round The Next Corner* Gollancz 1967

Humphrey Carpenter *O.U.D.S. A Centenary History of the Oxford University Dramatic Society* Oxford University Press 1985

John Casson *Lewis and Sybil* Collins 1972

Michael Darlow and Gillian Hodson *Terence Rattigan, The Man and his Work* Quartet Books 1979

Russell Davies (ed.) *The Kenneth Williams Diaries* Harper Collins 1993

Herbert Farjeon *The Farjeon Omnibus* Hutchinson

Clive Fisher *Noel Coward* Weidenfeld and Nicolson 1992

Kate Fleming *Celia Johnson* Weidenfeld and Nicolson 1991

Bryan Forbes *Ned's Girl, the Life of Edith Evans* Elm Tree 1977

John Gielgud *Early Stages* Macmillan 1939

Martin Green *Children of the Sun* Constable 1977

Ronald Harwood *Sir Donald Wolfit C.B.E. His Life and Work in the Unfashionable Theatre* Secker and Warburg 1971

Ronald Hayman *Robert Bolt* Heinemann 1969

Harold Hobson *Unfinished Journey* Weidenfeld and Nicolson 1978

Richard Huggett *Binkie Beaumont, Eminence Grise of the West End Theatre 1933-1973* Hodder and Stoughton 1984

Nicholas de Jongh *Not in Front of the Audience, Homosexuality on Stage* Routledge 1992

Charles Landstone *Off Stage* Elek 1953

Diana de Marly *Costume on the Stage 1660-1940* Batsford 1982

Norman Marshall *The Other Theatre* John Lehmann 1947

Kenneth More *More or Less* Hodder and Stoughton 1978

Robert Morley and Sewell Stokes *Responsible Gentleman* Heinemann 1966

Sheridan Morley *Gladys Cooper* Heinemann 1979

Allardyce Nicoll *English Drama, a Modern Viewpoint* Harrap 1968

Garry O'Connor *Ralph Richardson* Hodder and Stoughton 1982

John Osborne *A Better Class of Person* Faber and Faber 1981

Terence Rattigan *Collected Plays, Volumes Two and Three* Hamish Hamilton 1953, 1964.

Michael Redgrave *In My Mind's Eye* Weidenfeld and Nicolson 1983

Vanessa Redgrave *Vanessa* Hutchinson 1991

Peter Roberts (ed.) *The Best of Plays and Players* Methuen 1987

J.C. Trewin *Benson and the Bensonians* Barrie and Rockcliff 1960; *Dramatists of Today* Staples Press 1953

Simon Trussler *The Plays of John Whiting: an Assessment* Gollancz 1972

Kenneth Tynan *A View of the English Stage* Methuen 1975

Kenneth Williams *Just Williams* Dent 1985

T.C. Worsley *Fugitive Art* John Lehmann 1952

B.A. Young *The Rattigan Version* Hamish Hamilton 1986

Plays

Rodney Ackland *Absolute Hell* Oberon Books, 1990; *A Dead Secret* Samuel French, 1958

Robert Bolt *Flowering Cherry* Samuel French, 1958; *The Tiger and the Horse* Samuel French, 1961

John Bowen *I Love You Mrs Patterson* Evans Bothers, 1964

Wynyard Browne *Dark Summer* Evans Brothers, 1950; *The Holly and the Ivy* Evans Brothers, 1951; *A Question of Fact* Evans Brothers, 1955; *The Ring of Truth* Evans Brothers, 1960

N.C. Hunter *A Touch of the Sun* Warner-Chappell, 1958; *Waters of the Moon* English Theatre Guild, 1951

Errol John *Moon on a Rainbow Shawl* Faber and Faber, in *The Observer Plays* 1958

Terence Rattigan *The Deep Blue Sea* Samuel French, 1952

Tom Stoppard *Enter a Free Man* Faber and Faber, 1968

Christopher Taylor *The Wings of the Dove* Elek Books, 1964

Basil Thomas *Shooting Star* Deane and Sons Ltd., 1949

John Whiting *Marching Song* Samuel French, 1954.

Epilogue to the 2022 Edition

Frith Banbury died at home on 14th of May 2008, aged ninety-six, of cancer which struck swiftly.

The following day, his was the leading obituary in *The Times*, *The Daily Telegraph*, and *The Guardian*. In the latter Michael Billington wrote that Frith 'seemed to epitomise the glamour and style of The West End theatre in its 1940s and 50s heyday, yet . . . he was never a fully paid-up member of the theatrical establishment: he was much more eclectic in his tastes and adventurous in his outlook . . . He was a man of fascinating contradictions: a rebel against authority who yet believed strongly in theatrical discipline; an instinctive European who made his name directing quintessentially English middle-class plays: an embodiment of West End values who had a ravenous appetite for new writing.'

The Lost Summer, the Heyday of the West End Theatre, as this book was then called, had been published over thirteen years earlier when Frith had been eighty-three. I had assumed – very wrongly – that it would serve as an *envoi* to his career. Frith however had other plans.

He had already directed Edgar Wallace's *The Case of the Frightened Lady* at the Palace Theatre Watford in 1992 and was to withdraw through ill-health from a Chichester Festival production of Rodney Ackland's *After October* in 1997. In 1998 he directed Basil Thomas's *Shooting Star* at the Chester Gateway. At the Savoy Theatre in London, D.L. Coburn's *The Gin Game*, and lastly in 2003, Rodney Ackland's *The Old Ladies* (when he was ninety-one) which played Peterborough and Richmond.

In 2000 and rather to his embarrassment, Frith had been awarded the M.B.E. (he thought he had been offered a C.B.E.). He was worth more than that and he and the rest of us knew it. He asked me not to tell anyone!

The publication of *The Lost Summer* in 1995 (Nick Hern Books and Heinemann in the U.S.A) certainly put Frith back into the consciousness of many who worked in the theatre or watched it. Some actors and directors had not realised what a champion of new writing he had been, and some of the public (and not a few academics, who had accepted the superficiality of Kenneth Tynan's 'Froth Binbury',) realised that here was a man who – almost obsessed with the theatre – took his work seriously, and had promoted playwrights who would not otherwise have had such auspicious starts. And he had been trusted by some of the best actors of his time.

The book was reviewed prominently in all the main national newspapers (except *The Times*) and apart from *The Evening Standard*, whose critic was a friend of Peter Cotes and the *Daily Telegraph*, whose critic was irritated by an inaccurate reference to herself (corrected in the paperback,) all were full of praise. Sheridan Morley in *The Sunday Times*, and Ned Sherrin in *The Independent* were vivid and amusing as well as being complimentary.

I received a large postbag: from Frith's friends, so delighted that he and his work had been recognised and from theatregoers too, who remembered productions which had given pleasure or stirred them.

Only one – Professor Charles (Chuck) Nolte of the University of Minnesota – openly and actively disliked the book's structure and tone; while Paul Scofield wondered 'if we really needed to be told what Frith thought about his poor old nanny'. (p 9)

I was very lucky that Christopher Taylor, Frith's closest friend and colleague approved so heartily:

'I write to tell you that it's super. The construction is cunning, the selection of the material is wise and I agree with most of your views (by the time I've taken the book at a leisurely stroll, I suspect I'll have been persuaded to agree with *all* of them).

'It should prove a seminal work in the century's theatre history, and I haven't said how enviable is the quality of the actual writing.' (13.3.95)

I was indeed lucky in Christopher's opinion for Frith, irritated beyond measure that I had only shown him the manuscript at the last possible moment (a few days before publication) had decided to teach me a lesson.

He scrutinised the book for every fault, questioned some of the quotes and attitudes that I had attributed to him, and dictated over ten pages of 'corrections' (obediently typed up by his great-niece Ella Kenion) and dispatched them to The Harry Ransom Center of the University of Texas Austin, who on my advice, the year before, had bought his entire archive for £50,000. He also sent a copy to me. And I was enraged.

Much that he denied thinking or feeling was there on tape and it was evidence. But I was too angry and weary to fight back.

However he backtracked on one assertion which I did *not* have on tape. This was an account of the M.P. Woodrow Wyatt's visit on 16th of March

1954, concerning the impresario Binkie Beaumont's domination of West End Theatre. 'He questioned Frith closely as to Beaumont's professional integrity, repeated Peter Cotes's accusations mentioning him by name, and asked him point-blank whether there was any truth in his information that Beaumont employed only homosexuals.' (p 104)

Peter Cotes, who I had portrayed as the malign troublemaker of this episode was still alive. And Frith had insisted that Wyatt had not mentioned Cotes by name. I thus spent some uneasy weeks waiting for a nasty letter, which thankfully never arrived. However a colleague of mine from acting days, who turned out to be Peter Cotes's godson did write, not questioning my account, but mildly pointing out that his godfather had a kind, thoughtful, and loving side.

Through Julius Green's research for his 2015 book *Agatha Christie, A Life in Theatre*, it is now clear that the real force in the plot to overthrow Beaumont and his H.M. Tennent empire was *The Mousetrap* impresario, Sir Peter Saunders, unscrupulously using Peter Cotes as his front man and patsy.

Otherwise, I remember being annoyed over small things: that Frith had questioned the order of touring dates for *The Dark Summer*, which I had spent a long-time double checking. His corrections of my spelling of 'Ranyevskaya' (he thought it should be 'Ranevsky', being ignorant of the Russian liquid 'e') and that I had quoted the *actual* letters that Dame Edith Evans and Dame Sybil Thorndike had written to him over *Waters of the Moon* overacting affair (pp 116–117) which did not tally which his often retold dinner party anecdote!

I threw my copy of these notes into the wastepaper basket, but anyone interested can find them among the Frith Banbury Papers at the Ransom Center.

After he had simmered down, Frith wrote to me: 'My dear Charlie, I've now read it again and have no hesitation in saying that I think you have done a smashing job. It was a mistake on my part to try reading it as a novel. The overall style and tenor and context of the book is, as you say, more important than its incidentals. What's more I am delighted with the fact that the book is not all about me personally, partly because it *is* in a sense, even at those passages where it seems not to be, and anyway because that makes it so much more interesting than any of the theatre books that have been around lately. As for the selection of material, I think it's rather cunning, although there are naturally omissions, unavoidable I do see, that I would have liked to see here. As far as opinions go, I take no exception to any of them, though there are one or two I'd like to have clarified for me.

'Dear Charlie, I do hope you'll soon feel up to talking about it. I'd love to do that.

With love and thanks,
Frith (14.3.95)'

We were friends again for the rest of his life.

Writing about Frith's life and work was a privilege and it was fun. Obviously there were certain things which I felt that I couldn't say in 1995, that I am able to now: Sir Ralph Richardson's reaction on being told that Wendy Hiller was to succeed Celia Johnson in *Flowering Cherry*, 'Oh God no! She's like a female Charles Laughton,' when Dame Wendy was very much alive. Or Bobby Fleming, asking with mock innocence – after I had spent some time trying to persuade him of my belief in reincarnation – 'Does that mean that Frith Banbury might come back as a good director?'

What did the book get right and where were its predictions wrong?

The enormous Terence Rattigan revival and re-evaluation in Britain, had not taken place in 1995. Today it is clear that Rattigan was one of the greatest English-language playwrights of the twentieth century. I said that Rodney Ackland's *The Pink Room* was 'the only really great modern play that Frith ever directed'. And I was wrong. *The Deep Blue Sea* was the greatest new play that he directed.

The case of Rodney Ackland remains much as it did in 1995. He has his champions and adherents but he has never become mainstream. In the year *The Lost Summer* was published there was an excellent production of *Absolute Hell* at The National Theatre with Dame Judi Dench, directed by Anthony Page. In 2016, there was an impressive and finely acted *After October*, directed by Oscar Toeman at the Finborough Theatre.

About the National Theatre's 2018 production of *Absolute Hell*, the less said the better. As I lamented to one of our leading theatre critics, 'No one will ever do Rodney's plays again.' His reply was, 'well certainly not for a very long time.'

It is sad that the warm heart and the ironic nuance of Wynyard Browne remains unappreciated. Perhaps the only production that this book's enthusiasm really engendered was Sam Walter's (hero of the Orange Tree, Richmond) 2009 revival of *The Ring of Truth*. This play I claimed as 'The best English comedy to have been written in the twenty-three years between *Blithe Spirit* in 1941 and *Entertaining Mr. Sloane* in 1964'. In spite of being agreeably acted and skillfully directed (by Auriol Smith) it was plainly not that.

The most interesting case is perhaps that of N.C. Hunter, about whose plays I was fairly lukewarm.

Never having had a successful American production in his lifetime, his plays have found a champion in Jonathan Bank and his then assistant Jesse Marchese, and a home with the Mint Theatre Company at The Beckett Theatre Off Broadway. After successfully producing Hunter's unperformed *A Picture of Autumn* in 2013, Austin Pendleton's production of *A Day by the Sea* in 2016 was a superbly acted and paced piece of ensemble playing. And it justly received glorious reviews (a Southwark Playhouse production in London the following year, was less happily cast).

I believe I was right in saying, 'None of N.C. Hunter's plays are connected much to an outside world, and thus they have dated very little. Living so far from the capital, he writes a pure kind of English quite free of contemporary jargon or slang. The action could be quite easily updated a decade without any difference being made. And the best parts he wrote were for the middle-aged or old'.

In an ideal world, Jonathan Bank plans to produce another of Hunter's plays.

In 2012 Errol John's *Moon on a Rainbow Shawl* had a truly wonderful production at The National Theatre (by Michael Buffong) in association with the Talawa Theatre Company. It was given its pre-eminence as the best of all Caribbean plays.

My pronouncement that television had killed small-scale intimate revue in the theatre was certainly wrong. In the last twenty-five years, there has been a plethora of these in the West End and regions, and most of them deservedly very successful.

When I first wrote this book, I felt as if I had a battle to fight: recognition of those playwrights whose reputation had been set aside by the emergence of the Royal Court and the Angry Young Men of the mid-1950s. Matters are sorted. Reputations are even now. And *The Lost Summer* helped with that. How wonderful that, in the middle of the twentieth century, our theatre could produce both Rattigan and Pinter.

Frith Banbury received a lot of attention when the book was first published. As Christopher Taylor said to me in 1996, 'You've certainly given him a very good year!' And I was glad, if I had.

When Frith died, I telephoned the friend who had introduced us, who was by then an old man living in Derbyshire. I didn't want him to hear of it first from the next day's papers.

'I didn't love him,' said Edward Mace. 'But I'm very glad that I knew him'.

That was how I felt at the time too.

I now think of Frith Banbury with the greatest affection and gratitude. Writing this at the peak of the Covid-19 pandemic, with theatres around the world closed, I know that I would speak for Frith in the profoundest and most passonate hope that the theatre which he loved in all its forms, and served in the best way he could, would come alive and flourish again.

Charles Duff
The Charterhouse 2021

Index